Yoga Upaniṣad Series *Volume 3*

Yoga Darśana Upaniṣad

Ancient Insight into the System of Aṣṭāṅga Yoga

Original Sanskrit text with
Transliteration, Translation and Commentary

Swāmī Satyadharma Saraswatī

Sannyāsī Śrimukti (Ruth Perini)

Dedication

To all friends, practitioners and teachers of yoga, and to all seekers of spiritual wisdom, regardless of time or place, creed, gender, age or race.

CONTENTS

		page
Introduction		9
Invocation		18

FIRST SECTION: Aṣṭāṅga yoga is the sādhana of the jivanmukta.

Verse		
1	Dattātreya, avatar and illumined teacher	19
2	The worthy disciple	22
3	The disciple's request	24
4, 5	The eight limbs of yoga	25
6	The ten yamas, or yogic disciplines	27
7, 8	Ahiṃsā, non-violence	29
9, 10	Satyam, truth	32
11, 12	Asteya, honesty	34
13, 14a	Brahmacarya, abstinence	36
14b, 15a	Dayā, kindness	38
15b, 16a	Ārjavam, straight-forwardness	40
16b, 17a	Kṣamā, patience	42
17b, 18	Dhṛti, equanimity	44
19	Mitāhāra, moderate diet	47
20 to 23a	Śauca, cleanliness	49
23b to 25	The way to know supreme consciousness	52

SECOND SECTION: Knowledge of The Ten Niyamas, inner disciplines

Verse		
1, 2a	Ten niyamas	55
2b to 4a	Tapas, austerity	57
4b to 6a	Santoṣa, contentment	60
6b	Āstikya, faith in the higher reality	62
7	Dāna, giving freely	63
8	Worship of Īśwara	65
9	Vedānta śravana, hearing the knowledge of truth	67

10	Hrīḥ, remorse or shame	70
11	Mati, faith in the vedic teaching	72
12 to 16	Japa, repetition of the mantra	75

THIRD SECTION: Nine Āsanas

Verse		
1, 2a	Nine major āsanas	78
2b, 3a	Swastikāsana, the auspicious pose	80
3b, 4a	Gomukhāsana, the cow face pose	82
4b, 5	Padmāsana, the lotus pose	84
6	Vīrāsana, the hero pose	86
6i to iii	Siṃhāsana, the lion pose	88
7, 8a	Bhadrāsana, the gracious pose	90
8b to 10a	Muktāsana, liberated pose	92
10b to 12a	Mayurāsana, the peacock pose	95
12b, 13a	Sukāsana, the easy pose	97
13b, 14	Benefits of mastering āsana	99

FOURTH SECTION: The Subtle Body

Verse		
1, 2	Center of fire and triangle of śakti	101
3 to 5a	Root of the nāḍīs	104
5b to 8	Enumeration of the nāḍīs	106
9, 10	Brahma and suṣumnā nāḍīs	108
11 to 13a	Kuṇḍalinī	110
13b to 17	Location of the major nāḍīs	113
18 to 23a	Termination of the major nāḍīs	116
23b to 30a	Ten prāṇas	119
30b to 34	Functions of the prāṇas	122
35 to 39a	Deities relating with the nāḍīs	125
39b, 40a	Lunar and solar movement in the nāḍīs	127
40b to 43a	Uttarāyan and dakṣiṇāyan	128
43b to 47	Equinox and eclipse	131
48 to 56	Inner pilgrimage places	134
57 to 59	Vision of Śiva within oneself	139
60 to 63	Absorption in Brahma	141

FIFTH SECTION: Prāṇāyāma

Verse		
1 to 4	Purification of the nāḍīs	144
5 to 10	Nāḍī śodhana prāṇāyāma	147
11, 12	Signs of nāḍī purification	152
13, 14	Purification of the Self	154

SIXTH SECTION: Aspects of Prāṇāyāma

Verse		
1, 2	Description of prāṇāyāma	156
3 to 9	Prāṇāyāma with praṇava	158
10 to 12a	Benefits of the practice	162
12b, 13	Components of prāṇāyāma	164
14 to 20	Perfection of prāṇāyāma	166
21 to 32a	Prāṇāyāma eradicates disease	170
32b to 43a	Ṣaṇmukhi mudrā controls prāṇa	175
43b, 44a	Signs of the conquest of vāyu	181
44b to 51	Dawning of vairagya and removal of disease and sin	183

SEVENTH SECTION: Pratyāhāra

Verse		
1 to 4a	Description of pratyāhāra	187
4b to 8	Pratyāhāra by focusing on prāṇa	191
9, 10a	Benefits of pratyāhāra	195
10b to 12	Pratyāhāra by focusing on prāṇa (method 2)	197
13, 14	Pratyāhāra according to vedānta	201

EIGHTH SECTION: Dhāraṇā

Verse		
1 to 6	Pañca bhūta dhāraṇā, concentration on the five elements	203
7 to 9	Dhāraṇā on the Self	210

NINTH SECTION: Dhyāna

Verse		
1, 2	Meditation on Brahma with attributes	213
3 to 5	Meditation on Brahma without attributes	216
6	Fruits of Meditation	219

TENTH SECTION: Samādhi

Verse		
1 to 5	Nature of samādhi	221
6 to 12	Only Brahma remains	225
13	Epilogue	229

APPENDICES

1. Sanskrit text 231
2. Pronunciation Guide 253
3. Continuous Translation 255

About the Author 277
About the Translator 278

Introduction

Veda is a Sanskrit word meaning ‘knowledge’. In the context of the Vedas, it means ‘revealed knowledge which is *śruti*, ‘heard’ from within, not taught. These ancient spiritual texts or hymns, through which we can learn much of the perceptions and insights of the early vedic seers, are grouped into four *samhitas* or collections: *Rig Veda, Yajur Veda, Sāma Veda* and *Atharva Veda.* They were revealed to enlightened beings 3,000 to 4,500 years ago or more (the Rig-Veda contains astronomical references describing occurrences in 5,000 to 3,000 BCE), and transmitted orally by the sages from generation to generation within brahmin families.

The four Vedas were considered to be divine revelations, and each word was carefully memorised. This was to ensure accurate transmission, but also because each syllable was considered to have spiritual power, its source being the supreme, eternal sound. This was a mammoth task, as there are 20,358 verses in the four Vedas, approximately two thousand printed pages. They were composed in fifteen different metres, which demanded perfect control of the breath. Georg Feuerstein describes them as ‘a composite of symbol, metaphor, allegory, myth and story, as well as paradox and riddle’ and their composers as ‘recipients and revealers of the invisible order of the cosmos [with] inspired insights or illumined visions’1.

Rig Veda

The Rig Veda is the oldest spiritual text in the world and still regarded as sacred, containing 1,028 hymns or songs of 10,589 verses in praise of the divine (*rig* or *ric* meaning ‘praise’). Each hymn is recognised as a *mantra*, a sacred sound vibration, which releases energy from limited material awareness, thus expanding the consciousness. It is also the earliest surviving form of Sanskrit. The illumined seers composed the hymns while established in the highest consciousness, thus able to commune with luminous beings of the higher realms. There are about 250 hymns in praise of *Indra*, the divine force behind the ocean, heavens, thunder, lightning, rain and the light of the sun; 200 of *Agni*, born of the Sun, becoming the god of sacrificial fire, and over 100 of *Soma*, who gives immortality, and who is connected to the Sun, Moon, mountains, rivers and oceans. Others are dedicated to *Varuna*, who protects cosmic order; the *Ashvins*, supreme healers; *Ushas*, goddess of the dawn; *Aditi*, goddess of eternity; and *Saraswati*, goddess of the Vedas and of music and the arts.

Yajur Veda

The hymns of the Yajur-Veda, Veda of Sacrifice, consist of sacrificial formulas or prayers, including those of an internal or spiritual nature, which are chanted by the *adhvaryu* (priest), who performs the sacrifice. About a third of its 1,975 verses are taken from the Rig Veda. The rest are original and in prose form.

Sāma Veda

The Sāma Veda, Veda of Chants, gives instructions on the chanting of vedic hymns. The majority of its 1,875 verses are from the Rig Veda; only 75 verses are original. Many of the hymns were sung by special priests during sacrificial rites. Some are still sung today.

Atharva Veda

The Atharva Veda, named after the seer Atharvan, whose family were great seers in vedic times, contains 731 hymns of 5,977 verses, about one fifth of which are from the RigVeda. Much of the Atharva Veda consists of magical spells and charms for gaining health, love, peace and prosperity, or taking revenge on an enemy. Possibly for this reason, the Atharva Veda was either not accepted by the orthodox priesthood, or not given the same standing as the other Vedas.

The vedic people and their culture

The vedic people lived for over 2,500 years mainly along the banks of the Saraswati River, which was located in Northern India between the modern Ravi and Yamuna Rivers down to what is now the desert of Rajasthan. The Saraswati River dried up in about 1,900 BCE due to tectonic upheavals. Other areas of habitation included the Ganges River and its tributaries, rivers in Afghanistan (previously called Gandhara), the Himalayas and Mount Kailash in Tibet.

The vedic people had a complex multi-tiered view of the universe, in which humankind, nature and the divine are intertwined and interrelated. They had a deep knowledge of the oceans, mountains, deserts and forests of the physical world, as well as of the subtle worlds of deities and different levels of consciousness. People lived in cities or villages or were nomads, and were fully engaged in worldly life. They were an agrarian people, yet also had herds of cattle, horses and camels. Cities were constructed of stone, bricks and metal. They built chariots and ships. They were skilled workers in gold, metal, clay, stone, wood, leather and wool, and showed a very high standard in arts, crafts, astrology, medicine, music, dance and poetry.

After the Vedas

The Vedas were the foundation for the later revelations (*śruti*) in the *Brāhmaṇas* (ritual texts), the *Āranyakas* (texts on rituals and meditation for forest-dwelling ascetics) and the *Upaniṣads* (esoteric texts). Later still, the Vedas were the basis for numerous works of remembered or traditional knowledge, known as *smṛti,* including the epics: i.e. the *Mahābhārata, Rāmāyaṇa* and *Purāṇas,* and the *Sūtras,* or threads of knowledge, e.g. *Yoga Sūtras.* All these texts contain many concepts and practices, which come directly from the four Vedas.

Upaniṣads

The word *upaniṣad* is comprised of three roots: *upa* or 'near', *ni* or 'attentively', and *sad,* 'to sit'. The term describes the situation in which these unique texts were transmitted. The students or disciples sat near the realized master and listened attentively, as he expounded his experiences and understanding of the ultimate reality. These teachings are said to destroy the ignorance or illusion of the spiritual aspirant in regard to what is self and non-self, what is real and unreal, in relation to the absolute and relative reality. Only disciples were chosen, who had persevered in *sādhana catuṣṭaya*, the four kinds of spiritual effort, viz. *viveka* (discrimination between the permanent and impermanent), *vairagya* (non-attachment), *ṣadsampatti* (six virtues of serenity, self-control, withdrawal of the senses, endurance, perfect concentration and strong faith) and *mumukṣutva* (intense desire for liberation).

The Upaniṣads are derived from the Āranyakas, because they were chanted in the forest (*āranya*) after the aspirant had retired from worldly life. They are recorded in the later form of Sanskrit used in the Brāhmaṇas, and considered the last phase of *śruti*, vedic revelation. The Upaniṣads are regarded as *vedānta*, the end of the Vedas, inferring that *vedānta* is the end or completion of all perceivable knowledge, as they guide the aspirant beyond the limited mind to the *ātman* (spiritual self) and thus to *mokṣa* (liberation). Each upaniṣad reflected the teachings and tradition of a realized master, and was connected with a specific Veda and vedic school. It is estimated that there are over 200 Upaniṣads, which have been divided into seven groups: *Major*, *Vedānta*, *Śaiva, Śakta, Vaiśnava, Sannyasa* and *Yoga.*

Yoga Upaniṣads

The twenty one Yoga Upaniṣads give an understanding of the hidden forces in nature and human beings, and describe esoteric yogic practices by which these forces can be manipulated and controlled. They emphasise that the inner journey to the one permanent reality, the *ātman*, is the essential one. Journeys to external places, such as holy sites and temples, as well as rituals and ceremonies, are not given importance. Their teachings give important information on the subtle body (*cakras, koṣas, prāṇa, kuṅḍalinī,* meditative states), and the tantric and yogic techniques, not given in the earlier upaniṣads, to attain them. Therefore, they are regarded as a significant integration of Vedanta and Tantra, which were previously considered incompatible. They are classified as 'minor' only because they postdate Adi Shankara.

Although their teachings actually predate Patañjali, the Yoga Upaniṣads were codified after the *Yoga Sūtras of Patañjali,* and form an important part of the classical yoga literature. However, they contain no references to Patañjali or his *Yoga Sūtras*. So, although the compilation of the Yoga Upaniṣads is post-Patañjali, the *vidyās*, or meditative disciplines, contained within them are pre-Patañjali. The Yoga Upaniṣads emerged at a time when the vedic and tantric cultures were coming together to share their knowledge. The wise thinkers from each culture sat down together and discussed how their insights and teachings could be combined in order to benefit humanity. Thus these upanisads combine the teachings of both tantra and yoga. It is evident in them that yoga leads to vedānta, and vedānta leads to yoga. However, they were written down by vedantic scholars and practitioners in order to show that these *vidyās* and related practices were not borrowed from Patañjali, but were known and practised from the ancient period.

Within the twenty-one Yoga Upaniṣads are six sub-groups which have their own main focus. The *Bindu Upaniṣads*, which include the *Amṛta-Bindu* (also known as the *Brahma-Bindu-Upaniṣad*), *Amṛta-Nada-Bindu*, *Nada-Bindu*, *Dhyāna-Bindu* and *Tejo-Bindu-Upaniṣads*, all concentrate on the bindu, the source or origin of all sound, and hence of creation. Bindu represents the transcendental sound manifested in the mantra *Aum*. The *Hamsa-Mantra*, *Soham*, is the main practice of the *Hamsa*, *Brahma-Vidya*, *Mahavakya* and *Paśupata-Brahma-Upaniṣads*. Concentration on *prāṇa*, the life force related to the process of inhalation and exhalation, brings the yogin to the knowledge of the transcendental self. The light of pure consciousness, which the enlightened irradiate is the theme of the *Advaya-Taraka* and *Maṅḍala-Brahmana-Upaniṣads*. The *Kṣurika-Upaniṣad* (*kṣurika* meaning 'dagger') emphasises non-attachment as a means to liberation. The sixth group, comprised of eight late Yoga Upaniṣads from 1200 to 1300 A.D., covers teachings related to hatha and kundalini yogas. They are the *Yoga-Kuṅḍalī, Yoga-Tattwa, Yoga-Śikhā, Varāha, Śāndilya, Tri-Śikhi-Brahmana, Yoga-Darśana* and *Yoga-Chūdāmani Upaniṣads.*

Yoga Darśana Upaniṣad

This concise and complete text on aṣṭāṅga yoga consists of the teachings given to the sage Sāmkṛti by his guru, Lord Dattātreya. The word *darśana* comes from the word *dṛś* 'to see'. *Yoga darśana* means an understanding or insight into the system of yoga. Sāmkṛti asks Dattātreya to describe the eight-limbed path of yoga, so that he can become a *jivanmukta,* liberated while still living. Dattātreya is regarded as an *avatāra*, a human manifestation of the divine, embodying the qualities of Brahma, Viṣṇu and Śiva.

There are ten sections in this upaniṣad, comprising 220 verses in total. In the first and second sections, Dattātreya describes the ethical foundation of yoga: *yama*, the rules of behaviour with others, and *niyama*, rules of personal discipline. The third section deals with the nine major *āsanas* and their benefits. They are *swastikāsana, gomukhāsana, padmāsana, vīrāsana, siṃhāsana, bhadrāsana, muktāsana, mayurāsana* and *sukhāsana.* The fourth section gives a description of the subtle body, also known as the pranic body, which gives energy and life to the physical body and all of its organs and systems. It includes the *nāḍīs*, *kuṅḍalinī*, the ten *prānas*, the inner pilgrimage sites, the vision of the inner Śiva, and absorption into the supreme consciousness through insight into Brahma. It also relates the circulation of the life force in the body to the course of the sun through the zodiac.

The fifth section is on *prāṇāyāma*, how to purify the *nāḍīs* through the practice of *nāḍī śodhana*, the signs of *nāḍī* purification, and finally knowledge of the true self. In the sixth section Dattātreya continues explaining the system of *prāṇāyāma* and combines the practice with the three components of *Aum*, or the *praṇava.* He outlines the effects and benefits of this practice, and further recommends *ṣanmukhi mudra* as a way to control *prāna.* The seventh section concerns *pratyāhāra*, the first stage of meditation, withdrawal of the senses. It gives techniques for inducing *pratyāhāra*, explains their benefits, and the effect of *pratyāhāra,* according to *vedānta.* The eighth section deals with the second stage of meditation, *dhāraṇā*, concentration. It begins with the practice of concentrating on the five elements, ether, air, fire, water and earth, and concludes with concentration on the self. These tantric teachings on *pratyāhāra* and *dhāraṇā* are unique, and will not be found in other texts on yoga or meditation.

The topic of the ninth section is *dhyāna*, spontaneous meditation, which arises only after *pratyāhāra* and *dhāraṇā* have been mastered. Here Dattātreya describes *dhyāna* on Brahma, both with attributes and without attributes, and then the results of this meditation. In section ten Dattātreya explains the nature of *samādhi*, the eighth limb of raja yoga, the realisation of the identity of the individual self with the supreme self.

In the current time, yoga has become a common household word, and the practices of yoga have proliferated around the world. Many kinds of yoga teacher training courses are offered in different countries and languages. Some are intensive and include the philosophy and psychology of yoga in the context of human experience. Others are short and give a very superficial explanation and experience of basic yoga postures. This translation and commentary on the Yoga Darśana Upaniṣad offers an essential key to the origin and background of yoga, which will give the modern student, practitioner and scholar a deeper understanding of the vast scope of yoga, and how the system and practices have evolved from ancient times.

It is our hope that by the sincere study of this and other classical texts on yoga, the modern practitioners and teachers will be able to connect with the roots of yoga, which go back in time to the very dawn of human civilization. By connecting with the antiquity of yoga, a new vision emerges in which one begins to see the highest aspirations that the yogis of old cherished in their hearts, not only for the peace and wellbeing of all, but for enlightenment and immortality.

References

Saraswati, Swami Satyadharma. *Yoga Chudamani Upanishad* (Yoga Publications Trust, Munger, Bihar, India, 2003)

Aiyar, N.K. *Thirty Minor Upanishads* (Parimal Publications, Delhi, India 2009)

Feuerstein, Georg and Kak, Subhash and Frawley, David. *In Search of the Cradle of Civilization* (Quest Books, Illinois, USA 2001)

1. *ibidem* p.20

Feuerstein, Georg. *The Yoga Tradition* (Hohm Press, Prescott, Arizona USA 2001

Frawley, David. *Gods, Sages and Kings* (Passage Press, Salt Lake City, Utah USA 1991)

दर्शनोपनिषत्

Darśanopaniṣat

आप्यायन्तु । इति शान्तिः

āpyāyantu iti śāntiḥ

Let these verses bring fulfilment.
Thus [there will be] peace.

प्रथमः खण्ड्ः

prathamaḥ khaṇdaḥ

First Section

जीवन्मुक्तिसाधनं अष्टाङ्गयोगः

jīvanmuktisādhanam aṣṭāṅgayogaḥ

Aṣṭāṅga yoga is the sādhana of the jivanmukta.

Verse 1: Dattātreya, avatar and illumined teacher

दत्तात्रेयो महायोगी भगवान्भूतभावनः ।

चतुर्भुजो महाविष्णुर्यागसाभ्राज्यदीक्षितिः ।।१।।

dattātreyo mahāyogī bhagavānbhūtabhāvanaḥ
caturbhujo mahāviṣnuryāgasābhrājyadīkṣitiḥ (1)

Anvay

mahāyogī: great *yogin*; *dattātreyaḥ*: *bhagavān*: blessed one; *bhāvanaḥ*: promotes the welfare of; *bhūta*: all living beings; *caturbujaḥ*: four-armed; *mahā-viṣnuḥ*: Great Viṣṇu; *dīkṣitiḥ*: initiated; *yoga-sā-bhrājya*: brilliance of *yoga.*

Translation

The great yogin, Dattātreya, [is] the blessed one [who] promotes the welfare of all living beings. The four-armed great Viṣṇu initiated [him] into the brilliance of yoga.

Commentary

Lord Dattātreya is referred to here in the first verse of this upaniṣad, because he is the seer, the teacher of this yoga, and also a great luminary in his own right. The verse describes him as the blessed one, who promotes the welfare of all living beings. Dattātreya is considered to be an *avatara*, or direct incarnation of the *Trimurti,* combining all the divine qualities of *Brahma* (lord of creation), *Viṣṇu* (lord of sustenance), and *Śiva* (lord of dissolution) in one divine or supreme being. The name Dattatreya is a combination of two words: *datta*, meaning 'that which is given' and *atreya,* referring to Rishi Atri, who was his physical father.

Dattātreya is still worshipped today in South India as a divine manifestation and many legends confirm his spiritual origin. Being a human vessel for the qualities of the three gods, Brahma, Viṣṇu and Śiva, he is said to be the blessed one, who promotes the welfare of all living beings. An ordinary person lives only for him or herself, and is incapable of blessing and promoting the welfare of all beings. Only a divine person, who is born with such an exalted aim, can live for the welfare of all others. Dattātreya is further described as a great yogi, because he was born in yoga, as a child of the great rishi and seer Atri and his wife Anasūya.

Dattātreya's mother, Anasūya, was considered to possess all the powers and knowledge of yoga that had been earned by her husband, due to her flawless character and moral excellence. She obtained Dattātreya as her third child due to a boon, which she received from the three deities, Brahma, Viṣṇu and Śiva, who had paid her a visit one day in her husband's absence just to check out her perfect moral reputation. When the three deities came to her door in the form of debonair young men, she invited them inside. As soon as they were seated, she immediately transformed them into tiny infants, took them on her lap, and suckled them at her breasts. After the three infant gods were nourished, she carried them outside, and transformed them back into their male forms. The three gods were so pleased by this experience that they offered Anasūya a boon, and she chose that all three of them should incarnate together as her third son, Dattātreya, who was born to her a year later.

The verse further states that Dattātreya was initiated into the highest, or illumined, yoga by Lord Viṣṇu himself. This implies that even a divine manifestation requires initiation into yoga, and Dattātreya received his initiation from the supreme godhead. Thus, as the seer of this upaniṣad, he is perfectly qualified to guide the yogic aspirants of all times into this comprehensive teaching on the system of aṣṭāṅga yoga.

Verse 2: The worthy disciple

तस्य शिष्यो मुनिवरः सांकृतिर्नाम भक्तिमान् ।
पप्रच्छ गुरुमेकान्ते प्राञ्जलिर्विनयान्वितः ।।२।।

tasya śiṣyo munivaraḥ sāmkṛtirnāma bhaktimān
papraccha gurumekānte prāñjalirvinayānvitaḥ (2)

Anvay

tasya: his; *bhaktimān*: devoted; *śiṣyaḥ*: disciple; *sāmkṛtiḥ*: sāmkriti; *nāma*: by name; *munivara*ḥ: best of ascetics; *papraccha*: asked; *guru*: spiritual teacher; *ekānte*: in solitude; *vinayānvitaḥ*: respectfully; *prāñjaliḥ*: his hands folded together in humility.

Translation

His devoted disciple, Sāmkṛti by name, who is the best of ascetics, asked his guru, in solitude, respectfully, his hands folded together in humility.

Commentary

This verse sets the background for the teaching given in this upanishad. The worthy disciple, Sāmkṛti, approaches the illumined master of yoga. The qualities that determine the worthiness of a disciple are herein enumerated: (i) he is devoted, (ii) he is ascetic, (iii) he approaches in solitude, (iv) he is respectful, and (v) he is humble. These are the necessary qualities for the spiritual seeker, who wishes to receive the highest teachings in yoga.

The first requisite is devotion, which is very difficult to find in most students of yoga today. Devotion means firm faith in, dedication to and love of higher consciousness. People may love the relations, things and places of the world, but they do not love the transcendent and luminous existence. Secondly, the ideal student should be ascetic by nature. This means that he or she is able to live simply, able to endure hardships, and does not have many requirements. The need for many things disturbs the mind and makes it unsuited to receive the higher teachings.

Thirdly, solitude is the main requisite for sādhana. This means that the worthy disciple approaches the master alone. He or she does not need to be surrounded and supported by a bevy of friends and relations. Fourthly, respect is an essential spiritual quality. In the absence of respect the subtle channel, which connects the teacher and the student, remains firmly closed. If this is the case, there can be no true teaching and no worthy recipient. Fifthly, humility is a necessary requisite, because it is the sign of one who has some mastery over the all powerful ego. When ego is dominant, the teachings will fall on deaf ears.

Verse 3: The disciple's request

भगवन्ब्रूहि मे योगं साष्टाङ्गं सप्रपञ्चकम् ।
येन विज्ञानमात्रेण जीवन्मुक्तो भवाम्यहम् ।।३।।

bhagavanbrūhi me yogaṃ sāṣṭāṅgaṃ saprapancakam
yena vijñānamātreṇa jīvanmukto bhavāmyaham (3)

Anvay
bhagavan: o Lord; *brūhi*: describe; *me*: me; *prapancakam*: in detail; *aṣṭāṅgam yogam*: eight-limbed *yoga*; *yena vijñānamātreṇa*: with this knowledge; *aham bhavāmi*: I shall become; *jīvanmuktaḥ*: *jīvanmukta*, liberated while living and embodied.

Translation
O Lord, describe to me in detail the eight-limbed yoga. With this knowledge, I shall become a *jivanmukta*.

Commentary
The ideal disciple approaches Lord Dattātreya, the illumined master, and asks him for the gift of yoga. Sāmkṛti, being a worthy aspirant, as the previous verse ascertains, requests a complete description of aṣṭāṅga yoga, the kingly yoga, also known as rāja yoga. This yoga is an integral and total science in itself, which includes eight limbs, encompassing all the stages and states of yoga. In times of old, this yoga was held in highest regard. Most aspirants were considered to be unfit for this teaching, and so it was kept secret. It could only be given to an aspirant, who showed signs of unusual intelligence and merit. Samkriti, being a such a disciple, requests this knowledge, so that he may become a *jivanmukta*, one who is liberated, even while living.

Verses 4 and 5: The eight limbs of yoga

सांकृते शृणु वक्ष्यामि योगं साष्टाङ्गदर्शनम् ।

अष्टङ्गोद्देशः

यमश्च नियमश्चैव तथैवासनमेव च ।।४।।

प्राणायामस्तथा ब्रह्मन्प्रत्याहारस्ततः ।

धारणा च तथा ध्यानं समाधिश्चाष्टमं मुने ।।५।।

sāmkṛte śṛṇu vakṣyāmi yogaṃ sāṣṭāṅgadarśanam
aṣṭaṅgoddeśaḥ
yamaśca niyamaścaiva tathaivāsanameva ca (4)
prāṇāyāmastathā brahmanpratyāhārastataḥ param
dhāraṇā ca tathā dhyānaṃ samādhiścāṣṭamaṃ mune (5)

Anvay

śṛṇu: listen; *sāmkṛte*: Sāmkriti; *vakṣyāmi*: I will explain; *darśanam*: system; *aṣṭa-aṅga yogam*: eight-limbed *yoga*; *aṣṭaṅga-uddeśaḥ*: Account of the Eight-Limbs; *yama*: self-restraints, rules of conduct; *ca*: and; *niyama*: personal discipline; *tathā*: then; *āsana*: steady meditative posture; *prāṇāyāma*: expansion of vital energy by means of the breath; *brahman pratyāhāra*: withdrawal of the senses; *param dhāraṇā*: complete *dhāraṇā*, concentration; *dhyānam*: meditation; *samādhi*: union with pure consciousness; *aṣṭamam*: eighth; *mune*: o Sage.

Translation

Listen, Sāmkriti, I will explain the system of the eight-limbed yoga. (Here follows) the account of the eight limbs: *Yama* and *niyama* and then *āsana* and *prāṇāyāma*, then *pratyāhāra*, then complete *dharana*, and then *dhyanam,* and *samadhi* is the eighth, oh Sage.

Commentary

Lord Dattātreya acknowledges Sāmkriti, who is also a sage in his own right, and begins by enumerating the eight limbs of yoga: (i) *yama*, external observances, (ii) *niyama*, internal disciplines, (iii) *āsana*, postures, (iv) *prāṇāyāma*, breath control, (v) *pratyāhāra*, introversion of the senses, (vi) *dhāraṇā*, concentration, (vii) *dhyāna*, meditation, and (viii) *samādhi*, transcendental consciousness.

Verse 6: The ten yamas, or yogic disciplines

दशविद्यमः
अहिंसा सत्यमस्तेयं ब्रह्मचर्यं दयार्जवम् ।
क्षमा धृतिर्मिताहारः शौचं वेति यमा दश ॥६॥

daśavidyamaḥ
ahimsā satyamasteyaṃ brahmacharyaṃ dayārjavam
kṣamā dhṛtirmitāhāraḥ śaucaṃ veti yamā daśa (6)

Anvay
vid: knowledge of; *daśa yamaḥ*: ten *yamas*; *ahimsā*: non-violence in thought and action; *satyam*: truth; *asteyam*: honesty; *brahmacaryam*: continence, diversion of energy from the senses to the higher consciousness; *dayā*: compassion; *arjavam*: straightforwardness; *kṣamā*: patience; *dhṛti*: equanimity; *mitāhāra*: balanced moderate diet; *śaucam*: cleanliness of body and mind; *veti*: are; *daśa*: ten; *yamāḥ*: *yamas.*

Translation
Knowledge of the ten yamas; *ahimsā*, *satyam*, *asteyam*, *brahmacaryam*, *dayā*, *arjavam*, *kṣamā*, *dhṛti*, *mitāhāra*, *śauca* are the ten *yamas*.

Commentary
This verse enumerates the ten yamas, or external disciplines, which formed the first limb of ashtanga yoga, at the time when this teaching was given. Other yoga systems and classical texts may advocate a different number of yamas. For example, the *Raja Yoga Sutras* of Patanjali, describe five yamas: (i) *ahimsā*, non-violence, (ii) *satya*, truthfulness in speech, (iii) *asteya*, honesty in action, (iv) *brahmacarya*, abstinence or moderation in sexual conduct, and (v) *aparigraha*, non-possessiveness.

The practice of yama is considered to be an important requisite for the higher stages of meditation, because it removes mental disturbance and dissipation, caused by negative interactions within the world. In order to progress in meditation, the mind must be free from these impurities and at peace within itself. The ten yamas recommended here are: (i) *ahiṃsā*, non-violence, (ii) *satya*, truthfulness in speech, (iii) *asteya*, honesty in action, (iv) *brahmacarya*, abstinence or moderation in sexual conduct, (v) *daya*, kindness or compassion, (vi) *arjava*, straightforwardness, (vii) kṣamā, patience, (viii) *dhṛti*, equanimity, (ix) *mitāhāra*, moderate and balanced diet, and (x) *śauca*, cleanliness of body and mind.

Verses 7 and 8: Ahiṃsā, non-violence

अहिंसा

वेदोक्तेन प्रकारेण विना सत्यं तपोधन ।

कायेन मनसा वाचा हिंसा हिंसा न चान्यथा ।।७।।

आत्मा सर्वगतो ऽच्छेद्यो न ग्राह्य इति या मतिः ।

मा चाहिंसा वरा प्रोक्ता मुने वेदान्तवेदिभिः ।।८।।

ahiṃsā
vedoktena prakāreṇa vinā satyaṃ tapodhana
kāyena manasā vācā hiṃsā hiṃsā na cānyathā (7)
ātmā sarvagato 'cchedyo na grāhya iti yā matiḥ
mā cāhiṃsā varā proktā mune vedāntavedibhiḥ (8)

Anvay
vinā: except; *prakāreṇa*: in the manner; *uktena*: declared; *veda*: in the Vedas; *tapodhana*: o austere one; *satyam*: truly; *na hiṃsā hiṃsā*: no violence at all; *kāyena*: in the body; *manasā*: in the mind; *vācā*: in speech; *ca*: and; *anyathā*: any other way; *ātmā*: *ātmā*, supreme spirit; *sarvagataḥ*: all-pervading; *acchedyaḥ*: indivisible; *na grāhya*: imperceptible; *mune*: o Sage; *yā matiḥ*: this authority; *proktā*: is stated; *vedānta-vedibhiḥ*: by those who know *vedānta*; *varā mā*: best authority; *ahimsā*: on *ahimsā,* non-violence.

Translation
Non-violence: Except in the manner declared in the Vedas, oh austere one, [there should] truly [be] no violence at all in body, speech and mind, or any other way. The *ātma* [is] all-pervading, indivisible [and] imperceptible. O Sage, this understanding is stated by those who know *vedānta*, [which is] the best authority on *ahimsā.*

Commentary
Ahiṃsā, non-violence, is given as the first of the ten yamas, which shows its significance. All religious and spiritual

teachings uphold the importance of non-violence. Violence of any kind is to be eschewed by a sincere aspirant, whether in thought, speech or action, because it disturbs the mind and makes any practice of yoga or meditation impossible. Violence relates and gives rise to many negative emotions, such as anger, fear, hatred and revenge. These emotions are so powerful that they may even outlive a person, and be carried on through the family line. Violence is a very powerful karma, which is very difficult to eradicate. One act of violence gives rise to another and another, and then the same act returns to harm the doer, sparking off further acts of violence.

For these reasons, ahiṃsā, or non-violence, is the first yama, upon which all the other yamas are based. As long as there is violence in a person's nature, the other yamas will not be established. In the absence of yama, the higher stages of aṣṭāṅga yoga cannot be attained. This verse states that there should 'truly' be no acts of violence at all, whether through body, speech or mind, or in any other way. For example, one may justify acts of violence, considering them to be necessary or right for the overall good. Or one may perpetrate violence through the agency of another, thinking one's own slate to be clean. In whatever way violence is committed, the karma of such acts will surround one like a haze of black smoke.

This haze is very difficult to purify and remove. We have all read the story of Milarepa, the great yogi from Tibet. His guru, Marpa, put him through long years of suffering and humiliation just to purify him of the violence he had done in his earlier life. Because, as long as that negative karma remained, Milarepa could neither receive nor practice the higher teachings, which related with the pure nature of consciousness. Milarepa was fortunate to have had such a great guru as Marpa, who patiently, year after year, caused him such suffering that his negative karma was completely expunged. When Milarepa was finally freed from the karma of violence, he entered *samādhi*, the transcendental state, and remained established in this state for the rest of his life.

The above verse also states that the *ātma*, the pure self, soul or spirit, residing within each person, is all-pervading, imperceptible and indivisible. The ultimate purpose of yoga is to unite with the ātma, even while living in the physical body. The word *yoga* itself is actually defined as this 'union'. Ahiṃsā, non-violence, is therefore, the first prerequisite of yoga. This is stated by those who know *vedanta*, the highest philosophy of the vedas, which is considered to be the best authority on ahimsa.

Verses 9 and 10: Satyam, truth

सत्यम्

चक्षुरादीन्द्रियैर्दृष्टं श्रुतं घ्रातं मुनीश्वर ।

तस्यैवोक्तिर्भवेत्सत्यं विप्र तन्नान्यथा भवेत् ।।९।।

सर्वं सत्यं परं ब्रह्म न चान्यदिति या मतिः ।

तञ्च सत्यं परं प्रोक्तं वेदान्तज्ञानपारगैः ।।१०।।

satyam
cakṣurādīndriyairdṛṣṭaṃ śrutaṃ ghrātaṃ munīśvara
tasyaivoktirbhavetsatyaṃ vipra tannānyathā bhavet (9)
sarvaṃ satyaṃ paraṃ brahma na cānyaditi yā matiḥ
tanca satyaṃ paraṃ proktaṃ vedāntajñānapāragaiḥ (10)

Anvay
munīśvara: o great Sage; *dṛṣṭaṃ*: [that which is] seen; *śrutam*: heard; *ghrātam*: smelt; *indriyaiḥ*: through the sense organs; *cakṣuḥ*: of the eyes; *ādi*: etc; *uktiḥ bhavet*: is said to be; *satyam*: *satyam*, truth; *vipra*: *Brahman*; *bhavet*: is; *na anyathā*: no different from; *tat*: that; *param satyam*: highest truth; *brahma*: *Brahman*, omnipresent principle of existence; *sarvam*: everywhere; *ca*: and; *na anyat*: not elsewhere; *yā matiḥ*: this understanding; *tanca*: leads to; *param satyam*: highest truth; *proktam*: as declared; *vedānta-jñāna-pāragaiḥ*: by those who have absorbed the wisdom of *vedānta.*

Translation
Truth: O great Sage, that which is seen, heard and smelt through the sense organs of the eyes etc is said to be *satyam,* as *Brahman* is no different from that. The highest truth is that *Brahman* is everywhere and not elsewhere. This understanding leads to the highest truth as declared by those who have absorbed the wisdom of *Vedānta*.

Commentary
Satyam, truth, is the second yama, described here to the sage, Sāmkṛti. That which is perceived by the senses, i.e., seen through the eyes, heard through the ears, tasted by the tongue, and so on, is said to be true. One can know that it is true by one's own cognition. In the same way, *Brahman,* the ever-expanding and luminous consciousness, is the ultimate truth, and this can be known through experience by one's inner awareness. The ultimate truth is that Brahman, the universal consciousness, is all-pervading; it is the substratum of existence, which pervades everything everywhere. Because Brahman is everywhere, it cannot be elsewhere; it cannot be in one place, but not in another. The understanding of the nature of Brahman leads to the highest truth, satyam. This has been declared by those learned ones, who have imbibed the wisdom of vedanta, the highest knowledge of the vedas.

Verses 11 and 12: Asteya, honesty

अस्तेयम्

अन्यदीये तृणे रत्ने कानञ्चने मौक्तिके ऽपि च ।

मनसा विनिवृत्तिर्या तदस्तेयं विदुर्बुधाः ।।११।।

आत्मन्यनात्मभावेन व्यवहारविवर्जितम् ।

यत्तदस्तेयमित्युक्तमात्मविद्भिर्महा मुने ।।१२।।

asteyam
anyadīye tṛṇe ratne kāñcane mauktike 'pi ca
manasā vinivṛttiryā tadasteyaṃ vidurbudhāḥ (11)
ātmanyanātmabhāvena vyavahāravivarjitam
yattadasteyamityuktamātmavidbhirmahā mune (12)

Anvay
manasā: mind; *vinivṛttiḥ*: is free of thoughts of; *ratne*: wealth; *anyadīye*: belonging to others; *tṛṇe*: sacrificial grass; *kāñcane*: gold; *ca*: and; *api*: also; *mauktike*: pearls; *yā budhāḥ*: these wise ones; *viduḥ*: know; *tad*: this; *asteyam*: *asteyam*, honesty; *mahā mune*: o Great Sage; *yat*: those; *vidbhiḥ*: who know; *ātma*: *ātma*, supreme spirit; *iti*: say; *bhavena*: by being; *ātmani*: in the *ātma*; *vivarjitam*: avoiding; *vyavahāra*: action; *anātma*: egoic self; *tad uktam*: this is said; *asteyam*: honesty.

Translation
Honesty: [When] the mind is free of thoughts of wealth, belonging to others, [such as] sacrificial grass, gold and pearls, the wise ones know this to be *asteyam*. O Great Sage, those who know the *ātma,* say that by being in the *ātma* [and] avoiding action, which arises from the ego, or lower self, this is said to be *asteyam.*

Commentary
Asteya, meaning honesty in ourself, in our life, and in our dealings with others, is the third yama. It is easy to be honest,

when the mind is free from desire for wealth and objects, which others may enjoy. But this is not the case for most people, including yoga aspirants. Generally, we are happy until we see that others possess more money or better things, than we do. Upon considering this lack, the mind becomes dissatisfied, and begins to plan, scheme and dream about how to acquire the desirable objects. In this verse, the objects that were valued by the people of old are enumerated, such as: sacrificial grass, gold and pearls. Sacrificial grass was valuable, because it was often used in vedic rituals. Gold and pearls were the main form of wealth in the early days, when coin and paper currency were unavailable.

A wise person would understand that desire for wealth and possessions has a very disturbing effect on the mind. In order to keep such thoughts at bay, he would therefore restrain the mind, and practice honesty in all dealings. This honesty was called asteya, and it is an essential quality for an aspirant of ashtanga yoga. The Bible also states that it is easier for a camel to pass through the eye of a needle, than for a dishonest man to pass through the gates of heaven.

In the above verse it further states that those who have realised the *ātma*, the higher self, which is pure consciousness, have said that asteya is achieved by establishing oneself in the ātma, and avoiding all thoughts and actions, which relate with the lower or ego self, which is known as *anātma*.

Verses 13 and 14a: Brahmacarya, abstinence

ब्रह्मचर्यम्

कायेन वाचा मनसा स्त्रीणं परिविवर्जनम् ।

ऋतौ भार्यां तदा स्वस्य ब्रह्मचर्यं तदुच्यते ।।१३।।

ब्रह्मभावे मनश्चागं ब्रह्मचर्यं परंतप ।१४।

brahmacaryam
kāyena vācā manasā strīṇaṃ parivivarjanam
ṛtau bhāryāṃ tadā svasya brahmacaryaṃ taducyate (13)
brahmabhāve manaścāgaṃ brahmacaryaṃ paraṃtapa (14a)

Anvay
parivivarjanam: avoiding; *strīṇam*: women; *kāyena vācā manasā*: in body, speech [and] mind; *svasya*: his own; *bhāryām*: wife; *ṛtau*: during her periods; *tadā*: then; *tad*: this; *ucyate*: is called; *brahmacaryam*: continence; *paramtapa*: o Supreme Ascetic; *manaḥ*: mind; *āgam*: attains; *brahmacaryam*: continence; *brahma-bhāve*: when absorbed in the Absolute.

Translation
Abstinence: Avoiding women in body, speech [and] mind, [and] his own wife during her periods, then this is called *brahmacarya*. O Supreme Ascetic, the mind attains *brahmacarya*, when absorbed in the Absolute.

Commentary
Brahmacarya, abstaining from improper sexual conduct, is the fourth yama. This is an important restraint for yogis, and was often understood as total abstinence of sexual interaction. This verse recommends that one should avoid contact with women in general, whether through body, speech or mind. However, one's own wife should only be avoided, when she is in her monthly courses. So, brahmacarya relates with moderate and ethical sexual

behavior, rather than total abstinence. In times of old, sexual relations and producing of progeny were duties incumbent on every husband and wife. And nearly every man and woman was obliged to marry from an early age. Total restraint was only considered appropriate for a renunciate, or *sannyasi*, who would have no wife.

The word brahmacarya has two roots: *brahma,* 'the ever-expanding luminous consciousness', and *acara-* 'to roam'. Hence, the term brahmacarya implies one who roams freely in the absolute consciousness. The verse also states that the mind achieves brahmacarya, when it is absorbed in the absolute consciousness. We generally associate the highest consciousness with the crown of the head; whereas the sexual act is triggered by the nether regions between the legs. Thus, the yogi who practices moderation and restraint in regard to sexual conduct is able to remain absorbed in the absolute consciousness. Otherwise, the awareness is drawn to the lower regions by involvement with the opposite sex.

Verses 14b and 15a: Dayā, kindness

दया

स्वात्मवत्सर्वभूतेषु कायेन मनसा गिरा ।।१४।।

अनुज्ञा या दया सैव प्रोक्ता वेदान्तवेदिभिः ।१५।

dayā

svātmavatsarvabhūteṣu kāyena manasā girā (14b)

anujñā yā dayā saiva proktā vedāntavedibhiḥ (15a)

Anvay

anujñā: kindness; *sarva-bhūteṣu*: towards all creatures; *kāyena manasā girā*: in body, thought [and] speech; *svātmavat*: towards oneself; *yā*: this; *eva*: indeed; *proktā*: is called; *dayā*: *dayā*, compassion; *saḥ*: the one; *vedānta-vedibhiḥ*: who knows *vedānta.*

Translation

Kindness towards all creatures in body, thought and speech, [as if] towards oneself, this is indeed called compassion by the one who knows *vedānta*.

Commentary

Dayā, compassion, is the fifth yama. In a world of escalating greed and contention, acts of kindness become more and more rare. Here, however, kindness is not just an isolated action, but a quality or nature, which can be developed through yogic practice and purification. Kindness is an attribute of *sattwa guṇa*, the balanced or pure quality of nature. Until we develop this quality in our life, acts of kindness will always alternate with acts of selfishness and subversion, which are the expressions of rajas and tamas guṇas.

It is normal for the three guṇas to express themselves in life. This is why the forces of darkness often overcome the force of light. The yogi is a person who strives to live in the light, as far as possible. One method for achieving this is to be kind and merciful to all beings. In this sense, kindness becomes a way of life, a way of thinking, speaking, and acting with awareness and sensitivity towards oneself and others. We should always treat others, as we ourselves would wish to be treated. Such kindness is called dayā, or compassion, by the saints and teachers of all spiritual traditions and religions, including vedānta.

Verses 15b and 16a: ārjavam, straight-forwardness

आर्जवम्

पुत्रे मित्रे कलत्रे च रिपौ स्वात्मनि संततम् ।।१५।।

एकरूपं मुने यत्तदार्जवं प्रोच्यते मया ।१६।

ārjavam

putre mitre kalatre ca ripau svātmani saṃtatam (15b)

ekarūpaṃ mune yattadārjavaṃ procyate mayā (16a)

Anvay

ārjavam: straight-forwardness; *mune*: o Sage; *samtatam*: continuously; *ekarūpam*: one form; *yattad*: whatsoever; *svātmani*: in oneself; *putre*: son; *mitre*: friend; *kalatre*: wife; *ca*: and; *ripau*: enemy; *procyate*: is proclaimed; *ārjavam*: straight-forwardness; *mayā*: by me.

Translation

Straight-forwardness: O Sage, continuously [viewing] the one form whatsoever in oneself, (in one's) son, friend, wife and enemy, is proclaimed by me as *ārjavam*.

Commentary

Arjavam means to be straight forward with oneself, and with all of one's associations and dealings in life. A straight person is able to see and accept things as they are, rather than as they could or should be. In thinking about how things could be, the mind becomes overworked and bent. There is often a very thin line between cleverness and crookedness. To be straight forward is an important requisite for the higher practices of yoga, because it enables one to remain in alignment with truth. Ultimately, truth relates with the one underlying substratum of existence, which we are all a part of. One who makes a habit of cleverness and deceit, will be unable to recognise this truth, whether in the relative or absolute sense.

The clever mind can never accept or rest in one view or one truth. It seeks to explore and adjust all the possible paths in order to find the best for its own purposes. In this pursuit, the mind deviates from the one and becomes lost in the many. For a person, who is not straight forward by nature, it is necessary to develop this quality by recognising the one truth and the tendency of the mind to deviate from it in thought, speech and behaviour. The above verse describes straight forwardness as the ability to perceive the one underlying form continuously in oneself, as well as in all of one's associations, i.e., one's children, friends, husband or wife, and even in one's enemies. In the absence of this quality, the mind becomes bent, and is not qualified to attain the highest yoga.

Verses 16b and 17a: Kṣamā, patience

क्षमा

कायेन मनसा वाचा शत्रुभिः परिपीडिते ।।१६।।

बुद्धिक्षोभनिवृत्तिर्या क्षमा सा मुनिपुङ्गव ।१७।

kṣamā

kāyena manasā vācā śatrubhiḥ paripīḍite (16b)
buddhikṣobhanivṛttiryā kṣamā sā munipuṅgava (17a)

Anvay

kṣamā: patience; *paripīḍite*: one is tormented; *kāyena*: in body; *manasā*: thought; *vācā*: speech; *śatrubhiḥ*: by enemies; *nivrittiḥ*: is free from; *kṣoba*: agitation; *buddhi*: in the mind; *sā*: that; *kṣamā*: patience; *munipungava*: o Eminent Sage.

Translation

Patience: [When] one is tormented in body, thought and speech by enemies, and is free from agitation in the mind, that [is] *kṣamā*, o Eminent Sage.

Commentary

Patience is a quality which was reflected more often in people of earlier times. Nowadays, we rarely find this quality in ourselves or in others around us. The fast pace, expectations and choices available in our modern lifestyle cause over-stimulation, stress and tension from an early age. Patience weakens under this constant onslaught. When we are constantly hurried and worried about the next meeting, activity or acquisition, impatience becomes our natural and immediate response. We cannot wait calmly for the outcome of one action before beginning the next.

Patience can only develop in a person, who is able to wait and remain calm, even in the midst of difficult and demanding situations. A person who is able to remain calm and accept how things unfold, without losing patience, is in control of the mind and senses. As soon as one becomes impatient, irritation sets in. At this moment, one loses control over the speech and mind, and begins to react in ways, which are often detrimental to oneself, and to others as well. Patience is the ability to maintain a calm, cool approach, regardless of what one may hope or expect. In this sense, patience is a yogic quality, which allows one to live in harmony with the present moment, and to deal with what may arise in the best and most appropriate manner.

The above verse refers to the degree of patience required in an intense situation, where one may be faced with enemies or imminent danger. At such moments, there will be an immediate response or reaction, which may be inappropriate or even harmful. We often react before thinking or realising what we are saying or doing, and whether or not it will be beneficial. A person who is able to remain patient, even in extreme situations, has understood this reactive nature, and learned to manage it physically, mentally and verbally. Such a person becomes fit for the higher practices of yoga, because he or she is able to live yoga and apply the attitude of yoga in daily life.

Patience is also very necessary for the serious practitioner, who undertakes a regular yoga practice, or sadhana. A person who is impatient in daily life, will definitely become impatient with his or her sadhana, and begin to doubt its efficacy. This is a great block in one's progress, because yoga unfolds in its own time. The practitioner, who becomes impatient, will be unable to continue the practice with a calm and steady mind. Hence the efforts made will ultimately yield no result. In this sense, the quality of patience is like a rock in the midst of a vast and fast flowing river. It allows the practitioner to take hold and remain steady and still, even though the water of life is flowing past all around at a very rapid rate.

Verses 17b and 18: Dhṛti, equanimity

धृतिः
वेदादेव विनिर्मोक्षः संसारस्य न चान्यथा ।।१७।।
इति विज्ञाननिष्पत्तिर्धृतिः प्रोकता हि वैदिकैः ।
अहमात्मा न चान्यो ऽस्मीत्येवमप्रच्युता मतिः ।।१८।।

dhṛtiḥ
vedādeva vinirmokṣaḥ saṃsārasya na cānyathā
iti vijñānaniṣpattirdhṛtiḥ proktā hi vaidikaiḥ (17b)
ahamātmā na cānyo 'smītyevamapracyutā matiḥ (18)

Anvay
iti: it is said; *vinirmokṣaḥ*: total liberation; *saṃsārasya*: from the cycle of birth, death and rebirth; *eva*: indeed; *vedāt*: through the Vedas; *ca na anyathā*: and not otherwise; *dhṛti*: equanimity; *proktā*: is said to be; *niṣpattih*: outcome; *vijñāna*: understanding; *vaidikaiḥ*: by those versed in the Vedas; *aham . . . asmi*: I am; *ātmā*: Self; *ca na anyaḥ*: and nothing else; *iti*: says he; *matiḥ*: whose faith; *apracyutā*: steadfast.

Translation
Equanimity: It is said that total liberation from the cycle of birth, death and rebirth comes indeed through the vedas, and not otherwise. Equanimity is said to be the outcome of this understanding, by those versed in the vedas. 'I am *ātman* and nothing else', says he, whose faith [is] steadfast.

Commentary
Mokṣa, or liberation, is the ultimate goal of human evolution and it is spoken of in all the classical texts of yoga, as well as the upanishads, vedas and tantras. Liberation means total freedom from all worldly associations and identifications, which form bondage, and prevent us from remembering and realising our absolute inner nature, which is pure consciousness, *ātman* or the self. As soon as we are born, our

awareness shifts from a totality of consciousness to an individual consciousness that is limited by body, mind and world. This shift of awareness from unlimited to limited, from truth to untruth, is the basic cause of bondage. Henceforth, we strengthen these bonds that limit us by continual identification and involvement in a limited world of name and form, and by believing in the permanent nature of its transient existence.

Those who study the philosophy of the vedas and upaniṣads, understand that the nature of pure consciousness is unbound and unlimited, because it is free from all worldly associations. It has no name or form. It is vast and vacuous, like the sky, without any beginning or end. The ancients experienced this pure consciousness and called it atman, the self. In relation to the universe and all existence, whether manifest or unmanifest, they called this *Brahman*, the ever expanding and illuminated consciousness. According to the teachings of yoga and the philosophy of the vedas, "I am atma/brahma"; this is the ultimate truth. When this truth is realised, we are liberated from the cycle of birth, death and rebirth, because the bonds, which hold us into this cycle, are rent asunder.

In the absence of this teaching and realisation, liberation cannot take place. The vedas and upanishads provide us with the teaching, but the practices of yoga are essential to give us the actual realisation or experience of this state, called mokṣa, or liberation.

Equanimity, the ability to maintain a calm and balanced state of mind, even in the midst of turbulence all around, is said here to be the outcome of this understanding, which is attained by those who study the vedas, and who also practice yoga. Intellectual understanding must be augmented by experiential realisation for total liberation to occur. A momentary liberation may take place at different times in our lives. But total liberation requires steadfast faith in the existence of the absolute consciousness. This faith is not born of intellect, but of experience. A person may hear about a foreign land, and read all about that land. But he will only know that place by going there himself and living there for some time. In the same way, study of the vedas must also be combined with the practice of yoga in order to have the experience of "I am ātman and nothing else."

Verse 19: Mitāhāra, moderate diet

मिताहारः

अल्पभृष्टाशनाभ्यां च चतुर्थांशा वशेषकम् ।

तस्माद्योगानुगुण्येन भोजनं मितभोजनम् ।।१९।।

mitāhāraḥ

alpabhṛṣṭāśanābhyāṃ ca caturthāṃśāvaśeṣakam

tasmādyogānuguṇyena bhojanaṃ mitabhojanam (19)

Anvay

mitāhāraḥ: balanced, moderate diet; *alpa-bhṛṣṭa-aśanām*: little, fried food; *ca*: and; *caturāṃśa*: one fourth; *aṣakam*: relatively; *avaśa*: empty; *tasmāt*: thus; *anuguṇyena*: suitable; *yoga*: yogic; *mitabhojanam*: diet.

Translation

Moderate diet: A balanced, moderate diet has little fried food and one fourth [of the stomach] relatively empty. [This is] thus a suitable yogic diet.

Commentary

Moderation in food is an important requisite of yoga. In the *Bhagavad Gita*, Sri Krishna states that the yogi should neither eat too much or too little. In yoga, balanced diet and practices are like the two wings of a bird. Just as a bird cannot fly on one wing only, a yogic practitioner cannot progress to spiritual heights by performing the practices alone. While the yoga practices may benefit those, who are unable to observe moderation in diet, their subtle effects will only be experienced by those, who follow a balanced diet regularly. The types of food recommended for yogic practitioners belong to the sattwic category, which includes fruits, vegetables, whole grains, and nuts and legumes. Dairy products were also recommended for yogis, because in ancient times the people kept their own cows and tended them with great care. The milk products produced by these cows were pure and free from harmful chemicals and residues.

The main criteria for yogic diet is that the food consumed should be easily and quickly digested. This is because a yogi needs more time for practice, and the stomach needs to be empty during these periods for optimum results. This verse, therefore, mentions that a yogic diet should have very little fried food, because food fried at high temperatures becomes dry, denatured and difficult to digest. The verse also mentions that the stomach should only be three fourths full after a meal, leaving one fourth empty, so that the digestion process is facilitated.

Mitahara, moderate diet, is a great discipline that requires vigilance and discrimination. The yogi who observes mitahara on a regular basis, over years, will be free from disease and discomfort. He or she will be able to delve deeply into the practices of yoga without experiencing imbalance, obstruction or negative effects.

Verses 20, 21, 22 and 23a: Śauca, cleanliness

शौचम्

स्वदेहमलनिर्मोक्षो मृज्जलाभ्यां महामुने ।

यत्तच्छौचं भवेद्बाह्यं मानसं मननं विदुः ।।२०।।

अहं शुद्ध इति ज्ञानं शौचबाहुर्मनीषिणः ।

अत्यन्तमलिनो देहो देही चात्यन्तनिर्मलः ।।२१।।

उभयोरन्तरं ज्ञात्वा कस्य शौचं विधीयते ।

ज्ञानशौचं परित्यज्य बाह्ये यो रमते नारः ।।२२।।

स मुढः काञ्चनं त्यक्त्वा लोष्टं गृह्णाति सुव्रत ।२३।

śaucam
svadehamalanirmokṣo mṛjjalābhyāṃ mahāmune
yattacchaucaṃ bhavedbāhyaṃ mānasaṃ mananaṃ viduḥ (20)
ahaṃ śuddha iti jñānaṃ śaucabāhurmanīṣinaḥ
atyantamalino deho dehī cātyantanirmalaḥ (21)
ubhayorantaraṃjñātvā kasya śaucaṃ vidhīyate
jñānaśaucaṃ partiyajya bāhye yo ramate naraḥ (22)
sa muḍhaḥ kāñcanaṃ tyaktvā loṣṭaṃ gṛhṇāti suvrata (23a)

Anvay
mahāmune: o Great Sage; *nirmokshaḥ*: removing; *mala*: dirt; *svadeha*: from one's body; *mṛj*: cleaning; *jalābhyām*: with water; *bāhyam*: external; *śaucam*: cleanliness; *viduḥ*: knowing; *mānasam*: mind; *mananam*: through reflection; *aham*: I am; *śuddha*: pure; *jñānam*: wisdom; *śauca*: *śaucam*, purity; *bāhuḥ-manīṣinaḥ*: of the very wise; *dehaḥ*: body; *atyanta*: completely; *malinaḥ*: impure; *ca*: and; *dehī*: embodied Self; *atyanta*: completely; *nirmalaḥ*: pure; *jñātvā*: to one who knows; *ubhayorantaram*: difference; *kasya śaucam*: which *śaucam*; *vidhīyate*: is prescribed; *suvrata*: o Virtuous One; *parityajya*: having abandoned; *jñāna-śaucam*: purification through meditation; *naraḥ*: man; *yaḥ*: who;

ramate: delights; *bāhye*: in the external; *muḍhaḥ*: fool; *saḥ gṛhṇāti*: who picks up; *loṣṭam*: lump of earth; *tyaktvā*: ignoring; *kāñcanam*: gold.

Translation
Cleanliness: O Great Sage, removing dirt from one's body and cleaning it with water is external cleanliness. Knowing the mind through reflection: 'I am pure', this wisdom is *śaucam* of the very wise. The body is completely impure, and the embodied Self [is] completely pure. To one who knows the difference, which *śaucam* is prescribed? O Virtuous One, having abandoned purification through meditation, the man who delights in the external [is] a fool, who picks up a lump of earth, ignoring the gold.

Commentary
Cleanliness is an important requisite of yoga. In fact, it is the first of the *niyamas*, or internal disciplines, recommended in rāja yoga by the sage Patanjali. It is also said that cleanliness is close to godliness. This verse clarifies that cleanliness may be external or internal. Most people bathe the physical body daily with water, which achieves external cleanliness. However, the yogi who regularly reflects on the mind, realises the inner purity of the self. The understanding that my inner self, my consciousness, is inherently pure results in internal cleanliness. This realisation that I am innately pure is the cleanliness of the wise yogis.

The nature of the physical body will always be impure, because of its elemental constitution and associations with the world, but the inner self, the consciousness, remains absolutely pristine and pure. So, the question is asked in regard to the yogi, who is able to discriminate between the outer body and the inner self, which form of cleanliness should be practised? The reply given here is the yogi, who takes pleasure in the external body and its experiences, abandoning meditation on the internal purity of the self, is a fool, who picks up a lump of earth and ignores the gold.

Verses 23b, 24 and 25: The way to know supreme consciousness

ब्रह्मात्मवेदनविधिः

ज्ञानामृतेन तृप्तस्य कृतकृत्यस्य योगिनः ।।२३।।

न चास्ति किंचित्कर्तव्यमस्ति वेन्न स तत्त्ववित् ।

लोकत्रये ऽपि कर्तव्यं किंचिन्नास्त्यात्मवेदिनाम् ।।२४।।

तस्मात्सर्वप्रयत्नेन मुने ऽहिंसादिसाधनैः ।

आत्मानमक्षरं ब्रह्म विद्धि ज्ञानात्तु वेदनात् ।।२५।।

brahmātmavedanavidhiḥ

jñānāmṛtena tṛptasya kṛtakṛtyasya yoginaḥ (23b)

na cāsti kiṃcitkartavyamasti venna sa tattvavit

lokatraye 'pi kartavyaṃ kiṃcinnāstyātmavedinām (24)

tasmātsarvaprayatnena mune 'hiṃsādisādhanaiḥ

ātmānamakṣaraṃ brahma viddhi jñānāttu vedanāt (25)

Anvay

brahmātmavedanavidhiḥ: way to know the Supreme Consciousness; *tṛiptasya*: satisfied; *amṛtena*: with the nectar; *jñāna*: of meditation; *ca*: and; *kṛta-kṛtyasya*: having fulfilled his duties; *yoginaḥ*: *yogin*, spiritual aspirant; *asti*: has; *na . . kiṃcit*: nothing more; *kartavyam*: to be done; *ven*: longing for; *sa*: he; *na . . asti*: is not; *tattvavit*: knower of *Brahma*; *ātmavedinām*: one who knows the Supreme Spirit; *asti*: there is; *na . . kiṃcit . . api*: nothing more; *kartavyam*: to be done; *lokatraye*: in the three worlds; *tasmāt*: therefore; *mune*: o Sage; *sarva-prayatnena*: with every effort; *ahiṃsā-ādi-sādhanaiḥ*: with *ahiṃsā* and other practices; *viddhi brahma*: know *Brahma*; *ātmānam-akṣaram*: as the imperishable Self; *jñānāt*: through meditation; *vedanāt*: through higher knowledge.

Translation

The way to know the supreme consciousness: Satisfied with the nectar of meditation and having fulfilled his duties, the yogin has nothing more to be done. Longing for something to do, he is not a knower of *Brahma*. For one who knows the supreme spirit, there is nothing more to be done in the three worlds. Therefore, o Sage, with every effort, with *ahiṃsā* and other practices, know *Brahma* as the imperishable self through meditation and higher knowledge.

Commentary

The last requisite given here in this teaching is the understanding of the way to *brahmātma vedana vidhi*, which means 'knowledge of the supreme consciousness'. This knowledge is both individual, atman, and cosmic, brahma. The supreme consciousness is not realised through work or practices, which relate with the mundane world. It is attained through deep meditation. Therefore, the practitioner, who aspires for the highest yoga, should work in the world to fulfil his or her duties and obligations in life, whether pertaining to family, society, or profession. Having achieved this, the yogi can then set aside more time for solitude to enter into the depths of meditation.

By the regular practice of meditation, the mind gradually settles and becomes quiet, in the same way that particles will settle in a glass of water, if the glass is left undisturbed. As the mind quietens, the awareness goes into deeper states of consciousness, where it becomes inundated with nectar, or bliss. Drinking this nectar of meditation, the yogi becomes satisfied, and does not feel the compulsion to go outside and do other things, which cause the senses to externalise and mingle in the affairs of the world. So, it is said that the yogi, who drinks the nectar of meditation, is satisfied and has nothing else to do.

This verse reiterates that the yogi, who still longs for somewhere to go and something to do, has not perfected meditation; he or she is not a knower of brahman, the ever-expanding consciousness. There is nothing more to be done in the three worlds for one who knows the supreme consciousness. Thus, the accomplished sadhaka is advised to make every effort to observe all the requisites of yoga, such as non-violence, truth, honesty, moderation in sexual life and diet, in order to smooth the path for immersion in deep meditation. In this way, the yogi will come to understand and to realise that the cosmic consciousness, brahma, is no different to one's own imperishable self, ātma. I am ātma-brahma.

इति प्रथमः खण्डः

iti prathamaḥ khaṇḍaḥ

Thus [ends] the first section.

द्वितीयः खण्डः

dvitīyaḥ khaṇḍaḥ

Second Section

दशविधनियमः

daśavidhaniyamaḥ

Knowledge of The Ten Niyamas, inner disciplines

Verses 1 and 2a: Ten niyamas

तपः सन्तोषमास्तिक्यं दानमीश्वरपूजनम् ।

सिद्धान्तश्रवणं चैव ह्रीर्मतिश्च जपो व्रतम् ।।१।।

एते च नियमाः प्रोक्तास्तान्वक्ष्यामि क्रमाच्छृणु ।२।

tapaḥ saṃtoṣamāstikyaṃ dānamīśvarapūjanam
siddhāntaśravaṇaṃ caiva hrīrmatiśca japo vratam (1)
ete ca niyamāḥ proktāstānvakṣyāmi kramācchṛṇu (2a)

Anvay

ete: these; *proktāḥ*: are called; *niyamāḥ*: *niyamas*, inner qualities; *śṛṇu*: listen; *vakṣyāmi*: I will describe; *tān*: these; *kramāt*: in order; *tapaḥ*: endurance; *saṃtoṣa*: contentment; *āstikyam*: devotion; *dānam*: giving freely; *īśvara-pūjanam*: worship of a Supreme Reality; *siddhānta-śravaṇam*: listening to the scriptures; *ca eva*: and also; *hrīḥ*: shame, remorse; *matiḥ*: desire for humility; *japaḥ*: repetition of *mantra*; *ca*: and; *vratam*: commitment.

Translation

These are called the *niyamas.* Listen, I will describe these in order: (i) self-discipline, (ii) contentment, (iii) devotion, (iv) giving freely, (v) worship of a supreme reality, (vi) listening to the scriptures, (vii) remorse, and also (viii) desire for humility, (ix) repetition of *mantra,* and (x) commitment.

Commentary

The ten *yamas*, or disciplines of yoga, described in section one of this teaching, comprise the first limb of raja yoga. These disciplines are necessary to manage and curb the outgoing tendencies of the mind and senses, and protect the practitioner from negative associations, which influence and disturb the mind. The ten niyamas, as outlined here in section two, are more internal disciplines, which allow the practitioner to gain control over the senses and manage the mind at a deeper level. These ten qualities are given in the following order: (i) *tapas*, austerity, endurance; (ii) *santosha*, contentment; (iii) *astika*, faith in the highest consciousness; (iv) *dana*, charity, giving to others; (v) *ishwara pooja*, worship of the highest consciousness; (vi) *siddhanta shravana*, listening to the scriptures; (vii) *hree,* remorse or shame; (viii) *mati*, desire for humility; (ix) *japa*, repetition of *mantra,* syllables or words of power; and (x) *vrata*, vow or commitment.

Verses 2b, 3 and 4a: Tapas, austerity

तपः

वेदोक्तेन प्रकारेण कृच्छ्रचान्द्रायणादिभिः ।।२।।

शरिरशोषणं यत्तत्तप इत्युच्यते बुधैः ।

को वा मोक्षः कथं केन संसारं प्रतिपन्नवान् ।।३।।

इत्यालोचनमर्थज्ञास्तपः शंसन्ति पण्डिताः ।४।

tapaḥ
vedoktena prakāreṇa kṛcchracāndrāyaṇādibhiḥ (2b)
śarīraśoṣaṇaṃ yattattapa ityucyate budhaiḥ
ko vā mokṣaḥ kathaṃ kena saṃsāraṃ pratipannavān (3)
ityālocanamarthajñāstapaḥ śaṃsanti paṇḍitāḥ (4a)

Anvay
śarīra-śoṣaṇaṃ: emaciating the body; *prakāreṇa*: in the manner; *vedoktena*: taught in the Vedas; *kṛcchra-cāndrāyaṇa-adibhiḥ*: such as the penances performed according to the moon's course; *iti ucyate*: is called; *tapaḥ*: *tapas*, austerity; *budhaiḥ*: by the wise; *kaḥ mokṣaḥ*: what is *moksha*, liberation; *katham*: how; *kena*: from where; *paṇḍitāḥ*: learned ones; *śaṃsanti*: declare; *arthajñāḥ-tapaḥ*: understanding the sense of *tapas*; *pratipannavān*: is obtained; *ālocanam*: by reflecting on; *samsāram*: cycle of birth and death.

Translation
Austerity: Emaciating the body in the manner taught in the vedas, such as the penances performed, according to the moon's course, is called *tapas*, austerity, by the wise. What is *mokṣa*, liberation? How [and] from where [does it come]? The learned ones declare [that] understanding the sense of *tapas* is obtained by reflecting on the cycle of birth and death.

Commentary

Tapas is the practice of self-induced hardship, austerity or penance. The word *tapas* relates with heat, fire and the process of burning. All impurities are removed by fire. Tapas is performed in order to heat and temper the body and mind, so that they may be purified and capable of withstanding the high powered energy, which arises at the time of spiritual awakening. When wood is burned, it slowly changes into ash, a pure residue. Similarly, when the body of the sadhaka is burned, it becomes thin, emaciated, light and pure.

The verse above mentions emaciating the body in the manner that was taught in the vedas. In vedic times, as in early Christian times, the practice of tapas, penance, was often undertaken in order to remove impurity and weakness, and bring one closer to the light. Different forms of tapas were prescribed in the vedas, but one of the most common methods was fasting. Here, the practice of fasting, according to the phases of the moon, is mentioned as an example. On the full moon day, the yogi would eat and drink no more than 14 mouthfuls. As the moon waned, this amount was reduced by one mouthful per day. So that, by the dark moon day, no food or drink would be taken. Then as the moon waxed, one mouthful would be added each day, until the full moon day was reached. Such practices were called tapas by the wise, and were considered essential to free one from the bondage of worldly attachment.

Freedom from worldly bondage is called *moksha,* liberation. In this verse the question is asked: what is moksha; how and where does it come from? Because most people, living in the world, do not realise that they are in bondage. So they do not understand liberation, or imagine that they could experience such a state. Therefore, the learned ones, who have realised the impermanent nature of life in this world and the futility of attachment to it, have declared that understanding the aim of tapas is obtained by reflection on the cycle of birth and death.

Every being that is born and exists in this world will ultimately pass away.

Verses 4b, 5 and 6a: Santoṣa, contentment

सन्तोष:

यदिच्छालाभतो नित्यं प्रीतिर्या जायते नृणाम् ।।४।।

तत्सन्तोषं विदुः प्राजज्ञाः परिज्ञानैकतत्परा: ।

ब्रह्मावलोकपर्यन्ताद्विरक्त्या यल्लभेत्प्रियम् ।।५।।

सर्वत्र विगतस्नेह: सन्तोषं परं विदुः ।६।

santoṣaḥ
yaddicchālābhato nityaṃ prītiryā jāyate nṛṇām (4b)
tatsaṃtoṣaṃ viduḥ prājñāḥ parijñānaikatatparāḥ
brahmāvalokaparyantādviraktyā yallabhetpriyam (5)
sarvatra vigatasnehaḥ saṃtoṣaṃ paraṃ viduḥ (6a)

Anvay

yā prītiḥ: when the joy; *jāyate*: arises; *nṛṇām*: in men; *lābhataḥ*: from obtaining; *yad icchā*: any desire; *nityam*: constant; *tat . . viduḥ*: this is known as; *santoṣaḥ*: contentment; *prājñāḥ*: wise; *ekatatparāḥ*: solely intent on; *parijñāna*: true insight; *viraktyā*: becoming indifferent to; *labhet*: obtaining; *yat priyam*: one's desire; *vigata-snehaḥ*: free from attachment; *sarvatra*: everywhere; *paryantāt*: until; *avaloka*: one has realised; *brahma*: Supreme Consciousness; *viduḥ*: is known as; *param santoṣam*: supreme *santoṣa.*

Translation

Contentment: When the joy [which] arises in men from obtaining any desire [is] constant, this is known as *santoṣa* by the wise [who are] solely intent on true insight. Becoming indifferent to obtaining one's desire, and free from attachment everywhere, until one has realised brahma, is known as the supreme santoṣa.

Commentary

Santoṣa means that inner contentment or satisfaction, which is not influenced by hankering for or obtaining external things. Normally people, living in the world, are constantly influenced by their desires. They see or hear about some person, place or thing, and they want that for themselves. They feel happy when their desires are obtained, and unhappy when their desires remain unfulfilled. Therefore, when the same happiness that is experienced from the fulfilment of desire becomes constant, irrespective of whether one's desire is obtained or not, this is known as santosha, by the wise. Such a wise person, having understood the nature of desire and its influence on the mind, aims only to attain insight into truth.

In the early stages of yogic practice, the aspirant must practice santosha, and try to develop this state of constant contentment, even when the mind may be swamped with desire and dissatisfaction. Later on, as the mind becomes calm and less affected by the influence of desire, the state of santosha comes and goes. The aspirant is able to understand and witness the state of mind while it is beleaguered by desire, and also when the mind is able to remain calm, regardless of the desire and its attainment. With the perfection of yoga, one gradually becomes indifferent to desires, and whether or not they are obtained. Such a yogi enjoys freedom from attraction and attachment in all situations in this world, until the highest state of consciousness is realised. This is the ultimate state of santoṣa.

Verse 6b: Āstikya, faith in the higher reality

आस्तिक्यम्

श्रौते स्मार्ते च विश्वासो यत्तदास्तिक्यमुच्यते ।।६।।

āstikyam

śraute smārte ca viśvāso yattadāstikyamucyate (6b)

Anvay

viśvāsaḥ: faith, trust; *śraute*: in the *śrutis*, revealed knowledge; *ca*: and; *smārte*: in the *smṛtis*, knowledge transmitted by memory; *ucyate*: is called; *āstikyam*: devotion, faith.

Translation

Faith in the higher reality: Faith in the *śrutis* and *smṛtis* is called *āstikyam.*

Commentary

The vedic tradition is based on two types of knowledge: (i) *śruti*, knowledge that is heard or revealed directly from the source, and (ii) *smṛti*, knowledge based on what has been remembered and passed down. Through these two channels, knowledge of the higher reality has been passed down from age to age. The *śrutis* are comprised of teachings that were heard directly from sages and yogis, who experienced them in their own sadhana and meditation. When the teachings were remembered or written and then passed down from generation to generation, they were known as smrti, which also means memory. Because śruti and smṛti comprise the body of vedic knowledge, which relates with the existence of a higher reality, the yogic aspirant must have faith in them. By listening to and studying these texts, one develops an understanding of the higher reality, which leads to *āstikya*, or faith. In the absence of this faith, the worldly tendencies remain dominant, and the higher stages of yoga are difficult to attain.

Verse 7: Dāna, giving freely

दानम्

न्यायार्जितधनं श्रान्ते श्रद्धया वैदिके जने ।

अन्यद्वा यत्प्रदीयते तद्दानं प्रोच्यते मया ।।७।।

dānam
nyāyārjitadhanaṃ śrānte śraddhayā vaidike jane
anyadvā yatpradīyate taddānaṃ procyate mayā (7)

Anvay
yat: when; *dhanam*: money; *arjita*: acquired; *nyāyā*: ethically; *pradīyate*: is given away; *śraddhayā*: with reverence; *anyat jane*: to another person; *śrānte*: distressed; *vā*: or; *vaidike*: versed in the Vedas; *tat*: this; *procyate*: is declared; *dānam*: *dānam*, giving freely; *mayā*: by me.

Translation
Giving freely: When money acquired ethically is given away with reverence to another person [who is] distressed or versed in the vedas, this is declared *dānam* by me.

Commentary
In order to progress in yoga and attain expansion of consciousness, one must be able to jump over the sense of I-ness or mine-ness. Ego is what confines the mind and consciousness within a limited, individual field. The consciousness can never expand, as long as it is confined by the limited barrier of ego. In the absence of ego, there is no I and other, just one ever-expanding existence. Therefore, *dāna*, giving freely for the sake of giving, is an important practice of yoga. Giving freely allows one to expand the boundaries of consciousness, which are held tightly in place by the ego. These are the boundaries of my life, my house, my job, my family, my friends, my assets, my expectations.

When there is a strong sense of I and mine, it becomes difficult to give anything freely to anybody, without wanting or expecting something in return. Giving with any form of expectation is not dana, because it further gratifies and expands the ego. The practice of yoga may have many outcomes, but ultimately it will lead to finer states of consciousness, which are not accessible to mind and ego. Thus, it is necessary to practice giving freely in order to release the sense of ego and pride that arise from attaining wealth and position.

The yoga aspirant, who is able to acquire wealth through honest and fair dealings, should also be able to give it away freely to another person, who may be in distress or need. It is further recommended to give to learned persons, i.e., those who are well versed in the vedas, because they are of a spiritual nature and often have no work or substantial income. One's attitude while bestowing wealth or gifts upon another is of supreme importance. The Bible speaks of giving in such a way that the left hand does not know what the right hand is doing. Similarly, the yoga aspirant should give without pride or expectation of recognition. Giving freely in order to help others is also a way to balance the karmas, and remove negativity and greed, which obstruct the access to higher yoga.

Verse 8: Worship of Īśwara

ईश्वरपूजनम्

रागाद्यपेतं हृदयं वागदुष्टा ऽनृतादिना ।

हिंसादिरहितं कर्म यत्तदीश्वरपूजनम् ।।८।।

īśvarapūjanam
rāgādyapetaṃ hṛdayaṃ vācaduṣṭā 'nṛtādinā
hiṃsādirahitaṃ karma yattadīśvarapūjanam (8)

Anvay
yat: when; *hṛdayam*: heart; *apetam*: free from; *rāga*: desire; *ādi*: etc; *vāc*: speech; *aduṣṭā*: not guilty; *anṛtādinā*: lying; *karma*: action; *rahitam*: devoid of; *hiṃsā*: violence; *ādi*; etc; *tat*: this; *īśvara-pūjanam*: *īśvarapūjanam,* worship of a Supreme Reality.

Translation
Worship of *Īśvara*: When the heart is free from desire etc, the speech is not guilty of lying [and the] action is devoid of violence etc, this is *īśvara pūja,* worship of Īśvara.

Commentary
In rāja yoga there is no mention of God, apart from the term *Īśvara*, which means the indestructible reality. Īśvara is indestructible, because it is unmanifest. It is the subtle reality behind the manifestation of all existence. Whatever is manifest is destructible, but being unmanifest, Ishwara is indestructible. How then does one worship the unmanifest reality, without giving it some manifest form or association, which is then destructible? The verse mentions three ways.

First, the yogic aspirant must have a pure heart, which is unruffled by desire and yearning for all the relations and objects of the world. *Raga*, or desire, gives birth to attraction. We become attracted to those things which we desire. The thought that "I want", becomes the predominant influence and takes precedence over all other ideas. From desire, *dweṣa*, or aversion, is born. I want this, but I definitely do not want that. From these two, desire and aversion, the whole mental play unfolds and the mind is never at peace. And then, fear arises, because I may not get what I want, and I may instead get what I do not want. Therefore, the stalwart devotee of Īśvara stands guard patiently at the doors of his or her heart to ensure that worldly desires do not gain entry. When the heart is filled with desire and passion, it becomes agitated and stressed. In this state, Īśvara cannot be worshipped.

Second, speech is an important means by which one can worship Īśvara. The devotee of Īśvara strives to purify this channel by speaking the truth, because Īśvara, the unmanifest reality, is the absolute truth. In order to worship truth, one must be ever truthful. Therefore, the speech must be constantly guarded, and not allowed to utter lies or any kind of untruth, which would turn one away from Ishwara.

Third, the devotee of Īśvara should embody the principle of non-violence in thought, word and deed. Violence of any kind begets violence, and this negative karma disturbs the mind deeply. The person of violent tendency is unfit for the worship of Ishwara, which is the fulfilment of yoga.

Verse 9: Vedānta śravana, hearing the knowledge of truth

सिद्धन्तश्रवणम्

सत्यं ज्ञानमनन्तं च परानन्दं परं ध्रुवम् ।

प्रत्यगित्यवगन्तव्यं वेदान्तश्रवणं बुधः ।।९।।

siddhantaśravaṇam
satyaṃ jñānamanantaṃ ca parānandaṃ paraṃ dhruvam
pratyagityavagantavyaṃ vedāntaśravaṇaṃ budhaḥ (9)

Anvay
iti: thus; *budhaḥ*: knowing; *param dhruvam*: ultimate permanence; *satyam*: truth; *jñānam-anantam*: infinite wisdom; *ca*: and; *para-ānandam*: supreme bliss; *avagantavyam*: to be perceived; *pratyak*: inwardly; *vedānta-śravaṇam*: hearing and internalising the wisdom of *vedānta.*

Translation
Hearing the knowledge of truth: Thus, knowing that the ultimate permanence of truth, infinite wisdom and supreme bliss is to be perceived inwardly is *vedānta śravaṇam.*

Commentary
Nowadays, there are many texts and commentaries available on the philosophy and teachings of vedānta. In ancient times, however, these teachings were not readily available in written form. They were accessed directly from the learned teacher or yogi, who spoke about them to their worthy students and disciples. The upaniṣads, which form the main body of vedānta, were all originally transmitted in this way. The word *upaniṣad* refers to those teachings, which were heard, while sitting in close proximity to the seer or teacher. So, *vedānta śravaṇa* means hearing the teaching of vedānta. The essence of these teachings is summed up here in three parts.

The first teaching relates to inner knowledge of the ultimate permanence of truth. Most people are materialists, because they believe in the knowledge and permanence of the external world. For them, this is truth. Vedānta speaks of two realities: the outer experience, which is relative truth, and the inner experience, which is absolute truth. Whatever can be known in this world is said to be relative truth, because it is impermanent. The entire manifest creation is impermanent, because it is subject to decay and destruction. Vedānta speaks of an ultimate reality, which is permanent, constant and indestructible. This permanent reality is the substratum that supports and sustains the manifest creation. Being uncreated, it is not experienced in the dimension of time, space and object. It can only be experienced and known from within, when the consciousness has transcended the body and mind, and all of the associations of the world.

The second teaching pertains to infinite knowledge. A person, who is born in the world today, is subjected to many long and arduous years of education, whereby knowledge is fed into the mind from outside and slowly ingested. This is empirical knowledge about the world; it is not wisdom, because it is neither experiential nor does it relate to the permanent truth. Vedanta is an esoteric philosophy, which is based on inner knowledge of the eternal truth of the ever-expanding consciousness. This knowledge is said to be infinite, while all other knowledge is relative and limited to time, space and object.

The third teaching is about supreme bliss. In the course of life in this world, a person is constantly subjected to varying states of happiness and sorrow, success and failure, praise and blame. Like a pendulum, one sways uncontrollably from one extreme to the other. That is because one depends on the outer world and relations for meaning and experience in life. Vedānta speaks of another happiness, which is permanent and enduring, because it is not of this world. *Paramānanda*, supreme bliss, is the quality of experience in the highest consciousness, when the awareness has completely transcended the world of name, form, and ideation. This happiness is absolute; it has no beginning and no end.

Verse 10: Hrīḥ, remorse or shame

ह्रीः

देवलौकिकमार्गेषु कुत्सितं कर्म यद्भवेत् ।

तस्मिन्भवति या लज्जा ह्रीः सैवेति प्रकीर्तिता ।।१०।।

hrīḥ

devalaukikamārgeṣu kutsitaṃ karma yadbhavet
tasminbhavati yā lajjā hrīḥ saiveti prakīrtitā (10)

Anvay

yad: when; *karma*: action; *kutsitam*: blameworthy; *deva-laukika-mārgeṣu*: according to the ways of the worlds of the gods; *tasmin*: then; *bhavati*: there is; *lajjā*: shame; *sā*: this; *prakīrtitā*: is called; *hrīḥ*: *hrī.*

Translation

Remorse: When action is blameworthy, according to the ways of the worlds of the gods, then there is remorse, and this [remorse] is called *hrīḥ*.

Commentary

Many people pride themselves on doing wrong things and getting away with them. They think they are very clever, until they are caught. However, doing the wrong thing requires one to think in the wrong way. This wrong thinking and wrong action make a person crooked, and a crooked person is not a suitable candidate for the higher practices of yoga. Of course, everybody makes mistakes and sometimes one does something very bad, which is really blameworthy. Actions of a destructive and harmful nature are against the humanitarian laws and are unacceptable, even in the worlds of the gods, or luminous beings. One who commits a crooked or shameful act, should be aware of the consequences and feel remorse or repentance. If a person is sincerely sorry and seeks forgiveness for his or her wrong actions, then it is understood that such actions should not happen again. In this case, it will still be possible to progress on the path of higher yoga.

Verse 11: Mati, faith in the vedic teaching

मतिः

वैदिकेषु च सर्वेषु श्रद्धा या सा मतिर्भवेत् ।

गुरुणा चोपदिष्तो ऽपि तन्त्र संबन्धवर्जितः ॥११॥

matiḥ

vaidikeṣu ca sarveṣu śraddhā yā sā matirbhavet

guruṇā copadiṣṭo 'pi tatra sambandhavarjitaḥ (11)

Anvay

sā śraddhā: that faith; *sarveṣu vaidikeṣu*: in all those versed in the Vedas; *bhavet*: is; *matiḥ*: *mati*; *ca api*: and if; *tantra*: system; *upadiṣṭaḥ*: is advised; *guruṇā*: by the *guru*; *sambandha*: connection; *varjitaḥ*: terminated.

Translation

Faith in the vedic teaching: That faith in all those teachings versed in the Vedas is *mati*. And if [another] system is advised by the guru, the connection [with him should be] terminated.

Commentary

The two main cultures and systems of spiritual teaching from early times were tantra and veda. Tantra was the earliest system, which developed during the time of *Gondwana,* before the great cataclysms of nature destroyed and reduced this enormous, equatorial continent to a tiny land mass in the south of the Indian subcontinent. The people of this culture were an ancient race known as the *Dravidians*. Later on, the *Aryan* people, who were a different race, developed the vedic system in the northern part of India. The Aryan people and way of life was guided by wise rishis, or seers, who were infused with *dharmic* ethics and principles. The Dravidian people were a psychic race and their culture was guided by kings, who revered power and were considered to be *adharmic*, not adhering to the ethical and universal principles of spiritual life,

During the early vedic period, these two peoples met and fought many battles for supremacy. However, the Aryan peoples were ultimately victorious, and forced the Dravidian culture into submission. Afterwards the Aryan thinkers and leaders studied the tantric system and held many discussions with the kings and teachers of the tantric traditions. The outcome of some of these discussions can be found in the teachings of the yoga upanishads, because yoga was originally a part of the tantric body of spiritual practices. Finally, those tantric teachings which were considered beneficial for the welfare and evolution of humanity were placed under the vedic umbrella, and became a part of *Sanatan Dharma*, the eternal principles of the vedic tradition. Those teachings which were considered to be unworthy were excluded.

In the above verse, the rishi of this upanishad says that the aspirant must have *mati*, faith in the teachings of the vedas only. If the guru expounds teachings from a non-vedic system, the connection with him or her should be terminated. What is meant here by 'another system' is tantra, and its many sub-divisions. The body of tantra, which had existed from ancient times was very vast, and included many unsavoury aspects, which were not considered to be honourable or acceptable by the vedic teachers and leaders, although there were also many positive and profound teachings and practices to be found within tantra as well.

Thus, as often happens in the absence of discrimination, the aspirant may be mislead by the negative components, not having developed a refined sense of judgement and understanding. Therefore, the yoga which was incorporated into the upanishads and henceforth taught as a vedic science was acceptable, while the rest of the system and culture of tantra was to be avoided. This explains why today we often find texts and teachers, who refer to yoga as a vedic science. But there are also those, who speak of yoga as a part of tantra, and we can also see the direct relationship that yogas, such as hatha yoga, kundalini yoga, japa yoga, have with tantra.

Verses 12 to 16: Japa, repetition of the mantra

जपः

वेदोक्तेनैव मार्गेण मन्त्राभ्यासो जपः स्मृतः ।

कल्पसूत्रे यथा वेदे धर्मशास्त्रे पुराणके ।।१२।।

इतिहासे च वृत्तिर्या स जपः प्रोच्यते मया ।

जपस्तु द्विविधः प्रोक्तो वाचिको मानसस्तथा ।।१३।।

वाचिकोपांशुरुच्चैश्च द्विविधः परिकीर्तितः ।

मानसो मननध्यानभेदाद्द्वैविध्यमाश्रितः ।।१४।।

उच्चैर्जपादुपांशुश्च सहस्रगुणमुच्यते ।

मानसश्च तथोपांशोः सहस्रगुणमुच्यते ।।१५।।

उच्चैर्जपश्च सर्वेषां यथोक्तफलदो भवेत् ।

निचैः श्रोत्रेण चेन्मन्त्रः श्रुतश्चेन्निष्फलं भवेत् ।।१६।।

japaḥ
vedoktenaiva mārgeṇa mantrābhyāso japaḥ smṛtaḥ
kalpasūtre yathā vede dharmaśāstre purāṇake (12)
itihāse ca vṛttiryā sa japaḥ procyate mayā
japastu dvividhaḥ prokto vāciko mānasastathā (13)
vācikopāṃśuruccaiśca dvividhaḥ parikīrtitaḥ
mānaso mananadhyānabhedāddvaividhyamāśritaḥ (14)
uccairjapādupāṃśuśca sahasraguṇamucyate
mānasaśca tathopāṃśoḥ sahasraguṇamucyate (15)
uccairjapaśca sarveṣāṃ yathoktaphalado bhavet
nīcaiḥ śrotreṇa cenmantraḥ śrutaścenniṣphalaṃ bhavet (16)

Anvay

mantra-abhyāsaḥ: practice of *mantra*, divine sound vibrations; *vedoktena mārgeṇa*: in the correct way of the *Vedas*; *smṛtaḥ*: is named; *japaḥ*: *japa*; *yathā*: according to; *kalpa sūtre*: manuals on sacrificial rites; *vede*: ancient knowledge revealed by the divine; *dharma śāstre*: teachings on worldly duties; *purāṇake*: vedic mythology; *ca*: and;

itihāse: great epics; *yā vṛittiḥ*: this method; *procyate*: is called; *japaḥ*: *japa*; *mayā*: by me; *tathā*: then; *proktaḥ*: it is said; *dvividhaḥ japaḥ*: two kinds of *japa*; *vācikaḥ*: vocal; *mānasaḥ*: mental; *vācikaḥ*: vocal; *parikīrtitaḥ*: is divided; *dvividhaḥ*: two kinds; *upāṃśuḥ*: whispered; *ca*: and; *uccaiḥ*: aloud; *mānasaḥ*: mental; *āśritaḥ*: uses; *dvaividhyam*: two kind; *bhedāt*: differentiating between; *manana*: reflection; *dhyāna*: deep meditation; *upāṃśuḥ*: whispered; *ucyate*: is said; *sahasra-guṇam*: a thousand times better; *uccaiḥ-japāt*: than *japa* [said] aloud; *tathā*: likewise; *mānasaḥ*: mental; *upāṃśoḥ*: than whispered; *yathā*: whereas; *ukta*: it is said; *bhavet*: is; *phaladaḥ*: rewarding; *sarveṣāṃ*: in all [instances]; *nīcaiḥ*: in a low voice; *śrutaḥ*: heard; *śrotreṇa*: by ear; *ca*: and; *bhavet*: it has; *niṣphalam*: no results.

Translation

Japa: The practice of *mantra* in the correct way of the vedas is known as *japa.* According to the *Kalpa Sūtras, Vedas*, *Dharma Śāstras*, *Purāṇas* and *Itihāsas*, this method is called japa by me. Then it is said there are two kinds of japa, vocal [and] mental. Vocal is divided into two kinds, whispered and aloud. Mental uses two kinds, differentiating between reflection [and] deep meditation. Whispered japa is said to be a thousand times better than japa [said] aloud. Likewise mental [japa] is said to be a thousand times better than whispered. Whereas it is said *ucchaiḥ japa* (uttered aloud) is rewarding in all [instances], *nīcaiḥ* japa (uttered in a low voice) is heard by the ear, and it has no results.

Commentary

The final verse in part two of this upanishad, which describes the ten niyamas, or inner disciplines of yoga, is a discussion on the practice of japa. The purpose of the niyama is to purify the aspirant from within, so that the further stages of aṣṭaṅga yoga may be effective. Japa yoga is a powerful practice, which utilises sound vibration to raise the quality of the internal resonance and thus bring about a profound purification of the entire inner being. However, mantra is also a universal science, which has been known and utilised down through the ages by all traditions, starting with tantra.

From ancient times, mantras have been invoked for a variety of reasons, such as acquisition of wealth, power and position, love and progeny, protection, cure for disease, etc. Therefore, the rishi has stipulated here that only the practice performed in the correct way, according to the vedas, should be used for japa by the practitioner of ashtanga yoga. He recommends only the method of japa, which is in accord with the *Kalpa Sūtras*, sacrificial texts, vedic texts, comprising the revealed knowledge, *Dharma Śāstras*, books containing knowledge of vedic rituals, *Purāṇas*, ancient texts, and *Itihāsas*, epics from early vedic times.

The rishi then proceeds to discuss the types of japa to be undertaken by the yogic aspirant. There are two types of japa: one is uttered aloud vocally and the other is silent or mental. Of the vocal type, there are also two types: one is repeated verbally aloud and the other is whispered softly in a kind of murmur that is audible within oneself alone. Of the mental japa, there are also two types: one is repeated silently during mental reflection, and the other is heard within during deep meditation.

Of the japa repeated aloud, whispered japa is said to be a thousand times better than the verbal japa. Similarly, mental or silent japa is a thousand times better than whispered japa. Furthermore, it is said that japa uttered aloud is beneficial at all times, but japa repeated in a low voice that is heard by the ears of others has no results.

इति द्वितीयः खण्डः
iti dvitīyaḥ khaṇḍaḥ
Thus [ends] the second section.

तृतीयः खण्डः

tṛtīyaḥ khaṇḍaḥ

Third Section

आसनानि नव

āsanāni nava

Nine Āsanas

Verses 1 and 2a: Nine major āsanas

स्वास्तिकं गोमुखं पद्मं वीरसिंहासने तथा ।
भद्रं मुक्तासनं चैव मयूरासनमेव च ।।१।।
सुखाससनाख्यं च नवमं मुनिपुङ्गव ।२।
svāstikaṃ gomukhaṃ padmaṃ vīrasiṃhāsane tathā
bhadraṃ muktāsanaṃ caiva mayūrāsanameva ca (1)
sukhāsanasamākhyaṃ ca navamaṃ munipuṅgava (2a)

Anvay

munipuṅgava: o Eminent Sage; *tathā*: thus; *svastikam*: auspicious; *gomukham*: c ow-face; *padmam*: lotus; *vīra*: hero; *siṃhāsane*: lion pose; *bhadram*: gracious; *muktāsanam*: liberated pose; *ca . . eva*: and indeed; *mayūrāsanam*: peacock pose; *ca*: and; *sukhāsana*: easy pose; *samākhyam*: is counted; *navamam*: ninth.

Translation

O Eminent Sage, thus [these nine *āsanas* are]: *swastikāsana*, the auspicious pose, *gomukhāsana*, the cow-face pose, *padmāsana*, the lotus pose, *vīrāsana*, the hero pose, *siṃhāsana*, the lion pose, *bhadrāsana*, the gracious pose, *muktāsana*, the liberated pose, and indeed the *mayurāsana*, the peacock pose, and *sukhāsana*, the easy pose, is counted as the ninth.

Commentary

It is interesting to note that, while āsana has become the main focus of yoga today, in early times, āsana was utilised for sitting. All the asanas listed here are postures used for meditation, with the exception of simhasana, gomukhasana and mayurasana. Simhasana was important to alleviate problems of the throat, gomukhasana to release tension in the shoulders, and mayurasana to maintain the digestion. The concept of aṣṭaṅga yoga was that the āsana must be firm, steady and comfortable, to enable deeper meditation to unfold. Modern day yogic aspirants are realising the importance of meditation, but they are unable to sit steadily in one posture without shifting the body every few minutes.

This inability to sit comfortably for extended periods of time impedes the practice of meditation and is considered to be an obstacle in yoga. For this reason, the whole progression of yoga āsana developed, including āsanas, for every possible type of bodily movement: forward, backward, sideways, upward, inverted, and balancing. When the progression of āsana is properly mastered, the aspirant should be able to remove the toxins, tensions and stiffness from the body, so that sitting in one posture for a long period of time becomes possible for the purpose of meditation.

Verses 2b and 3a: Swastikāsana, the auspicious pose

स्वस्तिकम्

जानूर्वारन्तरे कृत्वा सम्यक् पादतले उभे ।।२।।

समग्रीवशिरः कायः स्वस्तिकं नित्यमभ्यसेत् ।३।

svastikam
jānūrvārantare kṛtvā samyak pādatale ubhe (2b)
samagrīvaśiraḥ kāyaḥ svastikaṃ nityamabhyaset (3a)

Anvay
abhyaset: one should practise; *nityam*: always; *svastikam*: auspicious pose; *kṛtvā*: placing; *grīva*: neck; *śiraḥ*: head; *kāyaḥ*: body; *sama*: in alignment; *vāḥ*: trying to put; *jānū*: knees; *samyak*: exactly; *antare ubhe pādatale*: at both feet.

Translation
One should always practise the auspicious pose, placing the neck, head [and] body in alignment, trying to put the knees exactly parallel with both feet.

Commentary
Swastikāsana is considered to be an unlocked meditation asana. It is very similar to *siddhasana* (or *muktasana*) but the heels do not apply pressure to the perineum. For this reason, it may be more comfortable to maintain, but it will not raise the energy from the lower centres to the brain, as in siddhasana. The word *swastika* means 'auspicious' or 'favorable'. The swastika is a universal symbol, which has been used by many religions and traditions from ancient times. A common analogy of the swastika is that its four limbs represent the four directions of the world, which have one common center, consciousness. Therefore, this pose can

be considered as the one most auspicious for realising the unity of all existence.

Technique

Sit on the floor with both legs stretched forward. Bend the left knee and place the left foot near the right inner thigh. Bend the right knee and place the right toes in the space between the left thigh and calf. Grasp the toes of the left foot and pull them upward between the right calf and thigh. Adjust the body so that the head, neck and shoulders are in alignment with the spine. The knees should be parallel with the feet. Relax the whole body in the position.

Verses 3b and 4a: Gomukhāsana, the cow face pose

गोमुखम्

सव्ये दक्षिणगुल्फं तु पृष्ठपश्चा नियोजयेत् ।।३।।

दक्षिणे ऽपि तथा सव्यं गोमुखं तत्प्रचक्षते ।४।

gomukham

savye dakṣiṇagulphaṃ tu pṛṣṭhapaścā niyojayet (3b)
dakṣiṇe 'pi tathā savyaṃ gomukhaṃ tatpracakṣate (4a)

Anvay

niyojayet: one should place; *dakṣiṇa-gulpham*: right ankle; *savye*: on the left; *paścā*: behind; *pṛṣṭha*: back; *api tathā*: and then; *savyam*: left; *dakṣiṇe*: on the right; *tat pracakṣate*: this is called; *gomukham*: cow face pose.

Translation

One should place the right ankle on the left behind the back, and then the left on the right; this is called the cow face pose.

Commentary

In early times, most families possessed cows, and cow's milk was a main staple in the diet. Cow urine and manure were also considered to be pure and utilised in the home for promoting health and sanitation. So, it is not surprising that the yogis of old saw the cow's face in this posture. This posture removes stiffness and tension from the shoulders, neck and spine, and improves the breathing. For these reasons it was considered very useful as an adjunct to meditation.

Technique

Sit with both legs outstretched. Bend the left knee and bring the left foot under the right leg, towards the back, placing it beside the right buttock. Bend the right knee and bring the right foot over the top of the left leg, placing it beside the left buttock. The knees should be positioned so that the right knee is above the left. Hold the back straight.

Raise the right arm, so that the elbow is beside the head. The right hand should reach down over the right shoulder with the palm towards the spine. Stretch the left arm behind the back. Reach upward and grasp the left hand with the right. The back of the left hand should be in contact with the spine. Join the fingers of the two hands. Hold the spine erect with the head facing forward.

The āsana should be repeated to the other side, holding the final pose for the same length of time

Verses 4b and 5: Padmāsana, the lotus pose

पद्मम्
अङ्गुष्ठावधि गृहीयाधस्ताभ्यां व्युत्क्रमेण तु ॥४॥
ऊर्ध्वोरुपरि विप्रेन्द्र कृत्वा पादतलद्वयम् ।
पद्मासनं भवेत्प्राज्ञ सर्वरोगभयापहम् ॥५॥

padmam
aṅguṣṭhāvadhi gṛhīyādhastābhyām vyutkrameṇa tu (4b)
ūrdhvorupari viprendra kṛtvā pādataladvayam
padmāsanam bhavetprājña sarvarogabhayāpaham (5)

Anvay
viprendra: o Distinguished Brahman; *kṛtvā*: placing; *pādatala-dvayam*: both feet; *ūrdhva*: upwards; *ūrupari*: on the thighs; *gṛhīyāt*: one should hold; *aṅguṣṭha-avadhi*: ends of the big toes; *hastābhyām*: with the hands; *vyutkrameṇa*: turned up; *bhavet*: this is; *padmāsanam*: lotus pose; *hayāpaham*: which wards off; *sarva-roga*: all disease.

Translation
O Distinguished Brahman, placing (the soles of) both feet upwards on the thighs, one should hold the ends of the big toes with the hands turned up. This is the lotus pose, O Wise One, which wards off all disease.

Commentary
Padmāsana is considered to be the best meditative āsana, because it holds the body in a locked, upright position, even when the practitioner enters deep states of meditation, where the consciousness soars beyond the body. This is a perfectly balanced position, which is conducive to equanimity and stillness, and also facilitates the opening of *suṣumnā nādi*, the spiritual pathway at the center of the spinal column. In the

description given here, the big toes of both feet are held with the hands turned upward. This refers to the practice of *baddha padmāsana*, the locked lotus pose, which is an advanced practice. Most practitioners will find this asana too difficult to achieve today. Therefore, it was traditionally reserved for the few wise ones.

The verse further states that this practice wards off all disease. This is because of the prānic balance, which is maintained in the posture during prolonged meditation. According to yoga, disease arises due to imbalance in the prāṇas and nāḍīs, energy channels. By sitting in this posture regularly, these imbalances are corrected and the resulting diseases resolved. Crossing the arms behind the back further opens and extends the shoulders and chest cavity, activating the energies in this region. While grasping the big toes with the fingers creates a completely closed energy circuit, containing the energy within the body, so that there is no dissipation.

Technique
Sit with the legs stretched forward. Bend the right knee and place the right foot on top of the left thigh. The sole of the right foot should be turned upward and the heel in contact with the lower abdomen. Bend the left knee and place the left foot on top of the right thigh in the same way. Both knees should be in contact with the floor.

Stretch both arms behind the back and cross them, one over the other. Grasp the right big toe with the index finger and thumb of the right hand. Grasp the left big toe with the index finger and thumb of the left hand. The hands should rest with the palms turned upward.

Verse 6: Vīrāsana, the hero pose

वीरासनम्

दक्षिणेतरपादं तु दक्षिणोरुणि विन्यसेत् ।

ऋजुकायः समासीनो वीरासनमुदाहृतम् ।।६।।

vīrāsana
dakṣiṇetarapādaṃ tu dakṣiṇoruṇi vinyaset
rijukāyaḥ samāsīno vīrāsanamudāhṛtam (6)

Anvay
vinyaset: one should put; *dakṣiṇetara-pādam*: left foot; *dakṣiṇa-ūruṇi*: on the right thigh; *rijukāyaḥ*: straight body; *samāsīnaḥ*: comfortable; *udāhṛtam*: this is called; *vīrāsana*: hero pose.

Translation
One should put the left foot on the right thigh, the body straight and comfortable. This is called the hero pose.

Commentary
Vīrāsana, the hero pose, is an unlocked position. For this reason, it is not generally used for meditation, although it is an easy and comfortable pose, compared to the locked positions. The word *vīra* means 'valiant' or 'powerful', the 'power to subdue'. Vīrāsana is actually an abbreviation for *mahāvīrāsana.* The word *mahā* means 'great', and *Mahāvīra* is one of the names of Hanuman, the monkey god, who was a great hero in the ancient Indian epic, *Ramāyana.* Vīrāsana stabilises the energy in the lower enters and enables control over the sexual energy. It also increases the willpower and strengthens the body,

Technique
Sit with both legs outstretched. Bend the right knee and bring the right foot towards the back. Place the right foot beside the right buttock, with the right big toe tucked under the buttock.

Bend the left knee and place the left foot on top of the right thigh, with the sole facing upward.. The knees should be separated. Rest the hands on the knees in chin or jnana mudra. Hold the spine erect and the head and neck straight.

Verses 6i, ii and iii: Siṃhāsana, the lion pose

सिंहासनम्

गुल्फौ च वृषणस्याधः सीविन्यः पार्श्वयोः क्षिपेत् ।

दक्षिणं सव्यगुल्फेन दक्षिणेन तथेतरत् ।।६-१।।

हस्तौ जानौ समास्थाप्य स्वाङ्गुलींरिप्रसर्य च ।

व्यक्तवक्त्रो निरीक्षेत नासाग्रं सुसमाहितः ।।६-२।।

सिंहासनं भवेदेतत् पूजितं योगिभिः सदा ।।६-३।।

siṃhāsanam
gulphau ca vṛṣaṇasyādhaḥ sīvinyaḥ pārśvayoḥ kṣipet
dakṣiṇaṃ savyagulphena dakṣiṇena tathetarat (6.i)
hastau jānau samāsthāpya svāṅgulīṃriprasarya ca
vyaktavaktro nirīkṣeta nāsāgraṃ susamāhitaḥ (6.ii)
siṃhāsanaṃ bhavedetat pūjitaṃ yogibhiḥ sadā (6.iii)

Anvay
kṣipet: one should put; *gulphau*: ankles; *adhah*: under; *vṛṣaṇasya*: testes; *ca*: and; *pārśvayoḥ*: beside; *sīvinyaḥ*: perineum; *dakṣiṇam*: right one; *savya-gulphena*: with the left ankle; *tathetarat*: vice versa; *hastau*: hands; *samāsthāpya*: well-placed on; *jānau*: knees; *ca*: and; *riprasarya*: spreading; *sva-aṅgulīm*: one's fingers; *vyakta-vaktro*: with open mouth; *nirīkṣeta*: one should gaze at; *susamāhitaḥ*: intently; *nāsāgram*: tip of the nose; *etat*: this; *bhavet*: is; *siṃhāsanam*: lion pose; *pūjitam*: honoured; *sadā*: always; *yogibhiḥ*: by the *yogins.*

Translation
One should place the ankles under the testes and beside the perineum, the right one with the left ankle, [and] vice versa, hands well-placed on the knees and spreading one's fingers. With open mouth, one should gaze intently at the tip of the nose. This is the lion pose, honoured always by the yogins.

Commentary
There are two techniques for performing this pose. One is simhāsana, the lion pose, as described here, which is considered to be the main practice in the classical yoga texts. The other is *simhagarjanāsana*, the roaring lion pose, which is given as the variation. In simhāsana, the lion sits silently, waiting. This is the meditative attitude, which the yogi develops in order to enter deep states of consciousness. So, in this sense, simhasana is also a major meditation asana.

Simhāsana is a powerful posture, just as its namesake, the lion, is a powerful creature. The position of the feet in this posture creates a natural *mūla bandha* by placing maximum pressure on the perineum. The head is bent forward, inducing jālandhara bandha, the throat lock. The eyes are open with the gaze focused at the nose tip, further stimulating *mūla dhāra cakra.* The mouth is open wide, with the tongue extended outside, stimulating the throat and the *viśuddhi cakra.*

Technique
Kneel on the floor with both knees apart. Cross both feet at the ankles. Lower the buttock onto the crossed feet, so that the right ankle is under the left testes, and beside the perineum. The left ankle is under the right testes, beside the perineum. In women, the crossed ankles will press the right and left side of the vagina. The feet and ankles must be very flexible to achieve this position.

Place the palms of the hands on the knees and spread the fingers wide apart. Bend the head forward and focus the gaze on the nose tip, as in *nasikagra mudra.* Open the mouth wide and extend the tongue as far outside as possible.

Verses 7 and 8a: Bhadrāsana, the gracious pose

भद्रासनम्

गुल्फौ तु वृषणस्याधः सीविन्याः पार्श्वयोः क्षिपेत् ।

पार्श्वपादौ च पाणिभ्यां दृधं बद्धवा सुनिर्लिम् ।।७।।

भद्रासनं भवेदेतद्विषरोगविनाशनम् ।८।

bhadrāsanam

gulphau ca vṛṣaṇasyādhaḥ sīvinyaḥ pārśvayoḥ kṣipet
pārśvapādau ca pānibhyāṃ dṛdhaṃ baddhavā sunirlim (7)
bhadrāsanaṃ bhavedetadviṣarogavināśanam (8a)

Anvay

tu: conjunction; *kṣipet*: one should put; *gulphau*: ankles; *adhah*: under; *vṛṣaṇasya*: testes; *ca*: and; *pārśvayoḥ*: beside; *sīvinyaḥ*: perineum; *pādau*: legs; *pārśva*: out to the sides; *baddhavā*: holding; *dṛdham*: firmly; *ca*: and; *sunirlim*: still; *pānibhyām*: with the hands; *etat bhavet*: this is; *bhadrāsanam*: gracious pose; *vināśanam*: which removes; *viṣa*: poison; *roga*: disease.

Translation

One should put the ankles under the testes and beside the perineum, knees out to the sides, holding [them] firmly and still with the hands. This is the gracious pose, which removes poison [and] disease.

Commentary

The word *bhadra* means 'gentle', 'gracious' or 'blessed'. This asana automatically induces *mūla bandha*, the perineal lock, and is used for the awakening of *mūladhāra cakra*, the root psychic center. For this reason, it is also called *mūlabandhāsana* in some of the classical texts. It is an important posture for the conservation of sexual energy, and helps to tone the reproductive and eliminatory organs. For these reasons, it keeps the body free from toxic buildup in the lower regions and helps to avert disease. Bhadrāsana is an excellent meditation pose for the advanced practitioner, whose knees, ankles and feet are very flexible.

Technique

Sit with the legs outstretched. Bend the knees and bring the soles of the feet together. Draw the heels towards the body, so that the outside of the feet remain in contact with the floor. Place the palms of the hands on the floor beside the buttocks and press down, raising the buttocks onto the ankles. The ankles should be under the testes and beside the perineum, so that the heels press the perineum. The legs should be positioned out to the sides, with the knees in contact with the floor. Hold the knees firmly and still with the hands.

Verses 8b, 9 and 10a: Muktāsana, liberated pose

मुक्तासनम्
निपीड्य सीविनीं मूक्ष्मा दक्षिणेतरगुल्फतः ॥८॥
वामं याम्येन गुल्फेन मुक्तासनमिदं भवेत् ।
मेढ्रादुपरि मिक्षिप्य सव्यं गुल्फं ततोपरि ॥९॥
गुल्फान्तरं च संक्षिप्य मुक्तासनमिदं मुने ।१०।

muktāsanam
nipīḍya sīvinīṃ mūkṣmā dakṣiṇetaragulphataḥ (8b)
vāmaṃ yāmyena gulphena muktāsanamidaṃ bhavet
medhrādupari nikṣipya savyaṃ gulphaṃ tatopari (9)
gulphāntaraṃ ca saṃkṣipya muktāsanamidaṃ mune (10a)

Anvay
nipīḍya: pressing; *yām sīvinīm*: this perineum; *mūkṣmā*: gently; *dakṣiṇetara-gulphataḥ*: with the right ankle; *vāmam*: left; *yena gulphena*: with that ankle; *idam bhavet*: this is; *muktāsanam*: pose of liberation; *nikṣpya*: placing; *ca*: and; *savyam gulpham*: left ankle; *upari . . . tata-upari*: one above the other; *medhrāt*: penis; *saṃkṣipya*: placed; *gulphāntaram*: between the ankles; *idam*: this; *muktāsanam*: pose of liberation; *mune*: o Sage.

Translation
Pressing the perineum gently with the right ankle, [and the pubis] with the left ankle, this is the pose of liberation. Placing [the right ankle] and the left ankle one above the other, with the penis placed between the ankles, this [is] the pose of liberation, O Sage.

Commentary
Muktāsana, the liberated pose, is another name for *siddhāsana*. The word *siddha* means 'accomplished' or 'perfected'. It refers to one, who is accomplished in yoga

through the mastery of this pose. *Siddhāsana* and *padmāsana* are the two most important meditative poses. The other meditation poses are modifications, some of which may be practised more easily and others that are even more difficult. While *padmāsana* aims at achieving total balance of the prāṇas for the awakening of suṣumnā, *siddhāsana* activates the lower centers and redirects the reproductive energy upward to the brain to be used for higher meditation.

Siddhāsana also awakens *ājñā cakra,* the psychic center at the mid-brain, due to the connection between mooladhara and ajna. When ājñā cakra is awakened, the higher dimension of consciousness is experienced. For these reasons, sitting in siddhasana for prolonged periods is considered to bring about the meditative state in itself. Thus, siddhāsana can be called muktāsana, the pose of liberation.

Although *padmāsana* is considered by adepts to be the ultimate meditative posture, siddhāsana is easier to practise and to hold for long periods. The body is firmly locked in this posture and the feet are less likely to become numb. Siddhāsana prevents the blood pressure from falling too low, and keep nervous depression from occurring during meditation. It regulates the production of sexual hormones and is essential for those who wish to practice celibacy for spiritual enhancement.

Technique

Sit on the floor with both legs extended. Bend the right knee and place the sole of the right foot against the inner left thigh. Draw the right heel under the body, placing it beneath the genitals, so that it gently presses the perineum. Bend the left knee and place the left ankle on top of the right, so that both ankles are touching. Push the toes and the outer edge of the left foot into the space between the right calf and thigh. The left heel should press the center of the pubic bone, directly above the genitals. The genitals should lie in-between the two heels. Grasp the right toes and pull them up into the space between the left calf and thigh. Adjust the body in the posture, so that it is comfortable and the pressure of the heels is firmly applied. The legs are now locked, with the knees touching the floor.

Verses 10b, 11 and 12a: Mayurāsana, the peacock pose

मयूरासनम्

कूर्पराग्रे मुनिश्रेष्ठ निक्षिपेन्नाभिपार्श्वयोः ॥१०॥

भूम्यां पाणितलद्वन्द्वं निक्षिप्यैकाग्रमानसः ।

समुन्नतशिरःपादो दण्डवत् व्योम्नि संस्थितः ॥११॥

मयूरासनमेतत् स्यात् सर्वपापप्रणाशनम् ।१२।

mayurāsanam
kūrparāgre muniśreṣtha nikṣipennābhipārśvayoḥ (10b)
bhūmyāṃ pāṇitaladvandvaṃ nikṣipyaikāgramānasaḥ
samunnataśiraḥpādo daṇḍavat vyomni saṃsthitaḥ (11)
mayūrāsanametat syāt sarvapāpapraṇāśanam (12a)

Anvay

muniśreṣtha: o Esteemed Sage; *nikṣipet*: one should put; *kūrpara-agre*: elbows in front; *nābhi-pārśvayoḥ*: against the sides of the navel; *nikṣipya*: placing; *pāṇitala-dvandvam*: both hands; *bhūmyām*: on the ground; *ekāgramānasaḥ*: mind one-pointed; *śiraḥ*: head; *samunnata*: raised; *pādaḥ*: legs; *daṇḍavat*: straight; *saṃsthitaḥ*: placed; *vyomni*: in the air; *etat syāt*: this is; *mayūrāsanam*: peacock pose; *praṇāśanam*: remover of; *sarva-pāpa*: all negativity.

Translation

O Esteemed Sage, one should put the elbows in front against the sides of the navel, placing both hands on the ground, mind one-pointed, head raised, legs straight, placed in the air. This is the peacock pose, remover of all negativity.

Commentary

Mayurāsana, the peacock pose, is mentioned in this upanishad and in many classical texts on yoga, due to its powerful influence on the *manipura cakra* and the digestive system. The other postures mentioned in this section are all sitting postures, which reaffirms the verse given in *Hatha Yoga Pradipika*, that 'hatha yoga leads to raja yoga'. The purpose of including this major asana here may have been for health reasons. The Indian subcontinent is hot and humid for many months of the year. Continuous heat and humidity affect the metabolism, causing toxins and bacteria to proliferate.

In these conditions the digestive system may become a problem, especially for a yogi, who performs sitting practices for the greater part of the day. The verse describes the practice, and then states that it will remove all obstructions. Digestive and metabolic ailments are considered to be the mother of all disease. For the yogi they are a great impediment, because the core energy becomes weak and unbalanced, making it very difficult to continue or progress in sadhana. Mayurāsana massages the abdominal organs and stimulates the intestinal peristalsis. It removes toxins and develops mental and physical balance.

Technique
Kneel on the floor with the knees apart and the feet together. Lean forward and place the palms of the hands on the floor, in-between the knees, so that the fingers point backward. Bring the elbows and forearms together. Lean further forward, so that the abdomen rests on the elbows and the chest on the upper arms. Stretch both legs backward, so that they are together and straight. Slowly elevate the trunk and legs, until they are horizontal with the floor, Hold the head up, facing forward. In the final pose, the whole body is balanced only on the palms of both hands. The weight of the body is supported by the muscles of the abdomen, and not by the chest.

Verses 12b and 13a: Sukāsana, the easy pose

सुखासनम्

येन केन प्रकारेण सुखं धैर्यं च जायते ।।१२।।

तत् सुखासनमित्युक्तमशक्तस्तत् समाश्रयेत् ।१३।

sukhāsanam

yena kena prakāreṇa sukhaṃ dhairyaṃ ca jāyate

tat sukhāsanamityuktamaśaktastat samāśrayet (13a)

Anvay

yena kena prakāreṇa: by whatever way; *jāyate*: one becomes; *sukham ca dhairyam*: comfortable and steady; *tat iti uktam*: this is called; *sukhāsanam*: easy pose; *aśaktah*: one who is weak; *samāśrayet*: should resort to; *tat*: this.

Translation

By whatever way one becomes comfortable and steady, this is called the easy pose. One who is weak should resort to this.

Commentary

Sukhāsana, the easy pose, is the most basic cross-legged posture. Although it is the easiest and most relaxing meditation position for beginners and elderly practitioners, it is difficult to sustain for long periods. In sukhasana the legs may be crossed in any comfortable manner. Hence, it is not a locked posture, as were the other poses mentioned earlier, and it does not hold the body upright and still for long periods. Furthermore, the knees and thighs may not be directly on the floor, which is an important attribute of the classical meditation postures. When the knees and thighs remain above the floor, the whole body weight is supported by the buttocks, which causes backache to develop. When the knees and thighs rest firmly on the floor, there is a larger and steadier area of support.

Technique

Sit with both legs outstretched. Bend the right knee and place the right foot beneath the left thigh. Bend the left knee and place the left foot beneath the right thigh. Relax the arms by the sides and place the hands on the knees. Hold the head, neck, shoulders and back upright and straight.

Verses 13b and 14: Benefits of mastering āsana

आसनजयफलम्

आसनं विजितं येन जितं तेन जगत्त्रयं ।।१३।।

अनेन विधिना युक्तः प्राणायामं सदा कुरु ।।१४।।

āsanajayaphalam
āsanaṃ vijitaṃ yena jitaṃ tena jagattrayam (13b)
anena vidhinā yuktaḥ prāṇāyāmaṃ sadā kuru (14)

Anvay
phalam: result; *āsana-jaya*: mastery of *āsana*; *yena*: whoever; *āsanam vijitam*: victorious in *āsana*, meditative posture; *(yena*: that person;) *jitam*: victory; *jagat-trayam*: three worlds; *anena vidhinā*: according to this principle; *yuktaḥ*: one who is intent; *kuru*: should do; *sadā*: always; *prāṇāyāmam*: *prāṇāyāma*, breathing practices.

Translation
Result of mastery of āsana: Whoever is victorious in āsana attains victory over the three worlds. According to this principle, one who is intent [on āsana] should always do *prāṇāyāma.*

Commentary
According to this verse, the mastery of āsana gives one victory over the three worlds. For us, the three worlds can also be analogous with the body, energy and mind. Mastery of āsana gives flexibility, sensitivity and control over the physical body. It activates and rebalances the pranas, energies sustaining the body, and purifies, steadies and focuses the mind. Āsana should always be practiced before prāṇāyāma. When āsana is mastered, prāṇāyāma becomes very successful.

इति तृतीयः खण्डः
iti tṛtīyaḥ khaṇḍaḥ

Thus [ends] the third section.

चतुर्थः खण्डः

caturthaḥ khaṇḍaḥ

Fourth Section

देहप्रमाणम्

dehapramāṇam

The Subtle Body

Verses 1 & 2: Center of fire and triangle of śakti

शरीरं तावदेव स्यात् षण्णवत्यङ्गुलात्मकम् ।
देहमध्ये शिखिस्थानं तप्तजाम्बूनदप्रभम् ॥१॥
त्रिकोणं मनुजानां तु सत्यमुक्तं हि सांकृते ।
गुदात्तु द्व्यङ्गुलादूर्ध्वं मेढ्रात्तु द्व्यङ्गुलादधः ॥२॥

śarīraṃ tāvadeva syāt śaṇṇavatyaṅgulātmakam
dehamadhye śikhisthānaṃ taptajāmbūnadaprabham (1)
trikonaṃ manujānāṃ tu satyamuktaṃ hi sāṃkṛte
gudāttu dvyaṅgulādūrdhvaṃ medhrāttu dvyaṅgulādadhaḥ (2)

Anvay
śarīram: body; *syāt*: is; *eva*: *emphatic*; *tāvat*: of a size; *ātmakam*: consisting of; *śaṇṇavati-aṅgula*: ninety-six *aṅgulas*, width of one finger; *dehamadhye*: in the centre of the body; *śikhisthānam*: site of Agni; *prabham*: whose light; *tapta*: glows; *jāmbū-nada*: like gold from the Jāmbū river; *tu*: *conjunction*; *sāṃkṛte*: o Sāṃkṛti; *uktam*: there is; *satyam*: truly; *trikonam*: triangle; *hi*: here; *manujānām*: in men; *dvyangulāt*: two *angulas*; *ūrdhvam*: above; *gudāt*: anus; *tu*: and; *adhaḥ*: below; *medhrāt*: penis.

Translation
The body is of a size consisting of ninety-six *aṅgulas*. In the centre of the body [is] the site of *Agni*, whose light glows like gold from the Jambū river. O Sāṃkṛti, there is truly a triangle here in men. It is two aṅgulas above the anus and two aṅgulas below the penis.

Commentary
Here begins the description of the subtle body, which in yoga is said to be anterior to the physical body. The subtle body is also known as the pranic body, and gives energy, life and movement to the physical body with its multitude of organs and systems. The subtle body is described as 96 aṅgulas, or finger widths, which may be around 7 to 8 feet high. Although the subtle body is contained within the physical, it often extends beyond it. In yoga, the subtle, or pranic, body is considered to be very important, as all the practices work on it in various ways to rebalance and awaken it. At the center of this field is the *śikhistana*, the center of fire. In yoga, we also refer to this center as the *agni maṇḍala,* and it too plays an important role in the awakening of the subtle energies. This center is described here as glowing like gold, which may be compared to the reflection of the sun, while rising or setting over the Jamboo river.

Next, a triangle is described, which is located midway between the anal sphincter and the urinary organ, two finger widths in front of the anus and two finger widths behind the organ. The seer further emphasises that this triangle is 'truly' there although, as a part of the subtle body, it is invisible to the physical eye. This triangle is the symbol of *śakti*, creative potential, within the *mūladhara cakra*, the root psychic center, which is located two centimetres inside, just above this point. The *kuṇḍalinī śakti* is depicted as a tiny serpent within this triangle, coiled three and a half times around the smokey *śiva lingam*, symbol of consciousness. The triangle is also the symbol for the fire element, which is responsible for transformation. Originally, the sages had seen these symbols during deep meditation, and later passed them down to their disciples. Sāṃkṛti is the name of the worthy disciple or student, who receives these teachings directly from his master, the seer of this upanishad.

Verses 3, 4 and 5a: Root of the nāḍīs

देहमध्यं विजानीहि मानुजानां तु सांकृते ।
कन्दस्थानं मुनिश्रेष्ठ मूलाधारान्नवाङ्गुलम् ।।३।।
चतुरङ्गुलमायामविस्तारं मुनिपुङ्गव ।
कुक्कुटाण्डवदाकारं भूषितं तु त्वगादिभिः ।।४।।
तन्मध्ये नाभिरित्युक्तं योगज्ञैर्मुनिपुङ्गव ।५।

dehamadhyaṃ vijānīhi manujānāṃ tu sāṃkṛte
kandasthānaṃ muniśreṣṭha mūlādhārānnavāṅgulam (3)
caturaṅgulamāyāmavistāraṃ munipuṅgava
kukkuṭāṇḍavadākāraṃ bhūṣitaṃ tu tvagādibhiḥ (4)
tanmadhye nābhirityuktaṃ yogajñairmunipuṅgava (5a)

Anvay

sāṃkṛte muniśreṣṭha: o Sāṃkṛti, best of sages; *deha-madhyam vijānīhi manujānām*: in the centre of the human body; *kanda-sthānam*: site of the root of the *nāḍīs*; *nava-aṅgulam*: nine *angulas,* width of nine fingers; *mūlādhārāt*: from *mūlādhāra cakra,* pranic centre just below base of spine; *munipuṅgava*: o Esteemed Sage; *catur-aṅgulam-āyāma-vistāram*: four *aṅgulas* in length; *kukkuṭa-aṇḍavat-ākāram*: like the shape of a chicken egg; *bhūṣitam*: covered; *tvagādibhiḥ*: with skin etc; *iti-uktam*: it is said; *yoga-jñaiḥ*: wise ones; *nābhiḥ*: navel; *tan-madhye*: inside it.

Translation

O Sāmkṛti, best of sages, in the centre of the human body [is] the location of the root of the nāḍīs, nine aṅgulas from *mūlādhāra cakra*. O Esteemed Sage, it is four *aṅgulas* in length, like the shape of a chicken egg, covered with skin etc. O Esteemed Sage, it is said by the wise that the navel [is] inside it.

Commentary

In this verse the location of *kanda*, the root of the *nāḍīs*, or energy channels, is described as nine finger widths above mūlādhāra cakra. This would place it just below the manipura cakra in the center of the body. The kanda is said to be four finger widths long and oval shaped, like an egg. It is covered with a subtle membrane. The wise, who are able to see this phenomenon with their inner vision, have said that the navel lies within it. The navel is also the center of the solar plexus and many nerves and nāḍīs are connected with it.

Verses 5b to 8: Enumeration of the nāḍīs

नाडीपरिगणनम्

कन्दमध्यस्थिता नाडी सुषुम्नेति प्रकीर्तिता ।।५।।

तिष्ठन्ति परितस्तस्य नाडयो मुनिपुङ्गव ।

द्विसप्ततिसहस्राङि तासां मुख्याश्चतुर्दश ।।६।।

सुषुम्ना पिङ्गला तद्वदिडा चैव सरस्वती ।

पूषा च वरुणा चैव हस्तिजिह्वा यशस्विनी ।।७।।

अलम्बुसा कुहूश्चैव विश्वोदारा पयस्विनी ।

शन्खिनी चैव गान्धारा इति मुख्याश्चतुर्दश ।।८।।

nāḍīparigaṇanam
kandamadhyasthitā nāḍī suṣumneti prakīrtitā (5b)
tiṣṭhanti paritastasya nāḍayo munipuṅgava
dvisaptatisahasrāṇi tāsāṃ mukhyāścaturdaśa (6)
suṣumnā piṅgalā tadvadiḍā caiva sarasvatī
pūṣā ca varuṇā caiva hastijihvā yaśasvinī (7)
alambusā kuhūścaiva viśvadārā payasvinī
śaṅkhinī caiva gāndhārā iti mukhyāścaturdaśa (8)

Anvay

parigaṇanam: enumeration of; *nāḍī*: pranic channels; *sthitā*: situated in; *kanda-madhya*: centre of the *kanda*; *prakīrtitā*: is called; *suṣumnā*: *suṣumnā*; *paritas-tasya*: around it; *dvisaptati-sahasrāṇi*: seventy two thousand; *tāsām*: among which; *tiṣṭhanti*: are; *caturdaśa*: fourteen; *mukhyāḥ*: principal ones; *munipuṅgava*: o Esteemed Sage.

Translation

Enumeration of the nāḍīs: The nāḍī that is situated in the centre of the kanda is called suṣumnā. Around it are seventy two thousand nāḍīs, among which are the fourteen principal ones, o Esteemed Sage. The fourteen principal *nāḍīs* are called: *suṣumnā, piṅgalā,* also *iḍā*, and *sarasvatī, pūṣā* and *varuṇā,* as well as *hastijihvā, yaśasvinī, alambusā, kuhū* and also *viśvodārā, payasvinī, śaṅkhinī* and *gāndhārā.*

Commentary

This verse begins the description of the major nāḍīs, which originate at the kanda. Of the 72,000 nāḍīs, there are fourteen principal nāḍīs: *suṣumnā, iḍā* and *piṅgalā, sarasvatī, pūṣā, varuṇā, hastijihvā, yaśasvinī, alambusā, kuhū, viśvodārā, payasvinī, śaṅkhinī* and *gāndhārā*.

Verses 9 and 10: Brahma and suṣumnā nāḍīs

आसां मुख्यतमास्तिस्रस्तिसृष्वेकोत्तमोत्तमा ।
ब्रह्मनाडीति सा प्रोक्ता मुने वेदान्तवेदिभिः ।।९।।
पृष्ठमध्यस्थितेनास्था वीणादण्डेन सुव्रत ।
सह मस्तकपर्यन्तं सुषुम्ना सुप्रतिष्ठिता ।।१०।।

āsāṃ mukhyatamāstisrastisṛṣvekottamottamā
brahmanāḍīti sā proktā mune vedāntavedibhiḥ (9)
pṛṣṭhamadhyasthitenāsthā vīṇādaṇḍena suvrata
saha mastakaparyantaṃ suṣumnā supratiṣṭhitā (10)

Anvay

mukhyatamās: first of all; *āsām*: among them; *tisraḥ*: three; *uttama*: main ones; *tisṛṣu*: among the three; *ekā*: one; *uttamā*: main; *sā proktā*: this is called; *Brahmanaadee*: *brahma nāḍī*, main *nāḍī* through which *kuṇḍalinī* ascends; *vedānta-vedibhiḥ*: by those who know *vedānta*; *mune*: o Sage; *pṛṣṭha-madhya*: at the centre of the back; *supratiṣṭhitā*: straight; *vīṇā-daṇḍena*: as a *vīṇā* shaft; *asthā*: like a bone; *paryantam*: going right up to; *mastaka*: head.

Translation

First of all, among them, three [are] the main ones; among the three [there is] one main [nadi]. This is called *brahma nāḍī*, by those who know *vedānta*, o Sage. Suṣumna is at the centre of the back, straight as a *vīṇā* shaft, like a bone going right up to the head.

Commentary

Amongst the fourteen principal nāḍīs, three are major: *suṣumnā, iḍā* and *piṅgalā*. Of these three, *brahma nāḍī* is the most important. Interior to *suṣumnā*, are *citrini* and *brahma nāḍīs*. Together, these three *nāḍīs*: *brahma, citrini* and *suṣumnā*, connect the physical being with the psychic and spiritual dimensions. Brahma nāḍī is considered most important of the three, by those who know *vedānta*, because it is the pathway of the *kuṇḍalinī*. In the early times, when these teachings were passed down, only those who studied *vedānta* had knowledge of the subtle phenomena, and understood the significance of the nāḍīs and the kuṇḍalinī in relation to spiritual awakening.

In the majority of people, even today, the suṣumnā remains dormant. This ensures that the energy remains focused on the outer world, rather than awakening the inner potential. Of these three nāḍīs, *brahma* is the subtlest and the innermost. Brahma nāḍī is enveloped by citrini, alongside of which the *cakras* are located. Suṣumnā forms a sheath around citrini, and rises straight up the center of the spinal column to the crown of the head.

Verses 11, 12 and 13a: Kuṇḍalinī

कुण्डल्याः स्थानं स्वरूपं च
नाभिकन्दादधः स्थानं कुण्डल्या द्व्यङ्गुलं मुने ।
अष्टप्रकृतिरूपा सा कुण्डली मुनिसत्तम ।।११।।
यथावद्वायुचेष्टां च जलन्नादिनि नित्यशः ।
परितः कन्दपार्श्चेषु निरुध्यैव सदा स्थिता ।।१२।।
स्वमुखेन संवेष्टय ब्रह्मरन्ध्र मुखं मुने ।१३।

kuṇḍalyāḥ sthānaṃ svarūpaṃ ca
nābhikandādadhaḥ sthānaṃ kuṇḍalyā dvyaṅgulaṃ mune
aṣṭaprakṛtirūpā sā kuṇḍalī munisattama (11)
yathāvadvāyuceṣṭāṃ ca jalannādini nityaśaḥ
paritaḥ kandapārśceṣu nirudhyaiva sadā sthitā (12)
svamukhena saṃveṣṭaya brahmarandhra mukhaṃ mune (13a)

Anvay

sthānam: location; *ca*: and; *svarūpam*: qualities; *kuṇḍalyāḥ*: of the *kuṇḍalī*; *dvi-aṅgulam*: two *aṅgulas*; *adhaḥ*: below; *nābhi-kandāt*: root of the navel; *rūpā*: form; *aṣṭa-prakṛti*: eight elements of nature; *munisattama*: Most Venerable Sage; *nityaśaḥ*: constantly; *ādini*: one is consuming; *jalanna*: water and food; *ca*: and; *cestām*: movement; *vāyu*: air; *yathāvat*: just like; *sadā*: always; *sthitā*: located; *paritaḥ*: around; *kanda-pārśceṣu*: sides of the *kanda*; *eva*: *emphatic*; *nirudhya*: blocks; *brahmarandhra*: fontanelle; *mukham*: mouth; *saṃveṣṭaya*: surrounding; *svamukhena*: with her own mouth; *mune*: o Sage.

Translation

Location and qualities of the *kuṇḍalī*: The location of the kuṇḍalī is two aṅgulas below the root of the navel, o Sage. The kuṇḍalī [has] the form of the eight elements of nature, most venerable Sage. [When] one is constantly consuming water and food and the movement of air, just like [the kuṇḍalī] always located around the sides of the kanda, blocks the fontanelle mouth, surrounding [it] with her own mouth, o Sage.

Commentary

The location of of the kuṇḍalinī is given here as two finger widths below the navel, where the kanda is located. Other texts on kuṇḍalinī yoga locate the kuṇḍalinī at the mūlādhāra cakra, just above the perineum. The location of kuṇḍalinī at mūlādhāra is her unconscious abode, where she rests in her most primal state. Here the inner awareness remains grounded in the material world. Whereas, the kuṇḍalinī energy residing at the kanda is in a more dynamic state, ready to awaken and ascend. This is why some traditions recognise the navel or maṇipura cakra as the center for awakening, while others speak of kuṇḍalinī, residing at the mūlādhāra cakra.

The kuṇḍalinī has the form of the eight elements of nature. These are represented by the cakra, which she deposits on her descent down through the suṣumnā. First she deposits the three elements of mind: *buddhi* (intellect), *citta* (memory) and *ahaṃkāra* (ego), at *ājñā cakra*, at the top of the spinal column. Next she descends to *viśuddhi cakra*, behind the throat, and deposits the element of space. Then she descends to *anāhata cakra*, behind the heart, and deposits the element of air. Next she descends to *maṇipura cakra*, behind the navel, and deposits the element of fire. She continues on her journey down to *swādhiṣṭhāna cakra*, behind the pubis, and deposits the energy of water, and finally she descends to *mūlādhāra cakra*, above the perineum, and deposits the energy of earth.

These five elements: earth, water, fire, air and space, along with the three elements of mind: buddhi, citta and ahaṃkāra, make eight elements of nature, which all human beings are comprised of. These eight elements represent the evolution of the kuṇḍalinī energy from divine to material, which is the cause of creation. Having assumed the earthly form through the combination and permutation of these elements, one must constantly consume food and water, and breathe air. The continuous intake of these earthly elements blocks the *brahmarandhra*, the opening of the brahma nāḍī at the fontanelle, holding the spirit in the body, in the same way that the kuṇḍalinī blocks the opening of suṣumnā at the lower centers with her own mouth at the kanda.

Verses 13b to 17: Location of the major nāḍīs

नाडीस्थानानि

सुषुम्नाया इडा सव्ये दक्षिणे पिङ्गला स्थिता ।।१३।।

सरस्वती कुहूश्चैव सुषुम्नापार्श्वयोः स्थिते ।

गान्धारा हस्तिजिह्वा च इडायाः पृष्ठपूर्वयोः ।।१४।।

पूषा यशस्विनी चैव पिङ्गलापृष्ठपूर्वयोः ।

कुहाश्च हस्तिजिह्वाया मध्ये विश्वोदरा स्थिता ।।१५।।

यशस्विन्याः कुहार्मध्ये वरुणा सुप्रतिष्ठिता ।

पूषायाश्च सरस्वत्या मध्ये प्रोक्ता यशस्विनी ।।१६।।

गान्धारायाः सरस्वत्या मध्ये प्रोक्ता च शङ्खिनी ।

अलम्बुसा स्थिता पायुपर्यन्तं कन्दमध्यगा ।।१७।।

nāḍīsthānāni
suṣumnāyā iḍā savye dakṣiṇe piṅgalā sthitā (13b)
sarasvatī kuhūścaiva suṣumnāpārśvayoḥ sthite
gāndhārā hastijihvā ca iḍāyāḥ pṛṣṭhapūrvayoḥ (14)
pūṣā yaśasvinī caiva piṅgalāpṛṣṭhapūrvayoḥ
kuhāśca hastijihvāyā madhye viśvodarā sthitā (15)
yaśasvinyāḥ kuhārmadhye varuṇā supratiṣṭhitā
pūṣāyāśca sarasvatyā madhye proktā yaśasvinī (16)
gāndhārāyāḥ sarasvatyā madhye proktā ca śaṅkhinī
alambusā sthitā pāyuparyantaṃ kandamadhyagā (17)

Anvay

nāḍī-sthānāni: locations of the *nāḍīs,* psychic currents; *iḍā*: *iḍā*, current of energy between the left nostril and base of spine, influencing left side of body and right side of brain; *savye*: on the left; *suṣumnāyā*: of *suṣumnā*, central energy flow; *piṅgalā*: *piṅgalā*, current of energy between the right nostril and base of spine, influencing right side of body and left side of brain; *dakṣiṇe*: on the right; *sarasvatī kuhūḥ-ca-eva*: *sarasvatī* and also *kuhū* (new moon); *sthite*: are;

suṣumnā-pārśvayoḥ: on both sides of *suṣumnā*; *gāndhārā pṛṣṭha*: *gāndhārā* [is] at the back; *ca hastijihvā pūrvayoḥ*: and *hastijihvā* at the front; *iḍāyāḥ*: of *iḍā*; *pūṣā yaśasvinī ca eva*: *pūṣā* and also *yaśasvinī*; *piṅgalā-pṛṣṭha-pūrvayoḥ*: are at the back and front of *piṅgalā*; *ca*: and; *viśvodarā sthitā*: *viśvodarā* is located; *madhye*: between; *hastijihvāyā kuhoḥ*: *hastijihvā* and *kuhū*; *varuṇā supratiṣṭhitā*: *varuṇā* is fixed; *madhye*: between; *yaśasvinyāḥ kuhāḥ*: *yaśasvinī* and *kuhū*; *yaśasvinī proktā*: *yaśasvinī* is said; *madhye pūṣāyāḥ ca sarasvatyāḥ*: between *pūṣā* and *sarasvatī*; *śaṅkhinī proktā*: *śaṅkhinī* is said; *madhye gāndhārāyāḥ ca sarasvatyāḥ*: between *gāndhārā* and *sarasvatī*; *alambusā gā paryantam*: *alambusā* goes right up to; *pāyu*: anus; *kanda-madhya*: from the centre of the *kanda*.

Translation

Locations of the nāḍīs: iḍā is on the left of suṣumnā; piṅgalā is on the right. Sarasvatī and also kuhū are on both sides of suṣumnā. Gāndhārā is at the back and hastijihvā at the front of iḍā. Pūṣā is at the back and yaśasvinī at the front of piṅgalā. Viśvodarā is located between kuhū and hastijihvā. Varuṇā is fixed between yaśasvinī and kuhū. Yaśasvinī is said to be between pūṣā and sarasvatī. Śaṅkhinī is said to be between gāndhārā and sarasvatī. Alambusā goes right up to the anus from the kanda.

Commentary

This verse contains a very clear description of the location of the fourteen major nāḍīs in relation to suṣumnā, iḍā and piṅgalā. Suṣumnā rises straight up through the center of the spinal passage from a point just above the mūlādhāra cakra. Iḍā originates to the left of suṣumnā and piṅgalā to the right. Saraswatī and kuhū are also located to the left and right of suṣumnā. Gāndhārā is at the back of iḍā and hastijihvā is at the front. Pūṣā is at the back of piṅgalā and yaśasvinī is at the front. Viśvodarā is located in-between *kuhū* and hastijihvā. Varuṇā is in-between yaśasvinī and kuhū. Yaśasvinī is in-between pūṣā and sarasvatī. Śaṅkhinī is in-between gāndhārā and *saraswatī*. Alambusā goes from the kanda to the anus.

Verses 18 to 23a: Termination of the major nāḍīs

पूर्वभागे सुषुम्नाया राकायाः संस्थिताः कुहूः ।
अधश्चोर्ध्वं स्थिता नाडी याम्यनासान्तमिष्यते ।।१८।।
इडा तु सव्यनासान्तं संस्थिता मुनिपुङ्गव ।
यशस्विनी च वामस्य पादाङ्गुष्ठान्तमिष्यते ।।१९।।
पूषा वामाक्षिपर्यन्ता पिङ्गलायास्तु पृष्ठतः ।
पयस्विनी च याम्यस्य कर्णान्तं प्रोच्यते बुधैः ।।२०।।
सरस्वती तथा चोर्ध्वं गता जिह्वा तथा मुने ।
हस्तिजिह्वा तथा सव्यपादाङ्गुष्ठान्तमिष्यते ।।२१।।
शङ्खिनी नाम या नाडी सव्यकर्णान्तमिष्यते ।
गान्धारा सव्यनेत्रान्ता प्रोक्ता वेदान्तवेदिभिः ।।२२।।
विष्वोदराभिधा नाडी कन्दमध्ये व्यवस्थिता ।२३।

pūrvabhāge suṣumnāyā rākāyāḥ saṃsthitā kuhūḥ
adhaścordhvaṃ sthitā nāḍī yāmyanāsāntamiṣyate (18)
iḍā tu savyanāsāntam saṃsthitā munipuṅgava
yaśasvinī ca vāmasya pādāṅguṣṭhāntamiṣyate (19)
pūṣā vāmākṣiparyantā piṅgalāyāstu pṛṣṭhataḥ
payasvinī ca yāmyasya karṇāntaṃ procyate budhaiḥ (20)
sarasvatī tathā cordhvaṃ gatā jihvā tathā mune
hastijihvā tathā savyapādāṅguṣṭhāntamiṣyate (21)
śaṅkhinī nāma yā nāḍī savyakarṇāntamiṣyate
gāndhārā savyanetrāntā proktā vedāntavedibhiḥ (22)
viṣvodarābhidhā nāḍī kandamadhye vyavasthitā (23a)

Anvay

kuhūḥ saṃsthitāḥ: *kuhū* is located; *pūrvabhāge suṣumnāyā*: in the upper part of *suṣumnā*; *rākāyāḥ*: full moon; *nāḍī sthitā ūrdhvam ca adhaḥ*: *nāḍī* goes up and down; *yāmya-nāsāntam*: southern nostril; *tu*: now; *iḍā saṃsthitā*: *iḍā* is located at; *savya-nāsāntam*: left nostril; *munipuṅgava*: o Esteemed Sage; *ca yaśasvinī iṣyate*: and *yaśasvinī* goes to;

vāmasya pāda-aṅguṣṭhāntam: toes of the left leg; *pūṣā paryantā*: *pūṣā* [goes] right up to; *vāma-akṣi*: left eye; *tu pṛṣṭhataḥ piṅgalāyāḥ*: and is behind *piṅgalā*; *ca payasvinī procyate*: and *payasvinī* is said; *budhaiḥ*: by the wise; *yāmyasya karṇāntam*: to the left ear; *tathā*: then; *sarasvatī gatā*: *sarasvatī* goes; *ūrdhvam jihvā*: up to the tongue; *mune*: o Sage; *ca hastijihvā*: and *hastijihvā*; *iṣyate*: goes; *aṅguṣṭha-antam*: up to the toes; *savya-pāda*: left leg; *nāḍī nāma śaṅkhinī*: *nāḍī* called *śaṅkhinī*; *iṣyate*: goes; *savya-karṇa-antam*: up to the left ear; *gāndhārā proktā*: *gāndhārā* is said; *vedānta-vedibhiḥ*: by those versed in the Vedas; *savya-netra-antā*: up to the left eye; *nāḍī viṣvodarā-ābhidhā*: *nāḍī* named *viṣvodarā*; *vyavasthitā*: is situated; *kanda-madhye*: at the centre of the *kanda*.

Translation

Kuhū is located at the upper part of suṣumnā, the full moon. [This] nāḍī goes up and down the southern nostril. Now iḍā is located at the left nostril, o esteemed Sage, and yaśasvinī goes to the toes of the left leg. Pūṣā [goes] right up to the left eye and is behind piṅgalā, and payasvinī is said by the wise [to go] to the left ear. Then sarasvatī goes up to the tongue, o Sage, and hastijihvā goes up to the toes [of] the left leg. The nāḍī called śaṅkhinī goes up to the left ear; gāndhārā is said by those versed in the Vedas [to go] up to the left eye. The nāḍī named viṣvodarā is situated at the centre of the kanda.

Commentary

Kuhū rises to the upper part of suṣumnā, which glows like the full moon. Kuhū goes up and down the back of the throat, behind the nostrils. Iḍā terminates at the left nostril and piṅgalā at the right. Suṣumnā represents the balanced flow of both nostrils together. Yaśasvinī flows downward to the left toes. Pūṣā flows up the right side behind piṅgalā and crosses over to the left eye. Payasvinī goes up to the left ear. Sarasvatī goes to the tongue. Hastijihvā goes to the toes of the left foot. Śaṅkhinī goes to the left ear, and gāndhārā goes to the left eye. Viṣvodarā is at the center of the kanda.

The description of the ten major nāḍīs is found in several upaniṣads and classical texts, such as the *Śiva Swarodaya*. The yogis and rishis of old had originally seen these channels during their meditation, and later described what they had seen to their devotees and disciples. In the early times such instruction had to be remembered, as there were very few capable scribes. Hence, we find similarities as well as differences in regard to the names and placements of these subtle channels.

In the *Śiva Swarodaya*, for example, kuhū is located in the reproductive organs, so we can assume that it rises through the body to the upper part of suṣumnā. Again, yaśasvinī is said to flow down to the left toes in this text, while the *Śiva Swarodaya* describes it flowing up to the left ear. Pūṣā is said to terminate at the left eye in this text, while in *Śiva Swarodaya* it is the right ear. Hastijihvā goes to the left toes in this text, while *Śiva Swarodaya* states the right eye. Śaṅkhinī goes to the anal region, according to *Śiva Swarodaya*, and to the left ear, according to this text. Both texts mention that gāndhārā goes to the left eye.

Verses 23b to 30a: Ten prāṇas

नाडीषु वायुसञ्चरः
प्राणो ऽपानस्तथा व्यानः समानोदान एव च ।।२३।।
नागः कूर्मश्च कृकरो देवदत्तो धनंजयः ।
एते नाडीषु सर्वासु चरन्ति दश वायवः ।।२४।।
तेषु प्राणादयः पञ्च सुख्याः पञ्चसु सुव्रत ।
प्राणसंज्ञस्तथा ऽपानः पूज्यः प्राणस्तयोर्मुने ।।२५।।
आस्यनासिकयोर्मध्ये नाभिमध्ये तथा हृदि ।
प्राणसंज्ञो ऽनिलो नित्यं वर्तते मुनिसत्तम ।।२६।।
अपानो वर्तते नित्यं गुदमध्योरुजानुषु ।
उदरे सकले कट्यां नाभौ जङ्घे च सुव्रत ।।२७।।
व्यानः श्रोत्राक्षिमध्ये च कुकुद्भ्यां गुल्फयोरपि ।
प्राणस्थाने गले चैव वर्तते मुनिपुङ्गव ।।२८।।
उदानसंज्ञो विज्ञेयः पादयोर्हस्तयोरपि ।
समानः सर्वदेहेषु व्याप्य तिष्ठत्यसंशयः ।।२९।।
नागादिवायवः पञ्च त्वगस्थ्यादिषु संस्थिताः ।३०।

nāḍīṣu vāyusañcaraḥ
prāṇo 'pānastathā vyānaḥ samānodāna eva ca (23b)
nāgaḥ kūrmaśca kṛkaro devadatto dhanaṃjayaḥ
ete nāḍīṣu sarvāsu caranti daśa vāyavaḥ (24)
teṣu prāṇādayaḥ pañca sukhyāḥ pañcasu suvrata
prāṇasaṃjñastathā 'pānaḥ pūjyaḥ prāṇastayormune (25)
āsyanāsikayormadhye nābhimadhye tathā hṛdi
prāṇasaṃjño 'nilo nityaṃ vartate munisattama (26)
apāno vartate nityaṃ gudamadhyorujānuṣu
udare sakale katyāṃ nābhau jaṅghe ca suvrata (27)
vyānaḥ śrotrākṣimadhye ca kakudbhyāṃ gulphayorapi
prāṇasthāne gale caiva vartate munipuṅgava (28)
udānasaṃjño vijñeyaḥ pādayorhastayorapi

samānaḥ sarvadeheṣu vyāpya tiṣṭhatyasaṃśayaḥ (29)
nāgādivāyavaḥ pañca tvagasthyādiṣu saṃsthitāḥ (30a)

Anvay

sañcaraḥ: movement; *vāyu*: *prāṇa*, vital air; *prāṇa*: vital energy; *apāna*: downward energy; *vyāna*: energy pervading the whole body; *samāna*: sideways energy between navel and diaphragm; *udāna*: energy in arms, legs and head; *nāga*: energy for burping and hiccupping; *kūrma*: energy for movement of eyelids; *kṛkara*: energy for sneezing, coughing, hunger and thirst; *devadatta*: energy for yawning; *dhanaṃjaya*: energy for decomposition of dead body; *ete daśa vāyavaḥ*: those ten *prāṇas*; *caranti*: are circulating; *nāḍīṣu sarvāsu*: in all the *nāḍīs*; *teṣu*: of these; *pañca prāṇādayaḥ*: five *prāṇic* bodies; *sukhyāḥ*: most beneficial; *suvrata*: o Virtuous One; *pañcasu*: among [these] five; *saṃjñaḥ*: called; *tathā*: and; *pūjyaḥ*: is to be worshipped; *mune*: o Sage; *tathā*: thus; *anilaḥ*: vital air; *prāṇa-saṃjñaḥ*: called *prāṇa*; *vartate*: exists; *nityam*: continuously; *madhye*: within; *āsya*: face; *nāsikayoḥ*: nostrils; *nābhi*: navel; *hṛdi*: heart; *munisattama*: o Excellent Sage; *guda*: anus; *udare*: stomach; *nābhau*: navel; *sakale katyām ca jaṅghe*: each hip and thigh; *ujānuṣu*: up to the knees; *suvrata*: o Virtuous One; *śrotra-akṣi-madhye*: within the ears [and] eyes; *kukudbhyām*: from the shoulders; *ca ... api*: and ... also; *gulphayoḥ*: in the ankles; *ca . . . eva*: and even; *prāṇa-sthāne*: in the *prāṇic* area; *gale*: in the neck; *munipuṅgava*: o Esteemed Sage; *vijñeyaḥ*: is known; *pādayoḥ*: in the feet; *api*: also; *hastayoḥ*: in the hands; *asaṃśayaḥ*: without doubt; *tiṣṭhati vyāpya*: is contained; *sarva-deheṣu*: in the whole body; *pañca vāyavaḥ*: five *prāṇas*; *ādi*: beginning with; *saṃsthitāḥ*: are located; *tvag-asthi-ādiṣu*: in the skin, bones, etc.

Translation

The movement of prāṇa in the nāḍīs: *prāṇa, apāna, vyāna, samāna, udāna,* and also *nāga, kūrma, kṛkara, devadatta* and *dhanaṃjaya* are the ten prāṇas, circulating in all the nāḍīs. Of these, five prāṇas are the most beneficial, o Virtuous One. Among [these] five prāṇas, called prāṇa and apana, prāṇa is to be worshipped, o Sage. Thus the vital air called prāṇa exists continuously within the face, the nostrils, the navel [and] the heart, o excellent Sage. Apāna is continuously in the anus, stomach, navel, and each hip and thigh up to the knees, o Virtuous One. Vyāna is within the ears, eyes, from the shoulders and also in the ankles, and even in the pranic area in the neck, o esteemed Sage. Udāna is known in the feet [and] also the hands. Samāna is without doubt contained in the whole body. The five (minor) prāṇas, beginning with nāga are located in the skin, bones etc.

Commentary

These verses name the five major and five minor prāṇas. The locations given here may differ to those given in other classical texts. The five major prāṇas are: *prāṇa*, *apāna, vyāna, samāna*, and *udāna*. These five prāṇas continuously sustain the physical body with vitality and life. Of these five, prāṇa is considered to be the most important. It flows upward from the navel to the heart and in the nostrils. It supports the lungs and heart. Apāna flows downward from the navel to the anus, hips, thighs and knees. It sustains the reproductive and excretory organs. Vyāna flows in the region of the shoulders, neck and head, sustaining the sensory organs, such as ears, eyes, nose, tongue, as well as the nervous system and the brain. Udāna flows in the hands and feet. Samāna flows throughout the whole body. The five minor prāṇas, beginning with nāga, are said to be located in the skin and bones, etc.

Again, the location of the prāṇas is different, as per the *Śiva Swarodaya,* which says that *prāṇa* is at the heart, apāna in the excretory organs, samāna at the navel region, udāna at the throat, and vyāna pervades the whole body.

Verses 30b to 34: Functions of the prāṇas

वायुव्यापाराः
निःश्वासोच्छ्वासकासाश्च प्राणक्रम हि सांकृते ।।३०।।
अपानाख्यस्य वायोस्तु विण्मूत्रादिविसर्जनम् ।
समानः सर्वसामीप्यं करोति मुनिपुङ्गव ।।३१।।
उदान ऊर्ध्वगमनं करोत्येव न संशयः ।
व्यानो विवादकृत् प्रोक्तो मुने वेदान्तवेदिभिः ।।३२।।
उद्गारादिगुणः प्रोक्तो नागाख्यस्य महामुने ।
धनंजयस्य शोभादि कर्म प्रोक्तं हि सांकृते ।।३३।।
निमीलनादि कूर्मस्य क्षुधा तु कृकरस्य च ।
देवदत्तस्य विप्रेन्द्र तन्द्रीकर्म प्रकीर्तितम् ।।३४।।

vāyuvyāpārāḥ
niḥśvāsocchvāsakāsāśca prāṇakarma hi sāṃkṛte (30b)
apānākhyasya vāyostu viṇmūtrādivisarjanam
samānaḥ sarvasāmīpyaṃ karoti munipuṅgava (31)
udāna ūrdhvagamanaṃ karotyeva na saṃśayaḥ
vyāno vivādakṛt prokto mune vedāntavedibhiḥ (32)
udgārādiguṇaḥ prokto nāgākhyasya mahāmune
dhanaṃjayasya śobhādi karma proktaṃ hi sāṃkṛte (33)
nimīlanādi kūrmasya kṣudhā tu kṛkarasya ca
devadattasya viprendra tandrīkarma prakīrtitam (34)

Anvay
vāyu-vyāpārāḥ: functions of the vital airs; *niḥśvāsa*: sighing; *ucchvāsa*: exhalation; *ca*: and; *kāsāḥ*: coughing; *prāṇa-karma*: activity of *prāṇa*; *hi*: *emphatic*; *sāṃkṛte*: o Sāṃkṛti; *tu*: now; *viṇmūtrādi*: feces and urine etc; *visarjanam*: are evacuated; *vāyoḥ*: by the vital air; *apāna-ākhyasya*: called *apāna*; *samānaḥ*: *samāna*; *karoti*: acts; *sarva-sāmīpyam*: in this whole region; *munipuṅgava*: o Esteemed Sage; *eva na saṃśayaḥ*: for sure; *udānaḥ*: *udāna*; *karoti*: performs;

ūrdhvagamanam: upward movement; *vyānaḥ*: *vyāna*; *proktaḥ*: is said; *vedānta-vedibhiḥ*: by those who know *vedānta*; *kṛt*: to cause; *vivāda*: conflict; *mune*: o Sage; *nāgākhyasya*: the one called *nāga*; *proktaḥ*: is said; *guṇaḥ*: attributes; *udgāra*: belching; *ādi*: etc; *mahāmune*: o Great Sage; *proktam*: it is said; *dhanaṃjayasya*: dhanamjaya; *karma*: effect; *śobhādi*: lustre; *Hi*: *emphatic*; *Tu*: now; *kūrmasya*: *kūrma*; *nimīlana*: shutting the eyes; *ādi*: etc; *ca*: and; *kṛikarasya*: *kṛkara*; *kṣudhā*: hunger; *prakīrtitam*: it is stated; *devadattasya*: *devadatta*; *karma*: cause; *tandrī*: sleep; *viprendra*: o distinguished Brahman.

Translation

Functions of the prāṇas: Sighing, exhalation and coughing are the activity of prāṇa, o Samkriti. Now, feces and urine etc are evacuated by the vital air called apāna. Samāna acts in this whole region, o esteemed Sage. For sure udāna performs the upward movement. Vyāna is said by those who know vedānta to cause conflict [between them], o Sage. The one called *nāga* is said [to have] the attributes of belching etc, o great Sage. *Dhanaṃjaya* is said [to have] the effect [of] lustre, o Sāṃkṛti. Now *kūrma* [causes] shutting the eyes etc, and *kṛkara* [causes] hunger. It is stated that *devadatta* [is] the cause [of] sleep, o distinguished Brahman.

Commentary

Here the functions of the ten *prāṇas* are enumerated. Of the five major energies, prāṇa is the energy responsible for sighing, coughing and exhalation. Apāna is responsible for evacuation of faeces, urine, gas and wind, and the foetus at the time of birth. Samāna vitalises the entire body. Udāna flows upward and mobilises the hands and feet. Vyāna flows in the region of the shoulders, neck and head, and vitalises the senses and brain, causing conflict.

Of the five minor prāṇas, *nāga* is responsible for belching and hiccuping. *Dhanaṃjaya* gives lustre to the skin. *Kūrma* causes blinking and shutting of the eyes. *Kṛkara* causes hunger and *devadatta* is the cause of sleep.

Verses 35 to 39a: Deities relating with the nāḍīs

नाडीदेवताः

सुषुम्नायाः शिवो देव इडाया देवताहरिः ।

पिङ्गलाया विरिञ्चः स्यात् सरस्वत्या विराण्मुने ।।३५।।

पूषा ऽधिदेवता प्रोक्तो वरुणा वायुदेवता ।

हस्तिजिह्वाभिधायास्तु वरुणो देवता भवेत् ।।३६।।

यशस्विन्या मुनिश्रेष्ठ भगवान् भास्करस्तथा ।

अलम्बुसाया अबात्मा वरुणः परिकीर्तितः ।।३७।।

कुहोः क्षुद्देवता प्रोक्ता गान्धारी चन्द्रदेवता ।

शङ्खिन्याश्चन्द्रमास्तद्वत् पयस्विन्याः प्रजापतिः ।।३८।।

विश्वोदराभिधायास्तु भगवान् पावकः पतिः ।३९।

nāḍīdevatāḥ
suṣumnāyāḥ śivo deva iḍāyā devatā hariḥ
piṅgalāyā viriñcaḥ syāt sarasvatyā virāṇmune (35)
pūṣā 'dhidevatā prokto varuṇā vāyudevatā
hastijihvābhidhāyāstu varuṇo devatā bhavet (36)
yaśasvinyā muniśreṣtha bhagavān bhāskarastathā
alambusāyā abātmā varuṇaḥ parikīrtitaḥ (37)
kuhoḥ kṣuddevatā proktā gāndhārī candradevatā
śaṅkhinyāścandramāstadvat payasvinyāḥ prajāpatiḥ (38)
viśvodarābhidhāyāstu bhagavān pāvakaḥ patiḥ (39a)

Anvay

nāḍī-devataḥ: *nāḍī* deities; *śivaḥ*: Śiva; *syāt*: is; *deva*: god; *suṣumnāyāḥ*: of *suṣumna*; *hariḥ*: Hari; *devatā*: deity; *iḍāyāḥ*: of *iḍā*; *viriñcaḥ*: Virinca; *piṅgalāyāḥ*: of *piṅgalā*; *virāt*: Virat; *sarasvatyāḥ*: of *sarasvatī*; *mune*: o Sage; *adhidevatā*: Adhidevatā, Supreme Deity; *proktaḥ*: is said; *pūṣā*: *pūṣā*; *varuṇā*: Varuṇā; *vāyu-devatā*: deity of *vāyu*; *varuṇā bhavet*: Varuṇā is; *devatā*: deity; *Hastijihvā-abhidhāyāḥ*: of the one named Hastijihvā; *parikīrtitaḥ*: it is declared; *muniśreṣtha*: o distinguished Sage; *bhagavān bhāskaraḥ*: Bhagavān Bhāskara; *yaśasvinyāḥ*: of *yaśasvinī*; *tathā*: and; *varuṇaḥ abātmā*: Varuṇā [has] the nature; *alambusāyāḥ*: of *alambusā*; *devatā kuhoḥ*: deity of *kuhū*; *kṣut*: Hunger; *candra*: Moon; *proktā*: is called; *devatā gāndhārī*: deity of *gāndhārī*; *tadvat*: likewise; *śaṅkhinyāḥ candra*: *śaṅkhinī* has the Moon; *payasvinyāḥ prajāpatiḥ*: *payasvinī* Prajapati; *tu*: and; *viśvodara-abhidhāyāḥ*: the one named *viśvodara* has; *patiḥ*: lord; *bhagavān pāvakaḥ*: Bhagavān Pāvaka.

Translation
The nāḍī deities: Śiva is the deity of *suṣumnā*. Hari is the deity of *iḍā*, Virinca of *piṅgalā* and Virat of *sarasvatī*, o Sage. Adhidevata, the Supreme Deity, is said [to be for] *pūṣā* [and] Varuṇā, the deity of *vāyu*, is the deity of the one named *hastijihvā*. It is declared, o distinguished Sage, that Bhagavān Bhaskara [is the deity] of *yaśasvinī*, and Varuṇā [has] the nature of *alambusā*. The deity of *kuhū* is Hunger; the Moon is called the deity of *gāndhārī*. Likewise, *śaṅkhinī* has the Moon, *payasvinī* Prajapati and the one named *viśvodara* has the lord Bhagavan Pavaka.

Commentary
Śiva, the lord of transcendental consciousness, is the deity of *suṣumnā*. Hari, or Vishnu, the lord who maintains the creation, is the deity of *iḍā*. Virinca, or Brahma, the lord of creation, is the deity of *piṅgalā*. Virat, the brilliant lord of all manifest creation, is the deity of *saraswatī*. Adhidevata, the supreme *deva*, is the deity of *pūṣā*. Varuṇā, lord of waters, is the deity of *hastijihvā*. Bhaskara, lord of light, is the deity of *yaśasvinī*. Varuṇā relates to *alambusā*. The deity of *kuhū* is Hunger. The Moon is the deity of *gāndhārī*, as well as *śaṅkhinī*, Prajapati, lord of creation, is the deity of *payasvinī*, and Pavaka, or *Agni*, lord of fire, is the deity of *viśvodara*.

Verses 39b and 40a: Lunar and solar movement in the nāḍīs

नाडीषु चन्द्रसुर्यसञ्चारः
इडायां चन्द्रमा नित्यं चरत्येव महामुने ।।३९।।
पिङ्गलायां रविस्तद्वन्मुने वेदविदां वर ।४०।

nāḍīṣu candrasūryasañcāraḥ
iḍāyāṃ candramā nityaṃ caratyeva mahāmune (39b)
piṅgalāyāṃ ravistadvanmune vedavidāṃ vara (40a)

Anvay
sañcāraḥ: movement of; *candra*: Moon; *sūrya*: Sun; *nāḍīṣu*: in the *nāḍīs*; *candramā*: lunar energy; *eva*: *emphatic*; *nityam*: always; *carati*: does flow; *iḍāyām*: in *iḍā*; *mahāmune*: o Great Sage; *tadvat*: likewise; *raviḥ*: solar energy; *piṅgalāyām*: in *piṅgalā*; *vara mune*: o Excellent Sage; *vedavidām*: of those who know the Vedas.

Translation
The movement of the moon and sun in the nāḍīs: The lunar energy does always flow in *iḍā*, o Great Sage. Likewise, the solar energy [flows] in *piṅgalā*, o excellent Sage of those who know the Vedas.

Commentary
Iḍā nāḍī carries the mental energy and hence it is said to relate with the moon, or lunar flow of prana. Iḍā is predominant in the left side of the body and the right side of the brain. Piṅgalā nāḍī is responsible for the energy of life and movement. Hence it is said to relate with the sun, or the solar flow. Piṅgalā is predominant in the right side of the body and the left brain.

Verses 40b to 43a: Uttarāyan and dakṣiṇāyan

नाडीषु संवत्सरात्मकप्राणसूर्यसञ्चारः
पिङ्गलाया इडायां तु वायोः संक्रमणं तु यत् ।।४०।।
तदुत्तरायणं प्रोक्तं मुने वेदान्तवेदिभिः ।
इडायाः पिङ्गलायां तु प्राणसंक्रमणं मुने ।।४१।।
दक्षिणायनमित्युक्तं पिङ्गलायामिति श्रुतिः ।
इडापिङ्गलयोः संधि यदा प्राणः समागतः ।।४२।।
अमावास्या तदा प्रोक्ता देहे देहभृतां वर ।४३।

nāḍīṣu samvatsarātmakaprāṇasūryasañcāraḥ
piṅgalāyāḥ iḍāyāṃ tu vāyoḥ saṃkramaṇaṃ tu yat (40b)
taduttarāyaṇaṃ proktaṃ mune vedāntavedibhiḥ
iḍāyāḥ piṅgalāyāṃ tu prāṇasaṃkramaṇaṃ mune (41)
dakṣiṇāyanamityuktaṃ piṅgalāyāmiti śrutiḥ
iḍāpiṅgalayoḥ saṃdhi yadā prāṇaḥ samāgataḥ (42)
amāvāsyā tadā proktā dehe dehabhṛtāṃ vara (43a)

Anvay
samvatsarātmaka: yearly; *sañcāraḥ*: flow; *sūrya*: solar; *prāṇa*: energy; *nāḍīṣu*: in the *nāḍīs*; *tu*: now; *yat*: when; *vāyoḥ*: vital airs; *saṃkramaṇam*: move; *piṅgalāyāḥ*: from *piṅgalā*, right major pranic channel; *iḍāyām*: into *iḍā*, left major pranic channel; *tat*: that; *proktam*: is called; *uttarāyaṇam*: *uttarāyaṇam*, northern path; *vedāntavedibhiḥ*: by those who know *vedānta*; *mune*: o Sage; *tu*: however; *prāṇa*: *prāṇa*, vital energy; *saṃkramaṇam*: moving; *iḍāyām*: from *iḍā*; *piṅgalāyām*: into *piṅgalā*; *iti uktam*: is said to be; *dakṣiṇāyanam*: southern path; *iti śrutiḥ*: as it is stated in the Vedas; *piṅgalāyām*: about *piṅgalā*; *yadā*: when; *prāṇaḥ*: *prāṇas*, energies; *iḍāpiṅgalayoḥ*: of *iḍā* and *piṅgalā*; *saṃdhi samāgataḥ*: join; *tadā*: then; *amāvāsyā*: time of no moon, preceding the new moon; *proktā*: is said; *dehe*: in the body; *dehabhṛtām*: of living creatures; *vara*: o Eminent One.

Translation

The yearly flow of the solar (and lunar) energy in the nāḍīs: Now, when the vital airs move from piṅgalā into iḍā, that is called *uttarāyaṇam,* the northern path, by those who know vedanta, o Sage. However, the prāṇa moving from iḍā into piṅgalā is said to be *dakṣiṇāyanam*, the southern path, o Sage, as it is stated in the Vedas about piṅgalā. When the prāṇas of iḍā and piṅgalā join, then *amavasya* is said [to be] in the body of living creatures, o eminent One.

Commentary

Uttarāyaṇa is also known as the summer solstice. This path is active for six months of the year, from mid January to mid-July. *Dakṣiṇāyana* is the winter solstice, which is active from mid-July to mid January. The above verses explain that when the prāṇas move from piṅgalā into iḍā, that is uttarāyaṇa. When the prāṇas move from iḍā into piṅgalā, that is dakṣiṇāyana, as stated in the Vedas.

Uttarāyaṇa is also called the northern path, because the sun moves north for these six months.This is considered to be the path of illumination that leads towards liberation. Dakṣiṇāyana is called the southern path, because here the sun moves on its course towards the south. This path leads towards darkness and further association with the ancestors and relations.

The time of death is considered to be very relevant here, because the departing soul will journey on one of these two paths, depending on the time of year of passing. In the *Mahabhārata*, it is described how Bhīṣma Pitama waited for many long months, lying on a bed of arrows, so that he could pass on the northern path, during the time of uttarāyaṇa.

When the prāṇas of iḍā and piṅgalā merge, this is said to be *amavasya,* the time of the dark moon or no moon. During amavasya, suṣumnā becomes active. During this period there is no light from the sun or the moon. Amavasya occurs every month just before the new moon. However, the darkest night of the year is celebrated as *Śivarātri*, the night of Śiva, or transcendental consciousness, which falls in February/March. During the period of amavasya, suṣumnā is activated due to the merging of iḍā and piṅgalā. This is a powerful time for meditation, but will not be conducive for any other works.

Verses 43b to 47: Equinox and eclipse

मूलाधारं यदा प्राणः प्रविष्टः पण्डितोत्तम ।।४३।।
तदाद्यं विषुवं प्रोक्तं तापसैस्तापसोत्तम ।
प्राणासंज्ञो मुनिश्रेष्थ मूर्धानं प्राविशेद्यदा ।।४४।।
तदन्त्यं विषुवं प्रोक्तं तापसैस्तत्त्वचिन्तकैः ।
निःश्वासोच्छ्वासनं सर्वं मासानां संक्रमो भवेत् ।।४५।।
इडया कुण्डलीस्थानं यदा प्राणः समागतः ।
सोमग्रहणमित्युक्तं तदा तत्त्वविदां वर ।।४६।।
यदा पिङ्गलया प्राणः कुण्डलीस्थानमागतः ।
तदातदा भवेत् सूर्यग्रहणं मुनिपुण्गव ।।४७।।

mūlādhāraṃ yadā prāṇaḥ praviṣṭaḥ paṇḍitottama (43b)
tadādyaṃ viṣuvaṃ proktaṃ tāpasaistāpasottama
prāṇāsaṃjño muniśreṣṭha mūrdhānaṃ praviśedyadā (44)
tadantyaṃ viṣuvaṃ proktaṃ tāpasaistattvacintakaiḥ
niḥśvāsocchvāsanaṃ sarvaṃ māsānāṃ saṃkramo bhavet (45)
iḍayā kuṇḍalīsthānaṃ yadā prāṇaḥ samāgataḥ
somagrahaṇamityuktaṃ tadā tattvavidāṃ vara (46)
yadā piṅgalāyā prāṇaḥ kuṇḍalīsthānamāgataḥ
tadātadā bhavet sūryagrahaṇaṃ munipuṅgava (47)

Anvay

praviṣṭaḥ: enters; *mūlādhāram*: *mūlādhāra*, base *cakra*, seat of *kuṇḍalī*; *paṇḍitottama*: o Wise Pandit; *tat*: this; *proktam*: is called; *ādyam*: beginning; *viṣuvam*: equinox; *tāpasaiḥ*: by ascetics; *tāpasa-uttama*: o Excellent Ascetic; *yadā*: when; *prāṇāsaṃjñaḥ*: this *prāṇa*; *praviśet*: enters; *mūrdhānam*: crown of the head; *muniśreṣṭha*: o Esteemed Sage; *tat*: this; *proktam*: is called; *antyam*: end; *viṣuvam*: of the equinox; *tāpasaiḥ*: by ascetics; *tattva-cintakaiḥ*: who are conscious of the true reality; *sarvam māsānām*: every month; *bhavet*: there is; *saṃkramaḥ*: coming together; *niḥśvāsa-ucchvāsanam*: of the exhalation and inhalation; *yadā*: when; *prāṇaḥ*: *prāṇa*, vital energy; *samāgataḥ*: reaches; *kuṇḍalī-sthānam*: site of the *kuṇḍalī*; *iḍayā*: through *iḍā*; *tadā*: then; *iti uktam*: it is said; *somagrahaṇam*: eclipse of the moon; *tattva-vidām*: by the knowers of the true reality; *vara*: o Excellent One; *yadā*: when; *prāṇaḥ*: *prāṇa*, vital energy; *agataḥ*: enters; *kuṇḍalī-sthānam*: site of the *kuṇḍalī*; *piṅgalāyā*: through *piṅgalā*; *tadātadā*: then; *bhavet*: it is; *sūryagrahaṇam*: solar eclipse; *munipuṅgava*: o Esteemed Sage.

Translation

When the prāṇa enters mūlādhāra, o wise Pandit, this is called the beginning of the equinox by ascetics, o excellent Ascetic. When this prāṇa enters the crown of the head, o esteemed Sage, this is called the end of the equinox by ascetics who are conscious of the True Reality. Every month there is the coming together of the exhalation and inhalation. When the prāṇa reaches the site of the kundalini through iḍā, then it is said [to be] the eclipse of the moon by the knowers of the true reality, o excellent One. When the prāṇa enters the site of the kundalini through piṅgalā, then it is the solar eclipse, o esteemed Sage.

Commentary

The equinox represents a time of equal day and night. In the practice of yoga, equal day and night correspond to the balance of piṅgalā and iḍā nāḍīs. This balance of iḍā and piṅgalā at mūlādhāra sparks off the awakening of kuṇḍalinī. Symbolically, it relates with the beginning of the equinox. When the kuṇḍalinī rises up suṣumnā and enters *sahasrara cakra*, at the crown of the head, this is compared to the end of the equinox, by those who have experienced the true reality.

Every month, the exhalation and the inhalation merge, which externally represents the time of dawn and dusk, when there is no sun and no moon. Internally this time symbolises the awakening of suṣumnā, where the body and mind are transcended. This is why dawn and dusk are considered to be most auspicious for sādhana and meditation. When the prāṇa reaches kuṇḍalinī through iḍā nāḍī, there is a lunar eclipse. When the prāṇa reaches kuṇḍalinī through piṅgalā, there is a solar eclipse.

Verses 48 to 56: Inner pilgrimage places

अन्तस्तीर्थप्राशस्त्यम्

श्रीपर्वतं शिरःस्थाने केदारं तु ललाटके ।
वाराणसीं महाप्राज्ञ भ्रुवोर्घ्राणस्य मध्यमे ।।४८।।
कुरुक्षेत्रं कुचस्थाने प्रयागं हृत्सरोरुहे ।
चिदम्बरं तु हृन्मध्ये आधारे कमलालयम् ।।४९।।
आत्मतीर्थंसमुत्सृज्य बहिस्तीर्थानि यो व्रजेत् ।
करस्थं स महारत्नं त्यक्त्वा काचं विमार्गते ।।५०।।
भावतीर्थं परं तीर्थं प्रमाणं सर्वकर्मसु ।
अन्यथा ऽलिङ्ग्यते कान्ता अन्यथा ऽलिङ्ग्यते सुता ।।५१।।
तीर्थानि तोयपूर्णानि देवान् काष्ठादिनिर्मितान् ।
योगिनो न प्रपद्यन्ते स्वात्मप्रत्ययकारणात् ।।५२।।
बहिस्तीर्थात् परं तीर्थमन्तस्तीर्थं महामुने ।
आत्मतीर्थं महातीर्थमन्यत्तीर्थं निरर्थकम् ।।५३।।
चित्तमन्तर्गतं दुष्टं तीर्थस्नानैर्न शुध्यति ।
शतशो ऽपि जलैर्धौतं सुराभाण्डमिवाशुचि ।।५४।।
विशुवायनकालेषु ग्रहणे चान्तरे सदा ।
वाराणस्यादिके स्थाने स्नात्वा शुद्ध भवेन्नरः ।।५५।।
ज्ञानयोगपराणां तु पादप्रक्षालितं जलम् ।
भवशुद्ध्यर्थ मज्ञानां तत्तीर्थं मुनिपुङ्गव ।।५६।।

antastīrthaprāśastyam

śrīparvataṃ śiraḥsthāne kedāraṃ tu lalāṭake
vārāṇasīṃ mahāprājña bhruvorghrāṇasya madhyame (48)
kurukṣetraṃ kucasthāne prayāgaṃ hṛtsaroruhe
cidambaraṃ tu hṛnmadhye ādhāre kamalālayam (49)
ātmatīrthaṃsamutsṛjya bahistīrthāni yo vrajet

karastham sa mahāratnaṃ tyaktvā kācaṃ vimārgate (50)
bhāvatīrthaṃparaṃ tīrthaṃ pramāṇaṃ sarvakarmasu
anyathā 'liṅgyate kāntā anyathā 'liṅgyate sutā (51)
tīrthāni toyapūrṇāni devān kāṣṭhādinirmitān
yogino na prapadyante svātmapratyayakāraṇāt (52)
bahistīrthāt paraṃ tīrthamantastīrthaṃ mahāmune
ātmatīrthaṃ mahātīrthamanyattīrthaṃ nirarthakam (53)
cittamantargataṃ duṣṭaṃ tīrthasnānairna śudhyati
śataśo 'pi jalairdhautaṃ surābhāṇḍamivāśuci (54)
viśuvāyanakāleṣu grahaṇe cāntare sadā
vārāṇasyādike sthāne snātvā śuddho bhavennaraḥ (55)
jñānayogaparāṇām tu pādaprakṣālitaṃ jalam
bhāvaśuddhyarthamajñānāṃ tattīrthaṃ munipuṅgava (56)

Anvay

prāśastyam: praise; *antaḥ-tīrtha*: inner *tīrthas*, sacred places; *śrīparvatam*: Mt. Kailash; *śiraḥsthāne*: within the head; *tu*: *conjunction*; *kedāram*: Kedāra; *lalāṭake*: in the forehead; *vārāṇasīm*: Vārāṇasī; *Madhyame*: between; *bhruvoḥ*: eyebrows; *ghrāṇasya*: nose; *mahāprājña*: o Wise One; *kurukṣetram*: field of Kuru; *hṛnmadhye*: in the heart centre; *kamalālayam*: Kamalālaya; *ādhāre*: in the base; *bhāvatīrtham*: *bhāvatīrtha*, true nature of *tīrtha*; *param tīrtham*: highest *tīrtha*; *pramānam*: proof; *sarva-karmasu*: of all actions; *anyathā . . . anyathā*: either . . . or; *kāntā*: wife; *sutā*: daughter; *alingyate*: may be embraced; *yoginaḥ*: *yogins*; *kāranāt*: because of; *pratyaya*: understanding; *svātma*: Self; *na prapadyante*: do not need; *toyapūrnāni tīrthāni*: water *tīrthas*; *devān*: gods; *nirmitān*: made of; *kāṣṭha*: wood; *ādi*: or other; *antaḥ tīrtham*: inner *tīrtha*; *param tīrtham*: supreme *tīrtha*; *bahiḥ-tīrthāt*: than the external *tīrtha*; *mahāmune*: o Great Sage; *ātmatīrtham*: *tīrtha* of the soul; *mahātīrtham*: greatest *tīrtha*; *anyattīrtham*: another *tīrtha*; *nirarthakam*: useless; *duṣṭam*: dirt; *antargatam*: concealed in; *cittam*: mind; *na śudhyati*: cannot be cleansed; *snānaiḥ*: by baths; *tīrtha*: in *tīrthas*; *iva*: just as; *bhāndam*: container; *surā*: for alcohol; *aśuci*: impure; *api*: even though; *jalaiḥ-dhautam*: it has been washed; *śataśaḥ*: 100 times; *sadā*: always; *snātvā*: bathing; *vārāṇasī-ādike sthāne*: in Vārāṇasī and such places; *viśuva-ayanakāleṣu*: during all the solstices; *ca antare grahaṇe*: and other eclipses; *naraḥ*: a man; *bhavet*: becomes; *śuddhaḥ*: pure; *tu*: yet; *pāda-prakṣālitam jalam*: having his feet washed; *bhāva-śuddhi-artham*: for purity of mind; *tat-tīrtham*: that is the *tīrtha*; *ajñānām*: of the ignorant; *munipuṅgava*: o Esteemed Sage.

Translation

Praise of the inner *tīrthas: Mt. Kailash* [is] within the head, *Kedāra* [is] in the forehead, *Vārāṇasī* [is] between the eyebrows and the nose, o wise One. *Kurukṣetra* [is] within the chest. *Prayāga* moves up in the heart. Now, *Cidambara* [is] in the heart centre. *Kamalālaya* [is] in the base. Whoever goes to external tīrthas, abandoning the inner tīrtha, seeks a piece of glass, while disregarding the precious jewel lying in his hand. *Bhāvatīrtha* is the highest tīrtha [and] proof of all actions. Either the wife or the daughter may be embraced. Yogins, because of understanding the self, do not need water tīrthas [or] gods made of wood or other [materials]. The inner tīrtha [is] the supreme tīrtha, [higher] than the external tīrtha, o great Sage; the tīrtha of the soul is the greatest tīrtha; another tīrtha [is] useless. Dirt concealed in the mind cannot be cleansed by baths in tīrthas, just as a container for alcohol [is] impure, even though it has been washed a hundred times. Always bathing in Vārāṇasī and such places, during all the solstices and other eclipses, a man becomes pure. Yet, having his feet washed for purity of mind by masters of *jñāna yoga*, that is the tīrtha of the ignorant, o esteemed Sage.

Commentary

Tīrthas are holy places, where saints, yogis or divine manifestations have lived or stayed, and performed sādhana, meditation, or perhaps some miracle. Some ancient texts, containing spiritual wisdom may be buried there. A field of energy and/or higher consciousness may also be stored there for the benefit of mankind in ages to come. In India, up to the present day, there are thousands of tīrthas, some of which are known, but many of which are secret or unknown. Those tīrthas which are known have become the major pilgrimage sites, where tourists and pilgrims go to connect with the higher self. However, these verses are not referring to these external tīrthas, but to the internal tīrthas, which the yogi may manifest through his or her sādhana and attainment.

Mount Kailash, the abode of Śiva, is located internally at the crown of the head, where Śiva, the pure, transcendent consciousness resides. Kedāra is located at the forehead, where *soma cakra* is situated. Vārāṇasī is at *bhrukuṭi*, the trigger point of *ajña*, in-between the eyebrows and the nose. Kurukṣetra is located in the chest, at the heart, where *anahata cakra* is located. Prayāga, is the center of confluence at the manipura cakra, and it moves up into the heart. Cidambara is also at the heart center. Kamālalaya is at the base, where mūlādhāra cakra is located at the pelvic floor.
The above verse states that whoever visits the external tīrthas, disregarding the internal tīrthas, seeks pieces of glass, while precious jewels are lying in the hand.

Bhāvatīrtha, the seat of the soul, is the highest tīrtha, and the highest truth. Therefore, it is the proof of all actions. At this level, either the wife or the daughter may be embraced without any sense of guilt. Yogis, who have understood the self, do not require the blessing of water tīrthas, sacred ponds, rivers, lakes, or images of the gods made from wood or other materials. The inner tīrtha is supreme, and higher than the external tīrthas. The tīrtha of the soul is the greatest tīrtha, and all others are useless for the yogi. The dirt concealed in the mind cannot be cleansed by bathing in water tīrthas, just a a container for alcohol is impure, even if it is washed a hundred times.

The man who bathes in Vārāṇasī, and such tīrthas, during all the solstices and eclipses, becomes pure, because these places are steeped in spiritual energy. Yet, the man who has his feet washed for purity of mind by masters of jñāna yoga worships at the tīrtha of the ignorant.

Verses 57 to 59: Vision of Śiva within oneself

आत्मनि शिवदृष्टिः

तीर्थे दाने जपे यज्ञे काष्ठे पाषाणके सदा ।
शिवं पश्यति मूढात्मा शिवे देहे प्रतिष्ठिते ।।५७।।
अन्तःस्थं मां परित्यज्य बहिष्ठं यस्तु सेवते ।
हस्तस्थं पिण्डमुत्सृज्य लिहेत् कूर्परमात्मनः ।।५८।।
शिवमात्मनि पश्यन्ति प्रतिमासु न योगिनः ।
अज्ञानां भावनार्थाय प्रतिमाः परिकल्पिताः ।।५९।।

ātmani śivadṛṣṭiḥ
tīrthe dāne jape yajñe kāṣṭhe pāṣāṇake sadā
śivaṃ paśyati mūḍhātmā śive dehe pratiṣṭhite (57)
antaḥsthaṃ māṃ parityajya bahiṣṭhaṃ yastu sevate
hastasthaṃ piṇḍamutsṛjya lihet kūrparamātmanaḥ (58)
śivamātmani paśyanti pratimāsu na yoginaḥ
ajñānāṃ bhāvanārthāya pratimāḥ parikalpitāḥ (59)

Anvay
śiva-dṛṣṭiḥ: vision of Śiva; *ātmani*: in oneself; *mūḍhātmā*: unconscious self; *sadā*: always; *paśyati*: sees; *Śivam*: Śiva; *tīrthe*: in *tīrtha*; *dāne*: in charitable gifts; *jape*: in *japa*, repetition of *mantra*; *yajñe*: in *yajna*, sacrificial fire; *kāṣṭhe*: in movement of wind and cloud; *pāṣāṇake*: in stone [idols]; *Śive*: whereas Śiva; *pratiṣṭhite*: is established; *dehe*: in the body; *tu*: thus; *yaḥ*: whoever; *sevate*: worships; *bahiṣṭham*: external; *parityajya*: forsaking; *mām*: me; *antaḥstham*: internal; *lihet*: he licks; *ātmanaḥ*: his own; *kūrparam*: elbow; *utsṛjya*: having cast away; *piṇḍam*: food; *hastastham*: in his hand; *yoginaḥ*: *yogins*; *paśyanti*: see; *śivam-ātmani*: Śiva inside themselves; *na*: not; *pratimāsu*: in idols; *pratimāḥ*: idols; *parikalpitāḥ*: are designed; *arthāya*: for the benefit of; *ajñānām bhāvana*: ignorant people.

Translation

Vision of Śiva in oneself. The unconscious self always sees Śiva in tīrtha, charitable gifts, *japa*, *yajña*, movement of wind and cloud, stone [idols], whereas Śiva is established in the body. Thus, whoever worships the external, forsaking me, the internal, [is as if] he licks his own elbow, having cast away the food in this hand. The yogins see Śiva inside themselves, not in idols. Idols are designed for the benefit of ignorant people.

Commentary

Śiva is the essence of light, pure consciousness. This consciousness is within each of us, and is accessible to each of us. The unconscious self is the person, who does not know this, even in theory, and seeks Śiva in places and actions deemed holy, in the natural environment, and in temples and idols. Śiva is known as the destroyer, because he is established in the transcendental state, beyond ego and duality. Only when they are destroyed, can we connect with Śiva, the cosmic consciousness. Ādi Śankara, the great vedantist of the 8th century C.E., realized this in his poem *Nirvāna-Śatka,* where he says he is not the senses, nor the mind nor the elements; he says *śivo'ham*, identifying only with Śiva, *sat-cit-ānanda*, the bliss of living in the supreme consciousness. This is true liberation, not to be sought or attained in the external world.

Verses 60 to 63: Absorption in Brahma

ब्रह्मदर्शनेन ब्रह्मभावः

अपूर्वमपरं ब्रह्म स्वात्मानं सत्यमद्वयम् ।

प्रज्ञानघनमानन्दं यः पश्यति स पश्यति ।।६०।।

नाडीपुञ्जं सदासारं नरभावं महामुने ।

समुत्सृज्यात्मनात्मानमहमित्यवधारय ।।६१।।

अशरीरं शरीरेषु महान्तं विभुमीश्वरम् ।

आनन्दमक्षरं साक्षान्मत्वा धीरो न शोचति ।।६२।।

विभेदजनके ज्ञाने नष्टे ज्ञानबलान्मुने ।

आत्मनो ब्रह्मणो भेदमसन्तं किं करिष्यति ।।६३।।

brahmadarśanena brahmabhāvaḥ
apūrvamaparaṃ brahma svātmānaṃ satyamadvayam
prajñānaghanamānandaṃ yaḥ paśyati sa paśyati (60)
nāḍīpuñjaṃ sadā 'sāraṃ narabhāvaṃ mahāmune
samutsṛjyātmanā 'tmānamahamityavadhāraya (61)
aśarīraṃ śarīreṣu mahāntaṃ vibhumīśvaram
ānandamakṣaraṃ sākṣānmatvā dhīro na śocati (62)
vibhedajanake jñāne naṣṭe jñānabalānmune
ātmano brahmaṇo bhedamasantaṃ kiṃ kariṣyati (63)

Anvay

brahma-bhāvaḥ: absorption in Brahma; *brahma-darśanena*: through insight into Brahma; *yaḥ*: whoever; *paśyati*: sees; *Brahma*: Brahma; *apūrvam*: incomparable; *aparam*: unexcelled; *satyam*: true; *advayam*: non-dual; *ghanam*: full of; *prajñāna*: knowledge; *ānandam*: bliss; *saḥ*: he; *paśyati*: sees; *sva-ātmānam*: his own Self; *iti*: thus; *avadhāraya*: affirming; *ātmanā*: through the Self; *aham ātmānam*: I am the Self; *samutsṛjya*: having renounced; *nāḍī-puñjam*: mass of *nāḍīs*; *sadā*: ever; *asāram*: unimportant; *nara-bhāvam*: spirit of man; *mahāmune*: o Great Sage; *matvā*: having rejoiced in; *sākṣān*: with one's own eyes; *aśarīram*: bodiless;

śarīreṣu: within the body; *akṣaram*: imperishable; *ānandam*: bliss; *mahāntam*: great; *vibhum-īshvaram*: all-pervading *Īśvara*; *dhīraḥ*: wise one; *na śocati*: does not grieve; *jñāne*: knowledge; *janake*: which has generated; *vibheda*: distinctions; *naṣṭe*: is destroyed; *jñānabalān*: by the forces of wisdom; *mune*: o Sage; *asantam*: being no; *bhedam*: difference; *ātmanaḥ brahmanaḥ*: between the Self and Brahman; *kim*: what; *kariṣyati*: can it do.

Translation
Absorption in Brahman through insight into Brahma: Whoever sees Brahma [as] incomparable, unexcelled, true, non-dual, full of knowledge [and] bliss, he sees his own Self. Thus affirming 'Through the Self, I am the Self', having renounced the mass of nāḍīs [as] ever unimportant to the spirit of man, o great Sage, [and] having rejoiced with one's own eyes in the bodiless within the body [and] the imperishable bliss of the great all-pervading *Īśvara*, the wise one does not grieve. [When] the knowledge which has generated distinctions is destroyed by the forces of wisdom, o Sage, [there] being no difference between the Self and Brahman, what can it do?

Commentary
These verses refer to Brahma and Brahman. Brahman is the pure, ever-expanding totality of consciousness. Brahma is the lord and creator of all, whose being is the essence of Brahman. When we worship Brahma, who is one of Īśvara's trinity of Brahma, Viṣnu and Maheśvara (Śiva), we activate and connect with the vibration of Brahman, the supreme consciousness, the source of all. Our true Self and Brahma have the same qualities. The wise person identifies with these qualities only, and not the gross body. He/she remains in the state of bliss of Īśvara, and, unaffected by external circumstances, affirms *aham brahmāsmi,* I am Brahman.

इति चतुर्थः खण्डः

iti caturthaḥ khaṇḍaḥ

Thus [ends] the fourth section.

पञ्चमः खण्डः

pañcamaḥ khaṇḍaḥ

Fifth Section

Prāṇāyāma

Verses 1 to 4: Purification of the nāḍīs

नाडीशोधनम्
सम्यक्कथय मे ब्रह्मन् नाडीशुद्धिं समासतः ।
यया शुद्धया सदा ध्यायन् जीवन्मुक्तो भवाम्यहम् ।।१।।
साम्कृते शृणु वक्ष्यामि नाडीशुद्धिं समासतः ।
विध्युक्तकर्मसंयुक्तः कामसंकल्पवर्जितः ।।२।।
यमाद्यष्टाङ्गसंयुक्तः शान्तः सत्यपरायणः ।
स्वात्मन्यवस्थितः सम्यक् ज्ञानिभिश्च सुशिक्षितः ।।३।।
पर्वताग्रे नदीतीरे बिल्वमूले वने ऽथवा ।
मनोरमे शुचौ देशे मठं कृत्वा समाहितः ।।४।।

nāḍīśodhanam
samyakkathaya me brahman nāḍīśuddhiṃ samāsataḥ
yayā śuddhayā sadā dhyāyan jīvanmukto bhavāmyaham (1)
sāṃkṛte śṛṇu vakṣyāmi nāḍīśuddhiṃ samāsataḥ
vidhyuktakarmasaṃyuktaḥ kāmasaṃkalpavarjitaḥ (2)
yamādyaṣṭāṅgasaṃyuktaḥ śāntaḥ satyaparāyaṇaḥ
svātmanyavasthitaḥ samyak jñānibhiśca suśikṣitaḥ (3)
parvatāgre nadītīre bilvamūle vane 'thavā
manorame śucau deśe maṭhaṃ kṛtvā samāhitaḥ (4)

Anvay

nāḍī-śodhanam: purification of the *nāḍīs*; *brahman*: o Brahman; *kathaya*: describe; *me*: to me; *samyak*: exactly; *samāsataḥ*: succinctly; *nāḍī-śuddhim*: purification of the *nāḍīs*; *sadā*: always; *dhyāyan*: contemplating; *yayā śuddhayā*: through this purity; *aham bhavāmi*: I become; *jīvanmuktaḥ*: liberated while in this body; *sāṃkṛte*: o Sāmkṛti; *śṛṇu*: listen; *vakṣyāmi*: I will tell; *samāsataḥ*: concisely; *vidhyukta*: according to the ritual; *śāntaḥ*: serene; *saṃyuktah*: merged with; *aṣṭāṅga*: eightfold path; *ādi*: beginning with; *yama*: *yamas*, self-restraints; *parāyaṇaḥ*: highest aim; *satya*: truth; *ca*: and; *avasthitaḥ*: fixed; *sva-ātmani*: on their true self; *jñānibhiḥ*: the wise; *suśikṣitaḥ*: practise; *samyak*: correctly; *kṛtvā*: having made; *maṭham*: hut; *manorame*: in a pleasant; *śucau*: clean; *deśe*: place; *parvatāgre*: on a mountain peak; *nadītīre*: on the bank of a river; *bilvamūle*: at the base of a Bilva tree; *athavā*: or else; *vane*: in a forest; *samāhitaḥ*: one can withdraw the mind.

Translation

Purification of the nāḍīs: O Brahman, describe to me exactly [and] succinctly the purification of the nāḍīs, [so that] always contemplating through this purity, I become liberated while in this body. O Sāmkṛti, listen! I will tell you concisely of the purification of the nāḍīs, according to ritual and set actions [and] devoid of personal desires and wishes. Serene, merged with the eightfold path, beginning with the yamas, [their] highest aim truth, and fixed on their true self, the wise practise correctly. Having made a hut in a pleasant, clean place, on a mountain peak, on the bank of a river, at the base of a *bilva* tree, or else in a forest, one can withdraw the mind.

Commentary

Sāmkṛti asks the Rishi how to purify the nāḍīs, so that he can achieve liberation, while still living in the body, by always contemplating and perceiving life through this purity. Impurities in the nāḍīs are low pranic energies, which are the effects of mental cravings and exhausting tamasic and rajasic lifestyles. The Rishi replies that in order to purify the nāḍīs, one must remain serene, devoid of personal desires, and perfect the eightfold path, beginning with the yamas and niyamas, as described in sections one and two. The wise practise correctly, who are strongly motivated and concentrated on the true self, the inner Śiva or Brahma.

In order to purify the nāḍīs and achieve liberation, the sadhaka should construct a small hut in a clean, pleasant and tranquil place, where he/she can practise intensively without any distraction or disturbance. In times of old, such sites as a mountain peak, river bank, forest or the base of a bilva tree (sacred to Śiva) were deemed auspicious and favourable for this purpose. Practising in the home, town or city affects the intensity and ultimate outcome of the sādhana.

Verses 5 to 10: Nāḍī śodhana prāṇāyāma

आरभ्य चासनं पश्चात् प्राङ्मुखोदङ्मुखो ऽपि वा ।
समग्रीवशिरःकायः संवृतास्यः सुनिश्चलः ।।५।।
नासाग्रे शशभृद्बिम्बे बिन्दुमध्ये तुरीयकम् ।
स्रवन्तममृतं पश्येन्नेत्राभ्यां सुसमाहितः ।।६।।
इडया प्राणमाकृष्य पूरयित्वोदरस्थितम् ।
ततो ऽग्निं देहमध्यस्थं ध्यायन् ज्वालावलीयुतम् ।।७।।
बिन्दुनादसमायुक्तमग्निबीजं विचिन्तयेत् ।
पश्चाद्विरेचयेत् सम्यक् प्राणं पिङ्गलया बुधः ।।८।।
पुनः पिङ्गलया ऽपूर्य वह्निबीजमनुस्मरेत् ।
पुनर्विरेचयेद्धीमानिडयैव शनैः शनैः ।।९।।
त्रिचतुर्वासरं वा ऽथ त्रिचतुर्वारमेव च ।
षट्कृत्वो विचरेन्नित्यं रहस्येवं त्रिसंधिषु ।।१०।।

ārabhya cāsanaṃ paścāt prāṅmukhodaṅmukho 'pi vā
samagrīvaśiraḥkāyaḥ saṃvṛtāsyaḥ suniścalaḥ (5)
nāsāgre śaśabhṛdvimbe bindumadhye turīyakam
sravantamamṛtaṃ paśyennetrābhyāṃ susamāhitaḥ (6)
iḍayā prāṇamākṛṣya pūrayitvodarasthitam
tato 'gniṃ dehamadhyasthaṃ dhyāyan jvālāvalīyutam (7)
bindunādasamāyuktamagnibījaṃ vicintayet
paścādvirecayet samyak prāṇaṃ piṅgalayā budhaḥ (8)
punaḥ piṅgalayā 'pūrya vahibījamanusmaret
punarvrecayeddhīmāniḍayaiva śanaiḥ śanaiḥ (9)
tricaturvāsaraṃ vā 'tha tricaturvārameva ca
ṣaṭkṛtvo vicarennityaṃ rahasyevaṃ trisaṃdhiṣu (10)

Anvay

ca: and; *ārabhya*: having begun; *āsanam*: posture; *paścāt*: from the west; *prāṅmukhaḥ*: facing east; *api vā*: or even; *danmukhaḥ*: facing north; *grīva*: neck; *śiraḥ*: head; *kāyaḥ*:

body; *sama*: aligned; *saṃvṛtāsyaḥ*: covered; *suniścalaḥ*: immobile; *susamāhitaḥ*: with well-focussed mind; *nāsāgre*: on the nosetip; *paśyet*: one should see; *netrābhyām*: with one's own eyes; *turīyakam*: *turīya*, fourth state of consciousness; *sravantam-amṛtam*: flow of nectar; *śaśabhṛdvimbe*: in the crescent moon; *bindumadhye*: at *bindu*, psychic centre in the top back of the head; *ākṛṣya*: drawing in; *prāṇam*: vital energy; *iḍayā*: through *ida*; *pūrayitva . . . sthitam*: filling; *udara*: belly; *tataḥ*: then; *dhyāyan*: meditating on; *agnim*: fire; *avalīyutam*: arising from; *jvāla*: flames; *dehamadhyastham*: in the centre of the body; *vicintayet*: one should reflect upon; *bījam*: *bīja*, source; *agni*: *agni*, fire; *samāyuktam*: together with; *nāda*: *nāda*, subtle sound vibration; *bindu*: *bindu*; *paścāt*: next; *budhaḥ*: sage; *virecayet*: emits; *prāṇam*: *prāṇa*; *samyak*: completely; *piṅgalayā*: through *piṅgalā*, right nasal passage; *punaḥ*: then; *āpūrya*: inhaling; *piṅgalayā*: through *piṅgalā*; *anusmaret*: one should reflect upon; *vahi-bījam*: *bīja* of *agni*, seed sound of fire element; *punaḥ*: then; *dhīmān . . . eva*: with full awareness; *virecayet*: one should exhale; *śanaiḥ śanaiḥ*: very slowly; *iḍayā*: through *iḍā*; *vicaret*: one should practise; *ṣaṭkṛtvaḥ*: six times; *tricaturvāsaram*: three or four days; *vā atha*: or else; *tricaturvāram*: three or four times; *ca*: and; *nityam*: always; *rahasya*: in secret; *trisaṃdhiṣu*: at sunrise, noon and sunset.

Translation

And having begun āsana from the west, facing east or even facing north, neck, head [and] body aligned, [the body] covered [and] immobile, with well-focused mind on the nose tip, one should see with one's own eyes *turīya*, the flow of nectar in the crescent moon at *bindu*. Drawing the prāṇa in through iḍā, filling the belly, then meditating on the fire arising from the flames in the centre of the body, one should reflect upon the *bīja* of *agni*, together with the *nāda* of *bindu*. Next the sage emits the prāṇa completely through piṅgalā. Then, inhaling through piṅgalā, one should reflect upon the *bīja* of *agni*. Then, with full awareness, one should exhale very slowly through iḍā. One should practise six times for three or four days or else three or four times, and always in secret at sunrise, noon and sunset.

Commentary

In this verse, the practice of *nāḍī śodhana prāṇāyāma* is described. The purpose of nāḍī śodhana is to balance and purify the nāḍīs. Therefore, prāṇāyāma should always be preceded by āsana, which regulates and releases the pranic flows, preparing the system for prāṇāyāma. The verse says, having begun the practice with āsana, facing west, one should sit for prāṇāyāma. The posture for the prāṇāyāma practice should be perfectly aligned, as in the classical meditation postures, so that the neck, head and body are straight and facing either east or north. The body should be covered to avoid physical disturbance.

Technique

One should begin the practice by sitting quietly until the body becomes steady and still. At this point one should focus the mind on the breathing at the nose tip. As the breathing becomes slow and rhythmic, one should simultaneously direct the inner gaze towards *bindu visarga,* the psychic centre at the top back of the head. Here one should perceive the flow of *amṛta*, 'the nectar of life', falling from the crescent moon at *bindu*, with one's own inner eye. The flow of nectar from the crescent moon has also been termed *turīya* here. *Turīya* means the 'transcendental consciousness', which is the source of the nectar, which flows down into the body from the crescent moon at bindu.

Focusing on the nosetip to stimulate mūlādhāra cakra, one should perceive turīya, the fourth state of consciousness, beyond the three states of waking, dreaming and sleeping. Bindu is located above ajña cakra, at the top back of the head, where some brahmins leave a tuft of hair, tightened to maintain awareness of this point. It is said that bindu is in *ānandamaya koṣa* and that it is the source, where everything manifests and dissolves back into. According to tantra there is a minute secretion in a dip in the higher centres of the upper cortex of the brain. In this secretion is a point, which is the bindu visarga, 'falling of the drop'.

Bindu is represented by a crescent moon and a white drop, which symbolises the nectar that drips down from bindu to *viśuddhi cakra*. The crescent moon symbolises its relationship with the phases of the moon, just as the human mind and emotions are influenced by the phases of the moon. When bindu is activated, the secretion of nectar that it produces is enough to nourish and maintain the whole body.

Having completed the preparation, one should perform nāḍī śodhana prāṇāyāma for the purification of the nāḍīs. Slowly inhale through the left nostril and draw the prāṇa down through the iḍā nāḍī, filling the belly. Retaining the breath inside, one should meditate on the fire, arising from the flames at the center of maṇipura cakra, the navel center. At the same time one should reflect on the *bīja* mantra of fire, which is the sound *Ram,* along with the bīja mantra of *bindu*, which is the sound *Aum.*

Next the prāṇa should be exhaled slowly and completely from the right nostril through piṅgalā nāḍī. At the end of exhalation, one should inhale from the right nostril through the piṅgalā nāḍī, filling the belly, and again reflecting on the fire at manipura, and the bīja mantras *Ram* and *Aum.* Then one should exhale very slowly with awareness from the left nostril, through the iḍā nāḍī. This completes one round of nāḍī śodhana prāṇāyāma.

One should perform six rounds of the practice for three or four days, or else three or four rounds. The practice should always be done at the time of sunrise, midday and sunset, when suṣumnā nāḍī is active. At sunrise the mind is still in the dreaming state; at noon iḍā and piṅgalā flow equally, and the mind is tranquil; and at sunset, iḍā and piṅgalā come together in suṣumnā at ajña cakra. One should always perform higher practices of yoga in secret, so as not to be disturbed by the thoughts and energies of others.

Verses 11 and 12: Signs of nāḍī purification

नाडीशुद्धिचिह्नानि
नाडीशुद्धिमवाप्नोति पृथक्चिह्नोपलक्षितः ।
शरिरलघुता दीप्तिर्वहेर्जाठरवर्तिनः ।।११।।
नादाभिव्यक्तिरित्येतच्चिह्नं तत्सिद्धिसूचकम् ।
यावदेतानि सम्पश्येत्तावदेवं समाचरेत् ।।१२।।

nāḍīśuddhicihnāni
nāḍīśuddhimavāpnoti pṛthakcihnopalakṣitaḥ
śarīralaghutā dīptirvaherjāṭharavartinaḥ (11)
nādābhivyaktirityetacihnaṃ tatsiddhisūcakam
yāvadetāni saṃpaśyettāvadevaṃ samācaret (12)

Anvay
cihnāni: indications; *nāḍīśuddhi*: *nāḍī* purification; *avāpnoti*: one obtains; *nāḍī-śuddhim*: purification of the *nāḍīs*; *pṛthak*: different; *cihnāni*: signs; *upalakṣitaḥ*: are perceived; *laghutā*: lightness; *śarīra*: of the body; *diptiḥ*: radiance; *vaheḥ*: of fire; *vartinaḥ*: moving in; *jāṭhara*: digestive system; *iti*: it is said; *nāda-abhivyaktiḥ*: manifestation of *nāda*, primal subtle sound vibration; *etat cihnam*: the sign; *sūcakam*: indicating; *tat siddhi*: this *siddhi*, psychic power; *samācaret*: one should do the practices; *evam*: *emphatic*; *yāvat . . . tāvat*: until; *saṃpaśyet*: one recognises; *etāni*: these.

Translation
Indications of nāḍī purification: One obtains purification of the nāḍīs [when] different signs are perceived: lightness of the body, radiance of fire, moving in the digestive system. It is said the manifestation of *nāda* is the sign, indicating this *siddhi*. One should do the practices until one recognises these [signs].

Commentary

The practice of nāḍī śodhana purifies the iḍā and piṅgalā nāḍīs by the process of alternate nostril breathing. Iḍā and piṅgalā are the two major nāḍīs in the body, which influence and control all the others. Once the nāḍīs are purified, the prāṇas become regulated and balanced throughout the body. This results in the state of *prāṇottana*, the awakening of the prāṇas, and gives rise to the feeling of lightness in the body, the first sign of nāḍī purification.

In the above technique the inhalation is directed down to the belly, where maṇipura cakra, the center of fire, is located. The breath is then retained, while meditating on the fire arising from the flames at the center of maṇipura. At the same time one should reflect on the bīja mantra of fire, which is the sound *Ram*, With the purification of the nāḍīs and awakening of the prāṇas, the pranic storehouse, which is located at *maṇipura cakra*, begins to expand with vital energy and light. This radiance becomes more effusive, and can be felt moving in the digestive system, the second sign of nāḍī purification.

The manifestation of *nāda*, the subtle psychic or internal sounds, is the third sign that arises with the purification of the nāḍīs. These sounds may be heard at any time, but they are not caused by any external objects. They arise from the subtle field of consciousness, which is not in contact with the outside world. Such sounds as bells, conch, flute, vīna, thunder or rain may be heard. One may also hear the sounds of different bīja and mantra, such as Aum, *Aim, Hrīm,* etc. The ability to hear the inner nādas is a sign that the yogi has perfected the practice. One should continue to perform the practice until these signs appear.

Verses 13 and 14: Purification of the Self

स्वात्मशुद्धिः

अथवैतत् परित्यज्य स्वात्मशुद्धिं समाचरेत् ।

आत्मा शुद्धिः सदा नित्यः सुखरूपः स्वयंप्रभः ॥१३॥

अज्ञानमलपङ्कं यः क्षालयेज्ज्ञानतोयतः ।

स एव सर्वदा शुद्धो नान्यः कर्मरतो हि सः ॥१४॥

svātmaśuddhiḥ
athavaitat parityajya svātmaśuddhiṃ samācaret
ātmā śuddhiḥ sadā nityaḥ sukharūpaḥ svayaṃprabhaḥ (13)
ajñānamalapaṅkaṃ yaḥ kṣālayejjñānatoyataḥ
sa eva sarvadā śuddho nānyaḥ karmarato hi saḥ (14)

Anvay
sva-ātma-śuddhiḥ: purification of one's own self; *athavā*: or; *parityajya*: having ceased; *etat*: this; *samācaret*: one should practise; *ātmā*: *ātman*, True Self; *sadā*: always; *śuddhiḥ*: pure; *nityaḥ*: ever; *sukharūpaḥ*: delightful; *svayaṃprabhaḥ*: self-illumined; *yaḥ*: whoever; *kṣālayet*: is cleansed; *malapaṅkam*: of the dirt; *ajñāna*: of ignorance; *toyataḥ*: by the water; *jñāna*: of knowledge; *saḥ*: he; *eva*: indeed; *sarvadā*: completely; *śuddhaḥ*: pure; *na*: not; *rataḥ*: bound; *hi*: *emphatic*; *anyaḥ karma*: to other action.

Translation
Purification of one's own self: Or, having ceased this [practice], one should practise purification of one's own self. The *ātman* [is] always pure, ever delightful, and self-illumined. Whoever is cleansed of the dirt of ignorance by the water of knowledge, he is indeed completely pure and is not bound to other action.

Commentary
Once the nāḍīs have been purified, one should attain knowledge of the *ātman*, the true self, through inner

experience and meditation, and thus be released from the bondage of *karma*. Knowledge of the true self is *vidyā.* In the absence of this knowledge, one lives under the influence of *avidyā,* ignorance. Those who live in ignorance believe in the physical and material reality, and become blind to the subtle, inner truth. The verse states that whoever is cleansed of the dirt of ignorance by the water of knowledge, is pure and never bound by karma, action.

इति पञ्चमः खण्डः

iti pañcamaḥ khaṇḍaḥ

Thus ends the fifth section.

षष्ठ: खण्डः

ṣaṣṭha khaṇḍaḥ

Sixth Section

Aspects of Prāṇāyāma

Verses 1 and 2: Description of prāṇāyāma

प्राणायामलक्षणम्

प्राणायामक्रमं वक्ष्ये सांकृते शृणु सादरम् ।

प्राणायाम इति प्रोक्तो रेचपूरककुम्भकैः ।।१।।

वर्णत्रयात्मकाः प्रोक्ता रेचपूरककुम्भकाः ।

स एष प्रणवः प्रोक्तः प्राणायामश्च तन्मयः ।।२।।

prāṇāyāmalakṣaṇam
prāṇāyāmakramaṃ vakṣye sāṃkṛte śṛṇu sādaram
prāṇāyāma iti prokto recapūrakakumbhakaiḥ (1)
varṇatrayātmakāḥ proktā recapūrakakumbhakāḥ
sa eṣa praṇavaḥ proktaḥ prāṇāyāmaśca tanmayaḥ (2)

Anvay
prāṇāyāma-lakṣaṇam: description of *prāṇāyāma*; *sādaram*: respectfully; *sāṃkṛte*: Sāṃkṛti; *vakṣye*: I will speak of; *prāṇāyāma-kramam*: system of *prāṇāyāma*; *iti proktaḥ*: it is declared; *reca-pūraka-kumbhakaiḥ*: by means of exhalation, inhalation and breath retention; *proktāḥ*: are said; *ātmakāḥ*: to consist of; *varṇa-traya*: the three sounds; *eṣa proktaḥ*: this is called; *praṇavaḥ*: *praṇava*, AUM; *ca*: and; *mayaḥ*: is formed of; *tat*: this.

Translation
Description of prāṇāyāma: Listen respectfully, Sāmkṛti. I

will speak of the system of prāṇāyāma. It is declared [that] prāṇāyāma [is] by means of exhalation, inhalation and breath retention. Exhalation, inhalation and breath retention are said to consist of the three sounds; this is called *praṇava*, and prāṇāyāma is formed of this.

Commentary

Here the teacher asks the student, Sāmkṛti, to listen respectfully to his description of prāṇāyāma. The word respect is used here to emphasise the importance of understanding the practice. When there is respect, one listens more carefully, and is able to grasp even the subtle nuances. Prāṇāyāma consists of three parts: inhalation, retention and exhalation. These three components are said to resonate with three sounds: inhalation'A', retention 'U' and exhalation 'M'. These three sounds form the *praṇava, Aum.* Therefore, prāṇāyāma is formed by praṇava.

Verses 3 to 9: Prāṇāyāma with praṇava

इडया वायुमाकृष्य पूरयित्वोदरस्थितम् ।
शनैः षोडशभिर्मात्रैरकारं तत्र संस्मरेत् ।।३।।
पूरितं धारयेत् पश्चाच्चतुःषष्ट्या तु मात्रया ।
उकारमूर्तिमत्रापि संस्मरन् प्रणवं जपेत् ।।४।।
यावद्वा शक्यते तावद्धारयेज्जपतत्परः ।
पूरितं रेचयेत् पश्चान्मकारेणानिलं बुधः ।।५।।
शनैः पिङ्गलया तत्र द्वात्रिंशन्मात्रया पुनः ।
प्राणायामो भवेदेषः ततश्चैवं समभ्यसेत् ।।६।।
पुनः पिङ्गलया पूर्य मात्रैः शोडशभिस्तथा ।
अकारमूर्तिमत्रापि स्मरेदेकाग्रमानसः ।।७।।
धारयेत् पूरितं विद्वाण प्रणवं संजपन् वशी ।
उकारमूर्तिं स ध्यायन् चतुःषष्ठ्या तु मात्रया ।।८।।
मकारं तु स्मरन् पश्चाद्रेचयेदिडयानिलम् ।
एवमेव पुनः कुर्यादिडया पूर्य बुद्धिमान् ।।९।।

iḍayā vāyumākṛṣya pūrayitvodarasthitam
śanaiḥ ṣoḍaśabhirmātrairakāraṃ tatra saṃsmaret (3)
pūritaṃ dhārayet paścāccatuḥṣaṣṭyā tu mātrayā
ukāramūrtimatrāpi saṃsmaran praṇavaṃ japet (4)
yāvadvā śakyate tāvaddhārayejjapatatparaḥ
pūritaṃ recayet paścānmakāreṇānilaṃ budhaḥ (5)
śanaiḥ piṅgalayā tatra dvātriṃśanmātrayā punaḥ
prāṇāyāmo bhavedeṣa tataścaivaṃ samabhyaset (6)
punaḥ piṅgalayā pūrya mātraiḥ śoḍaśabhistathā
akāramūrtimatrāpi smaredekāgramānasaḥ (7)
dhārayet pūritaṃ vidvān praṇavaṃ saṃjapan vaśī
ukāramūrtiṃ sa dhyāyan catuḥṣaṣṭyā tu mātrayā (8)
makāraṃ tu smaran paścādrecayediḍayānilam
evameva punaḥ kuryādiḍayā pūrya buddhimān (9)

Anvay

ākṛṣya: drawing in; *vāyum*: *vāyu*, vital air; *iḍayā*: through *iḍā*; *pūrayitva . . . sthitam*: filling; *udara*: abdomen; *tatra samsmaret*: one should bring to mind; *akāram*: sound 'A'; *śanaiḥ*: slowly; *ṣoḍaśabhiḥ-mātraiḥ*: for sixteen *mātras*, units of time; *paścāt*: then; *dhārayet*: holding; *pūritam*: inhalation; *ccatuḥṣaṣṭyā mātrayā*: for sixty four *mātrās*; *api*: also; *samsmaran*: contemplating; *atra*: here; *ukāra-mūrtim*: form of 'U'; *japet*: one should repeat; *budhaḥ*: sage; *dhārayet*: should hold; *pūritam*: inhalation; *yāvat . . . tāvat*: as long . . . as; *śakyate*: he can; *tatparaḥ*: following; *japa*: repetition; *recayet*: he should expel; *paścāt*: then; *anilam*: vital air; *makāreṇa*: with the sound 'M'; *śanaiḥ*: slowly; *dvātriṃśat-mātrayā*: for thirty-two *mātrās*; *piṅgalayā*: through *piṅgalā*; *punaḥ*: again; *eṣa*: this; *bhavet*: is; *prāṇāyāmaḥ*: *prāṇāyāma*; *ca*: and; *tataḥ*: therefore; *samabhyaset*: one should practise; *evam*: correctly; *punaḥ*: again; *pūrya*: inhaling; *piṅgalayā*: through *piṅgalā*; *śoḍaśabhiḥ mātraiḥ*: for sixteen *mātrās*; *smaret*: one should concentrate on; *api*: also; *atra*: here; *akāra-mūrtim*: form of 'A'; *ekāgramānasaḥ*: with one-pointed attention; *vidvān*: knowledgeable one; *dhārayet*: should hold; *pūritam*: inhalation; *catuḥṣaṣṭyā mātrayā*: for sixty-four *mātrās*; *saṃjapan*: repeating; *vaśī*: powerfully; *praṇavam*: *praṇava*, AUM; *tu*: while; *dhyāyan*: meditating on; *ukāra-mūrtim*: form of 'U'; *paścāt*: then; *smaran*: concentrating on; *makāram*: M; *recayet*: he should expel; *anilam*: vital air; *iḍayā*: through *iḍā*; *pūrya*: inhaling; *buddhimān*: wise one; *punaḥ kuryāt*: one should repeat; *evameva*: in this way.

Translation

Drawing the breath in through iḍā, and filling the abdomen, one should bring to mind the sound 'A', [counting] slowly for sixteen *mātrās*. Then, holding the inhalation for sixty four mātrās, [and] also contemplating here the form of 'U', one should repeat the praṇava. The sage should hold the inhalation as long as he can; following the repetition [of the praṇava], he should then expel the vital air with the sound 'M' slowly for thirty-two mātrās through piṅgalā again. This is prāṇāyāma, and therefore, one should practise correctly. Again, inhaling through piṅgalā for sixteen mātrās, one should also concentrate here on the form of 'A' with one-pointed attention. The knowledgeable one should hold the inhalation for sixty-four mātrās, repeating powerfully the praṇava, while meditating on the form of 'U'. Then, concentrating on 'M', he should expel the vital air through iḍā. Inhaling through iḍā, the wise one should repeat [the process] in this way.

Commentary
The yoga upaniṣads recommend that nāḍī śodhana prāṇāyāma be combined with repetition of the pranaya, *Aum,* as well as the ratio of 16:64:32. This version of nāḍī śodhana should not be undertaken until one has mastered the basic practice, and slowly increased the ratio.

Technique
Slowly inhale through the left nostril, filling the abdomen, for 16 counts. Simultaneously repeat the first syllable of the praṇava, 'A', sixteen times mentally. Then hold the breath inside at the abdomen for 64 counts, mentally repeating the second sound of the praṇava, 'U', for 64 counts. If it is not possible to retain the breath inside for the full 64 counts, one should hold it for as long as possible, without incurring stress or discomfort. Then exhale the breath through the right nostril for 32 counts, mentally repeating the third syllable of praṇava, 'M'. It is very important that this prāṇāyāma practice should be performed correctly.

Now the first half of the round is complete. To perform the second half, inhale slowly down to the abdomen through the right nostril for the count of 16, with mental repetition of the sound 'A'. Hold the breath inside at the abdomen for the count of 64, mentally repeating the sound ‘U’, Finally exhale slowly through the left nostril for the count of 32, with repetition of the sound ‘M’. This completes one round of the practice. To begin the next round, one should inhale through the left nostril and follow the same procedure.

Verses 10 to 12a: Benefits of the practice

एवं समभ्यसेन्नित्यं प्राणायामं मुनीश्वर ।

एवमभ्यासतो नित्यं षण्मासाद् ज्ञानवान् भवेत् ।।१०।।

वत्सराद्ब्रह्मविद्वान् स्यात् तस्मान्नित्यं समभ्यसेत् ।

योगाभ्यासरतो नित्यं स्वधर्मनिरतश्च यः ।।११।।

प्राणसंयमनेनैव ज्ञानान्मुक्तो भविष्यति ।१२।

evaṃ samabhyasennityaṃ prāṇāyāmaṃ muniśvara
evamabhyāsato nityaṃ ṣaṇmāsād jñānavān bhavet 10)
vatsarādbrahmavidvān syāt tasmānnityaṃ samabhyaset
yogābhyāsarato nityaṃ svadharmaniratāśca yaḥ (11)
prāṇasaṃyamanenaiva jñānānmukto bhaviṣyati (12a)

Anvay

muniśvara: o Excellent Sage; *samabhyaset*: one should practise; *nityam*: regularly; *evam*: correctly; *abhyāsataḥ*: having practised; *bhavet*: one becomes; *jñānavān*: *jñāni*, endowed with wisdom; *ṣat-māsāt*: in six months; *syāt*: one will be; *brahmavidvān*: *brahmavit*, one who has reached the fourth of the seven stages of wisdom; *vatsarāt*: in a year; *tasmāt*: thus; *samabhyaset*: one should practise; *nityam*: continually; *yaḥ*: whoever; *nityam*: always; *rataḥ*: is engaged in; *yoga-abhyāsa*: practice of *yoga*; *ca*: and; *nirataḥ*: devoted to; *svadharma*: one's own true nature; *prāṇa-saṃyamanena*: by control of the *prāṇa*; *eva*: indeed; *bhaviṣyati*: will become; *muktaḥ*: liberated; *jñānāt*: through higher wisdom.

Translation

O excellent Sage, one should practise prānāyāma regularly [and] correctly. Having practised regularly [and] correctly, one becomes a *jñāni* in six months. One will be a *brahmavit* in a year. Thus one should practise continually. Whoever is always engaged in the practice of yoga and devoted to his *svadharma*, by control of the prāṇa, will indeed become liberated through higher wisdom.

Commentary

Prāṇayāma is a very subtle and powerful method.. Therefore, one should practise it regularly and correctly. By doing so, the yogic aspirant becomes a *jñāni* within six months, A jñāni is able to discriminate between the mind and the consciousness, the permanent and the impermanent, the inner truth and the outer experience. One who continues to practise for one year will become a *brahmavit*, knower of Brahman, the superconsciousness. Therefore, one should practise continuously. Whoever remains engaged in the practice of yoga and dedicated to his own inner path, will gain control over the prāṇa, vital force, and will become liberated through higher wisdom.

Verses 12b and 13: Components of prāṇāyāma

पूरकादिलक्षणम्
बाह्यादापूरणं वायोरुदरे पूरको हि सः ।।१२।।
संपूर्णकुम्भवद्वायोर्धारणं कुम्भको भवेत् ।
बहिर्विरेचनं वायोरुदराद्रेचकः स्मृतः ।।१३।।

pūrakādilakṣaṇam
bāhyādāpūraṇaṃ vāyorudare pūrako hi saḥ (12b)
saṃpūrṇakumbhavadvāyordhāraṇaṃ kumbhako bhavet
bahirvirecanaṃ vāyorudarādrecakaḥ smṛtaḥ (13)

Anvay
pūraka-ādi-lakṣaṇam: description of *pūraka* etc; *hi*: so; *āpūraṇam*: filling; *udare*: abdomen; *vāyoḥ*: with vital air; *bāhyāt*: from outside; *pūrakaḥ*: inhalation; *dhāraṇam*: holding; *vāyoḥ*: vital air; *vat*: as if; *saṃpūrṇa-kumbha*: in a full pot; *bhavet*: is; *kumbhaka:* retention; *bahirvirecanam*: expelling; *udarāt*: from the abdomen; *smṛtaḥ*: is called; *recakaḥ*: exhalation.

Translation
Description of *pūraka:* So, filling the abdomen with vital air from outside [is] pūraka. Holding the vital air as if in a full pot is *kumbhaka*. Expelling the vital air from the abdomen is called *recaka*.

Commentary
The three components of prāṇayāma are the three stages of the breathing process. *Pūraka* is inhalation. *Kumbhaka* is breath retention, as if holding the breath inside a pot. *Recaka* is exhalation. In normal breathing these three stages of breath go on automatically, day and night, throughout life. The main difference between prāṇayāma and normal breathing is the awareness of the breath and the ratios or counts. It is said that our lives, from birth to death, are measured by breaths. Every

automatic or normal breath is counted in the duration of life. However, when we switch over to breathing with awareness and ratio, as in prāṇayāma, this type of breath is not counted. Therefore, yogis who mastered the three components of prāṇayāma, were often very long lived, while others were not.

Verses 14 to 20: Perfection of prāṇāyāma

प्राणायामसिद्धयः

प्रस्वेदजनको यस्तु प्राणायामेषु सो ऽधमः ।
कम्पनं मध्यमं विद्यादुत्थानं चोत्तमं विदुः ।।१४।।
पूर्वपूर्वं प्रकुर्वित यावदुत्थानसंभवः ।
संभवत्युक्तमे प्राज्ञः प्राणायामे सुखी भवेत् ।।१५।।
प्राणायामेन चित्तं तु शुद्धिं भवति सुव्रत ।
चित्ते शुद्धे शुचिः साक्षात् प्रत्यग्ज्योतिर्व्यस्थितः ।।१६।।
प्राणाश्चित्तेन संयुक्तः परमात्मनि तिष्ठति ।
प्राणायामपरस्यास्य पुरुषस्य महात्मनः ।।१७।।
देहश्चोत्तिष्ठते तेन किंचिज्जज्ञानाद्विमुक्तता ।
रेचकं पूरकं मुक्त्वा कुम्भकं नित्यमभ्यसेत् ।।१८।।
सर्वपापविनिर्मुक्तः सम्यग्ज्ञानमवाप्नुयात् ।
मनोजवत्वमाप्नोति पलितादि च नश्यति ।।१९।।
प्राणायामैकनिष्ठस्य न किंचिदपि दुर्लभम् ।
तस्मात् सर्वप्रयत्नेन प्राणायामान् समभ्यसेत् ।।२०।।

prāṇāyāmasiddhayaḥ

prasvedajanako yastu prāṇāyāmeṣu so 'dhamaḥ
kampanaṃ madhyamaṃ vidyādutthānaṃ cottamaṃ viduḥ (14)
pūrvapūrvaṃ prakurvita yāvadutthānasaṃbhavaḥ
saṃbhavatyuktame prājñaḥ prāṇāyāme sukhī bhavet (15)
prāṇāyāmena cittaṃ tu śuddhiṃ bhavati suvrata
citte śuddhe śuciḥ sākṣāt pratyagjyotirvyasthitaḥ (16)
prāṇāścittena saṃyuktaḥ paramātmani tiṣṭhati
prāṇāyāmaparasyāsya puruṣasya mahātmanaḥ (17)
dehaścottiṣṭhate tena kiṃcijjñānādvimuktatā
recakaṃ pūrakaṃ muktvā kumbhakaṃ nityamabhyaset (18)
sarvapāpavinirmuktaḥ samyagjñānamavāpnuyāt

manojavatvamāpnoti palitādi ca naśyati (19)
prāṇāyāmaikaniṣṭhasya na kiṃcidapi durlabham
tasmāt sarvaprayatnena prāṇāyāmān samabhyaset (20)

Anvay

prāṇāyāma-siddhayaḥ: perfection of *prāṇāyāma*; *tu*: now; *saḥ . . . yaḥ*: he who; *janakaḥ*: produces; *prasveda*: perspiration; *vidyāt*: is; *adhamaḥ*: lowest; *kampanam*: trembling; *madhyamam*: middle; *ca*: and; *viduḥ*: most accomplished one; *utthānam*: levitates; *uttamam*: highest; *yāvat*: when; *prakurvita*: this is done; *pūrvapūrvam*: repeatedly; *utthāna-saṃbhavaḥ*: highest stage; *saṃbhavati*: is attained; *prājñaḥ*: wise one; *bhavet*: becomes; *sukhī*: joyful; *prāṇāyāme*: in *prāṇāyāma*; *suvrata*: o virtuous one; *prāṇāyāmena*: through *prāṇāyāma*; *bhavati*: there is; *śuddhim*: purification of; *cittam*: mind; *citte śuddhe*: when the mind is purified; *śuciḥ*: bright; *pratyagjyotiḥ*: inward light; *sākṣāt*: clearly; *vyasthitaḥ*: established; *saṃyuktaḥ*: having united; *prāṇāḥ*: *prāṇā*s; *cittena*: with the mind; *tiṣṭhati*: he rests; *paramātmani*: in the Supreme Spirit; *asya*: this; *prāṇāyāma-parasya*: supreme *prāṇāyāma*; *puruṣasya*: spirit; *mahātmanaḥ*: of the Great Soul; *dehaḥ*: body; *uttiṣṭhate*: rises; *ca . . tena*: and thus; *vimuktatā*: loss of; *kimcit-jñānāt*: any knowledge; *muktvā*: leaving; *recakam*: exhalation; *pūrakam*: inhalation; *abhyaset*: he should practise; *kumbhakam*: breath retention; *nityam*: regularly; *vinirmuktaḥ*: released from; *sarva-pāpa*: all sins; *avāpnuyāt*: he obtains; *samyak-jñānam*: correct knowledge; *āpnoti*: he gains; *manojavatvam*: swiftness of thought; *ca*: and; *palita*: grey hair; *ādi*: etc; *naśyati*: disappears; *na kiṃcidapi*: nothing; *durlabham*: hard to obtain; *eka-niṣṭhasya*: for one singularly intent on; *tasmāt*: thus; *samabhyaset*: one should practise; *prāṇāyāmaan*: *prāṇāyāmas*; *sarvaprayatnena*: with total effort.

Translation

Siddhis of prāṇāyāma: He who produces perspiration is at the lowest [level] of prāṇāyāma. Trembling is the middle [stage], and the most accomplished one [who] levitates is the highest. When this is done repeatedly, the highest stage is attained, [and] the wise one becomes joyful in prāṇāyāma. O virtuous One, through prāṇāyāma there is purification of the mind. When the mind is purified, the bright inward light is clearly established. Having united the prāṇās with the mind, he rests in the supreme spirit. This supreme prāṇāyāma [is] the spirit of the great soul. The body rises and thus [there is] loss of any [mundane] knowledge. Leaving exhalation and inhalation, he should practise breath retention regularly. Released from all sins, he obtains correct knowledge. He gains swiftness of thought and grey hair etc disappears. Nothing [is] hard to obtain for one who is singularly intent on prāṇāyāma. Thus, one should practise prāṇāyāma with total effort.

Commentary

Prāṇāyāma is a very important practice in yoga. It rebalances the prāṇās and the nervous system and prepares the body and mind for higher yogas. Here the results or perfections of prāṇāyāma are enumerated. The first result that arises from prāṇāyāma is perspiration. The practice causes the body to become heated. This perspiration is different to ordinary perspiration, and should not be washed off directly, but rather wiped off with a soft, clean cloth.

In the next stage of prāṇāyāma, trembling arises due to activation of the prāṇās, nāḍīs and nerves. In the third stage, when the practice is mastered, the prāṇās expand throughout the body and there is the experience of lightness. In this stage the body may levitate easily. When these three stages are practised repeatedly, the highest stage is attained. The accomplished one becomes joyful during prāṇāyāma practice.

Through correct mastery of prāṇāyāma, the mind is purified. When the mind is purified, a bright internal light becomes established. This light is a symbol of the pure consciousness, the light of the soul. Having united the prāṇās with the mind through the practice of prāṇāyāma, the yogi rests in the supreme spirit. This level of prāṇāyāma is not a physical practice, but an expression of the consciousness of the highest soul. When the body rises, all mundane knowledge disappears. At this point, leaving inhalation and exhalation, one should focus on kumbhaka, breath retention, regularly.

By the mastery of prāṇāyāma, one is released from all negative karmas, or actions. One attains correct knowledge and swiftness of thought. Grey hair and other signs of old age disappear. Nothing is difficult to acquire for one who is able to focus one pointedly on prāṇāyāma. Therefore, one should practise prāṇāyāma with total dedication and effort.

Verses 21 to 32a: Prāṇāyāma eradicates disease

रोगनिवर्तकप्राणायामभेदाः

विनियोगान् प्रवक्ष्यामि प्राणायामस्य सुव्रत ।
संध्ययोर्ब्रह्मकाले ऽपि मध्याह्ने वाथवा सदा ॥२१॥
बाह्यं प्राणं समाकृष्य पूरयित्वोदरेण च ।
नासाग्रे नाभिमध्ये च पादाङ्गुष्ठे च धारणात् ॥२२॥
सर्वरोगनिर्मुक्तो जीवेद्वर्षशतं नरः ।
नासाग्रधारणाद्वापि जितो भवति सुव्रत ॥२३॥
सर्वरोगनिवृत्तिः स्यान्नाभिमध्ये तु धारणात् ।
शरीरलघुता विप्र पादाङ्गुष्ठनिरोधनात् ॥२४॥
जिह्वया वायुमाकृष्य यः पिबेत् सततं नरः ।
श्रमदाहविनिर्मुक्तो योगी नीरोगतामियात् ॥२५॥
जिह्वया वायुमाकृष्य जिह्वामूले निरोदहयेत् ।
पिबेदमृतमव्यग्रं सकलं सुखमाप्नुयात् ॥२६॥
इडया वायुमाकृष्य भ्रूवोर्मध्ये निरोधयेत् ।
यः पिबेदमृतं शुद्धं व्याधिभिर्मुच्यते हि सः ॥२७॥
इडया वेदतत्त्वज्ञ तथा पिङ्गलयैव च ।
नाभौ निरोधयेत्तेन व्याधिभिर्मुच्यते नरः ॥२८॥
मासमात्रं त्रिसन्ध्यायां जिह्वयारोप्य मरुतम् ।
अमृतं च पिबेन्नाभौ मन्दंमन्दं निरोधयेत् ॥२९॥
वातजाः पित्तजा दोषा नश्यन्त्येव न संशयः ।
नासाभ्यां वायुमाकृष्य नेत्रद्वन्द्वे निरोधयेत् ॥३०॥
नेत्ररोगा विनश्यन्ति तथा श्रोत्रनिरधनात् ।
तथा वायुं समारोप्य धारयेच्छिरस्थितम् ॥३१॥

शिरोरोगा विनश्यन्ति सत्यमुक्तं हि सांकृते ।३२।

roganivartakaprāṇāyāmabhedāḥ

viniyogān pravakṣyāmi prāṇāyāmasya suvrata
saṃdhyayorbrahmakāle 'pi madhyāhne vāthavā sadā (21)
bāhyaṃ prāṇaṃ samākṛṣya pūrayitvodareṇa ca
nāsāgre nābhimadhye ca pādāṅguṣṭhe ca dhāraṇāt (22)
sarvaroganirmukto jīvedvarṣaśataṃ naraḥ
nāsāgradhāraṇādvā 'pi jito bhavati suvrata (23)
sarvaroganivṛttiḥ syānnābhimadhye tu dhāraṇāt
śarīralaghutā vipra pādāṅguṣṭhanirodhanāt (24)
jihvayā vāyumākṛṣya yaḥ pibet satataṃ naraḥ
śramadāhavinirmukto yogī nīrogatāmiyāt (25)
jihvayā vāyumākṛṣya jihvāmūle nirodhayet
pibedamṛtamavyagraṃ sakalaṃ sukhamāpnuyāt (26)
iḍayā vāyumākṛṣya bhrūvāmadhye nirodhayet
yaḥ pibedamṛtaṃ śuddhaṃ vyādhibhirmucyate hi saḥ (27)
iḍayā vedatattvajña tathā piṅgalayaiva ca
nābhau nirodhayettena vyādhibhirmucyate naraḥ (28)
māsamātraṃ trisandhyāyāṃ jihvayāropya marutam
amṛtaṃ ca pibennābhau mandaṃmandaṃ nirodhayet (29)
vātajāḥ pittajā doṣā naśyantyeva na saṃśayaḥ
nāsābhyāṃ vāyumākṛṣya netradvandve nirodhayet (30)
netrarogā vinaśyanti tathā śrotranirodhanāt
tathā vāyuṃ samāropya dhārayecchirasthitam (31)
śirorogā vinaśyanti satyamuktaṃ hi sāmkṛte (32a)

Anvay

bhedāḥ: various; *nivartaka*: eradicate; *roga*: disease; *suvrata*: o Virtuous One; *pravakṣyāmi*: I will explain; *viniyogān*: uses; *prāṇāyāmasya*: of *prāṇāyāma*; *sandhyayoḥ*: at dawn and dusk; *brahmakāle*: before sunrise; *madhyāhne*: at noon; *vāthavā*: or else; *sadā*: at all times; *samākṛṣya*: inhaling; *bāhyam prāṇam*: external *prāṇa*; *udareṇa*: abdomen; *pūrayitva*: full; *ca*: and; *dhāraṇāt*: by concentrating; *nāsāgre*: on the nose tip; *nābhimadhye*: navel; *pādāṅguṣṭhe*: big toe; *nirmuktaḥ*: released; *sarva-roga*: from all disease; *naraḥ*: man; *jīvet*: can live; *varṣaśatam*: hundred years; *bhavati*: can be; *jitaḥ*: conquered; *dhāraṇāt*: by holding; *nāsāgra*: at the nose tip; *sarva-roga*: all diseases; *nivṛttiḥ syāt*: disappear; *tu*: when; *dhāraṇāt*: it is held; *nābhimadhye*: at the navel; *nirodhanāt*: if it is confined to; *pādāṅguṣṭha*: big toe; *vipra*: o Wise One; *śarīra*: body; *laghutā*: light; *naraḥ*: man; *yaḥ*: who; *satatam*: continuously; *pibet*: drinks; *vāyum*: vital air; *ākṛṣya*: having drawn in; *jihvayā*: through the tongue; *yogī*: *yogin*; *iyāt*: attains; *nīrogatām*: good health; *nirmuktaḥ*: free of; *śrama*: fatigue; *havi*: heat; *ākṛṣya*: drawing in; *vāyum*: vital air; *jihvayā*: through the tongue; *nirodhayet*: holding; *jihvāmūle*: at its (the tongue's) root; *pibet*: one should drink; *amṛtam*: nectar; *avyagram*: steadily; *āpnuyāt*: obtaining; *sakalam*: total; *sukham*: happiness; *ākṛṣya*: drawing in; *vāyum*: vital air; *iḍayā*: through *iḍā*; *nirodhayet*: holding; *bhrūvormadhye*: at the eyebrow centre; *yaḥ*: whoever; *pibet*: drinks; *śuddham*: pure; *amṛtam*: nectar; *hi*: surely; *mucyate*: will be freed; *vyādhibhiḥ*: from sickness; *vedatattvaña*: O you, who understands the essence of the Veda; *piṅgalayā eva*: or even through *piṅgalā*; *nirodhayet*: holding; *nābhau*: at the navel; *tena*: then; *naraḥ*: man; *mucyate*: will be freed; *vyādhibhiḥ*: from sickness; *aropya*: inhaling; *marutam*: air; *jihvayā*: through the tongue; *trisandhyāyām*: at these three points; *pibet*: he should drink; *amṛtam*: nectar; *ca*: and; *nirodhayet*: hold; *mandaṃmandam*: very gradually; *nābhau*: at the navel; *eva na saṃśayaḥ*: without doubt; *doṣāḥ*: disorders; *vātajāḥ pittajāḥ*: caused by *vāta* (wind) and *pitta* (bile); *naśyanti*: disappear; *ākṛṣya*: after drawing in; *vāyum*: *vāyu*; *nirodhayet*: retaining; *netradvandve*: in both eyes; *tathā* . . . *tathā*: the more . . . the more; *dhārayet*: he holds; *vāyum*: breath; *cirasthitam*: for a long time; *samāropya*: having placed; *netra-rogāḥ*: diseases of the eyes; *vinaśyanti*: be annihilated; *śrotra*: ears; *nirodhanāt*: destroyed; *śiro-rogāḥ*: diseases of the head; *uktam hi*: I declare this; *satyam*: truth; *sāmkṛte*: o Sāmkṛti.

Translation

The various prāṇāyāmas [which] eradicate disease: O

virtuous One, I will explain the uses of prāṇāyāma at dawn and dusk, before sunrise, at noon, or else at all times. Inhaling the external prāṇa [until] the abdomen [is] full, and by concentrating on the nose tip, navel or the big toe, released from all disease, a man can live a hundred years. [Prāṇa] can be conquered by holding it at the nose tip, o virtuous One. All diseases disappear, when it is held at the navel. If it is confined to the big toe, o wise One, the body [becomes] light. The man who continuously drinks the vital air, having drawn it in through the tongue, is a yogin [who] attains good health, free of fatigue and heat. Drawing the vital air in through the tongue [and] holding [it] at its root, one should drink the nectar steadily, [thus] obtaining total happiness.

Drawing the vital air in through iḍā [and] holding it at the eyebrow centre, whoever drinks pure nectar will surely be freed from sickness. O you, who understands the essence of the Veda, [drawing the breath in] through iḍā, or even through piṅgalā, and holding it at the navel, then a man will be freed from sickness. Inhaling the air through the tongue at [these] three points for a whole month, he should drink the nectar and hold it very gradually at the navel. Without doubt the disorders caused by *vāta* and *pitta* disappear, after drawing in the vāyu [and] retaining [it] in both eyes. The more he holds the breath for a long time, having placed [it there], the more will diseases of the eyes be annihilated, [and diseases of] the ears destroyed. Diseases of the head will be annihilated. I declare this the truth, o Sāmkṛti!

Commentary

Prāṇāyāma is a means to extend the internal fields of prāṇa, and in this way many diseases can be resolved. Most disease is due to excess or deficiency of prāṇa. The best times to practice prāṇāyāma are before sunrise, at dawn, at noon, and at dusk. If this is not possible or practical, it can also be performed at any other time. The method of prāṇāyāma described here is very basic. One should inhale slowly and deeply through both nostrils, drawing the breath downward into the abdomen until it is full. Holding the breath inside, one should concentrate on either the nose tip, the navel or the big toe. By this practice a person may be freed from all disease and live for 100 years.

By focusing the awareness at the nose tip, while holding the breath inside, one can control the prāṇa. The nose tip forms a bridge, connecting the three major nāḍīs, iḍā, piṅgalā and suṣumnā. Therefore, by concentrating at this point, while holding the breath inside, the prāṇas can be controlled. By focusing at the navel, all diseases disappear. The navel is related with manipura cakra, where the pranic storehouse is located. When the awareness is focused at this center, the prāṇas expand and disease disappears. When the awareness is focused at the big toe, the body becomes very light, and is capable of moving easily and quickly, because the energy is held in the proximity of the feet.

Next, the cooling methods of prāṇāyāma, performed with the mouth open, are described. By continuously drawing the breath in through the open mouth, over the tongue, the yogi is freed from heat and fatigue, and attains good health. The second cooling method involves drawing the breath in through the tongue, which is curled around to form a tube. At the end of inhalation, the breath should be held at the root of the tongue. In this way one should drink the nectar steadily, obtaining total happiness. *Lalana cakra*, a minor center, which holds the nectar, is located at the root of the tongue. When this practice is mastered, the nectar becomes profuse and the experience of bliss is ongoing.

Verses 32b to 43a: Ṣaṇmukhi mudrā controls prāṇa

षण्मुखीमुद्राभ्यासादिना वायुजयः

स्वसतिकासनमास्थाय समाहितमनास्तथा ।।३२।।

अपानमूर्ध्वमुत्थाप्य प्रणवेन शनैः शनैः ।

हस्ताभ्यां धारयेत्सम्यक् कर्णादिकरणानि च ।।३३।।

अङ्गुष्ठाभ्यां मुने श्रोत्रे तर्जनीभ्यां तु चक्षुसि ।

नासापुटावथान्याभ्यां प्रच्छादया कारणानि वै ।।३४।।

आनन्दाविर्भवो यावत् तावन्मूर्धनि धारयेत् ।

प्राणः प्रयत्यनेनैव ब्रह्मरन्ध्रं महामुने ।।३५।।

ब्रह्मरन्ध्रं गते वायौ नादश्चोत्पदयते ऽनघ ।

शङ्खध्वनिनिभश्चादौ मध्ये मेघध्वनिर्यथा ।।३६।।

शिरोमध्यगते वायौ गिरिप्रस्रवणं यथा ।

पश्चात् प्रीतो महाप्रज्ञ साक्षादात्मन्मुखो भवेत् ।।३७।।

पुनस्तज्ज्ञाननिष्पत्तिर्योगात् संसारनिह्नुतिः ।

दक्षिणोत्तरगुल्फेन सेवनं पीड्येत् स्थिरम् ।।३८।।

सव्येतरेण गुलफेन पीड्येट्बुद्धिमान् नरः ।

जान्वोरधः स्थितां सन्धिं स्मृत्वा देवं त्रियम्बकम् ।।३९।।

विनायकं च संस्मृत्य तथा वागीश्वरीं पुनः ।

लिङ्गनालात् समाकृष्य वायुमप्यग्रतो मुने ।।४०।।

प्रणवेन नियुक्तेन बिन्दुयुक्तेन बुद्धिमान् ।

मूलाधारस्य विप्रेन्द्र मध्ये तं तु निरोधयेत् ।।४१।।

निरुध्य वायुना दीप्तो वह्निरूहति कुण्डलीम् ।

पुनः सुषुम्नया वायुर्वह्निना सह गच्छति ।।४२।।

एवमभ्यसतस्तस्य जितो वायुर्भवेद्भृशम् ।४३।

ṣaṇmukhīmudrābhyāsādinā vāyujayaḥ
svastikāsanamāsthāya samāhitamanāstathā (32b)
apānamūrdhvamuṭṭhāpya praṇavena śanaiḥ śanaiḥ
hastābhyāṃ dhārayetsamyak karṇādikaraṇāni ca (33)
aṅguṣṭhābhyāṃ mune śrotre tarjanībhyāṃ tu cakṣuṣi
nāsāpuṭāvathānyābhyāṃ pracchādya kāraṇāni vai (34)
ānandāvirbhavo yāvat tāvanmūrdhani dhārayet
prāṇaḥ prayatyanenaiva brahmarandhraṃ mahāmune (35)
brahmarandhraṃ gate vāyau nādaścotpadyate 'nagha
śaṅkhadhvaninibhaścādau madhye meghadhvaniryathā (36)
śiromadhyagate vāyau giriprasravaṇaṃ yathā
paścāt prīto mahāprājña sākṣādātmanmukho bhavet (37)
punastajjñānaniṣpattiryogāt saṃsāranihnutiḥ
dakṣiṇottaragulphena sevanaṃ pīḍyet sthiram (38)
savyetareṇa gulphena pīḍyetbuddhimān naraḥ
jānvoradhaḥ sthitāṃ sandhiṃ smṛtvā devaṃ triyambakam (39)
vināyakaṃ ca saṃsmṛtya tathā vāgīśvarīṃ punaḥ
liṅganālāt samākṛṣya vāyumapyagrato mune (40)
praṇavena niyuktena binduyuktena buddhimān
mūlādhārasya viprendra madhye taṃ tu nirodhayet (41)
nirudhya vāyunā dīpto vahnirūhati kuṇḍalīm
punaḥ suṣumnayā vāyurvahninā saha gacchati (42)
evamabhyasatastasya jito vāyurbhavetbhṛśam (43a)

Anvay

vāyu-jayaḥ: control of *vāyu*; *ābhyāsādināḥ*: through the practice of; *ṣaṇmukhī-mudrā*: attitude where apertures of head are closed to facilitate internalising; *āsthāya*: seated in; *svastikāsanam*: auspicious pose; *manāḥ*: mind; *samāhita*: steady; *tathā*: then; *utthāpya*: raising; *apānam*: *apāna*, downward energy; *śanaiḥ śanaiḥ*: very slowly; *praṇavena*: with *praṇava*, sacred sound *Aum*; *dhārayet*: he should cover; *samyak*: completely; *karṇa*: ears; *ca*: and; *ādi-karaṇāni*: other sense organs; *hastābhyām*: with his hands; *vai pracchādya*: having well-covered; *karaṇāni*: sense organs;

mune: o Sage; *aṅguṣṭhābhyām*: with the thumbs; *śrotre*: on the ears; *tarjanībhyām*: with the index fingers; *cakṣuṣi*: on the eyes; *atha*: then; *anyābhyām*: with two others; *nāsāpuṭau*: on the nostrils; *dhārayet*: he should hold; *prayatyanena eva*: with effort; *mūrdhani*: at the roof of the palate; *tāvat*: until; *āvirbhavaḥ*: he experiences; *ānanda*: bliss; *brahmarandhram*: *brahmarandhra*, opening in the crown of the head; *mahāmune*: o Great Sage; *Gate Vāyau*: when the *vāyu* reaches; *nādah*: *nāda*, subtle sound of *Aum*; *utpadyate*: comes forth; *anagha*: o Faultless One; *ca*: and; *adau*: that; *nibhaḥ*: is like; *dhvani*: sound; *śaṅkha*: of a conch; *madhye*: inside; *yathā*: like; *meghadhvaniḥ*: thunder; *vāyu śiro-madhya-gate*: when the *vāyu* goes inside the head; *yathā*: like; *prasravanam*: waterfall; *giri*: coming down from the mountains; *paścāt*: afterwards; *bhavet*: there is; *prītaḥ*: delight; *sākṣāt*: in the sight of; *mukhaḥ*: appearance of; *mahāprājña*: o Great Wise One; *yogāt*: when he is in possession of; *punaḥ*: again; *tat jñāna*: that knowledge; *niṣpattiḥ*: which has come forth; *nihnutiḥ*: [there is] repudiation of; *saṃsāra*: the material world; *pīḍyet*: he should press; *sevanam*: suture; *sthiram*: firmly; *dakṣiṇa-uttara-gulphena*: with right and left ankles; *buddhimān naraḥ*: wise man; *pīḍyet*: should press; *savyetareṇa gulphena*: with right ankle; *smṛtvā*: contemplating; *sthitam*: its site; *sandhim*: at the junction; *adhaḥ*: above; *jānvoḥ*: knees; *ca tathā*: and then; *punaḥ*: also; *saṃsmṛtya*: meditating on; *devam*: deities; *Triyambakam*: Triyambaka (Śiva); *vināyakam*: Vināyaka (remover of obstacles; Gaṇeśa); *vāgīśvarīm*: Vāgīśvarī (deity of speech; Sarasvatī); *apyagrataḥ*: drawing from the front; *vāyum*: vital air; *mune*: o Sage; *samākṛṣya*: having contracted; *liṅganālāt*: urethra; *niyuktena*: united with; *praṇavena*: *praṇava*, Aum; *bindu*: *bindu*, source of Aum; *buddhimān*: wise one; *nirodhayet*: should hold; *tam*: it; *madhye*: in the centre; *mūlādhārasya*: of *mūlādhāra,* base cakra, seat of *kuṅḍalinī*; *viprendra*: o Chief of Brahmins; *nirudhya*: having been restrained; *vāyunā*: by the *vāyu*; *dīptaḥ vahniḥ*: brilliant fire; *rūhati*: ascends;

kuṅḍalīm: *kuṅḍalī*; *punaḥ*: then; *saha*: together with; *vāyuḥ-vahninā*: fire of *vaayu*; *gacchati*: it goes; *suṣumnayā*: through *suṣumnā*, central current of energy; *evam*: thus; *tasya abhyasataḥ*: with his regular practice; *bhavet*: he becomes; *bhṛśam*: definitely; *jitaḥ vāyuḥ*: conqueror of *vāyu*.

Translation

Control of *vāyu* through the practice of *ṣaṇmukhī mudrā*: Seated in *swastikāsana*, the mind steady, then, raising the *apāna* upwards very slowly with *praṇava*, he should completely cover the ears and other sense organs with his hands. Having covered the sense organs well, o Sage, with the thumbs on the ears, the index fingers on the eyes [and] then two others on the nostrils, he should hold the *prāṇa* with effort at the roof of the palate until he experiences the bliss of the *brahmarandhra*, o Great Sage. When the vāyu reaches the brahmarandhra, the *nāda* comes forth, o Faultless One, and that is like the sound of a conch, inside like thunder. When the vāyu goes inside the head, [it is] like a waterfall coming down from the mountains. Afterwards there is delight in the sight of the appearance of the *ātman,* o Great Wise One. When he is again in possession of that knowledge, which has come forth, there is repudiation of the material world. He should press the suture firmly, with the right and left ankles. The wise man should press with the right ankle, contemplating its site at the junction above the knees, and then also meditating on the deities Triyambaka, Vināyaka and Vāgīśvarī. Drawing vāyu from the front, o Sage, having contracted the urethra, united with praṇava and *bindu*, the wise one should hold it in the centre of *mūlādhāra*, o Chief of Brahmins. Having been restrained by the vāyu, the brilliant fire ascends the *kuṅḍalī;* then, together with the fire of vāyu, it goes through *suṣumnā*. Thus, with his regular practice, he definitely becomes the conqueror of vāyu.

Commentary

Ṣaṇmukhī mudrā is an important practice for raising the

prāṇa and awakening the *kuṅḍalinī*. The word ṣaṇmukhī has two roots: *ṣan* or *ṣat* means 'six', and *mukhī* means 'gates'. Here the sitting āsana is swastikāsana, which is an unlocked meditation pose. The word *swastika* means 'auspicious'.

Technique
Sit with both legs stretched in front of the body. Bend the left knee and place the sole against the inside of the right thigh, so there is no contact between the heel and the perineum, Then bend the right knee and place the right foot between the left thigh and calf muscle, so that there is no contact between the heel and the pubic bone. Seated in swastikāsana, allow the body to become still, and the mind to become steady.

Then inhale slowly, reversing the flow of the *apāna* energy (which normally flows downward from the waist to the pelvic floor). Raise the energy of apāna together with the breath and the flow of *Praṇava*, or the *Aum* sound, from the *mūlādhāra cakra*, at the perineum, to the *viśuddhi cakra*, behind the throatpit. Holding the breath inside, one should raise the arms, so that the hands are in front of the face and the elbows are pointing sideways. Close the six gates, using the five fingers of the hands. The inner flap of the ears can be pressed closed with the two thumbs. The two eyes can be closed with the index fingers. The two nostrils can be closed with the middle fingers. The mouth can be closed with the ring fingers above the upper lip and the little fingers below the lower lip.

Having closed the sensory organs well with the fingers of both hands, the prāṇa should be held with effort at the roof of the palate, until the bliss of *brahmarandhra*, or *suṣumnā*, is experienced. When the prāṇa enters the brahmarandhra, then the *nāda*, subtle sound, comes forth. First, that sound may be like the conch, then like thunder. When the prāṇa enters the head region, it sounds like a waterfall, coming down from the mountains. Afterwards, there is delight in the appearance of the *ātman*, pure consciousness, or pure self. When the yogi is again in possession of that inner knowledge, which has come forth from the experience of nāda, subtle sound, and ātma, pure self, there is rejection of the material world with all of its identifications and roles.

At this time he should pull up on the urethra and the anal sphincter, performing *vajroli* and *aświnī* mudras, and press the pubis firmly with the right and left ankles. He should press the right ankle, contemplating the junction just above the right knee, and meditate on the deities: *Triyambaka* (*Mrityunjaya*), *Vināyaka* (*Gaṇeṣa*)and *Vāgeśvarī* (*Saraswatī*). Drawing *vāyu* from the front, having contracted the urethra, united with *praṇava* and *bindu*, the wise one should hold the energy at the centre of mūlādhāra. Having been restrained by the vāyu, the kuṅḍalīni ascends the suṣumnā together with the fire of vāyu. Thus, by regular practice of ṣaṇmukhī mudrā, the yogi definitely conquers the vāyu.

Verses 43b and 44a: Signs of the conquest of vāyu

वायुजयचिह्नानि
प्रस्वेदः प्रथमः पश्चात् कम्पनं मुनिपुङ्गव ।।४३।।
उत्थानं च शरीरस्य चिह्नमेतज्जिते ऽनिले ।४४।

vāyujayacihnāni
prasvedaḥ prathamaḥ paścāt kampanaṃ munipuṅgava (43b)
utthānaṃ ca śarīrasya cihnametajjite 'nile (44a)

Anvay
prathamaḥ: at first; *prasvedaḥ*: excessive perspiration; *paścāt*: then; *kampanam*: trembling; *munipuṅgava*: o Esteemed Sage; *ca*: and; *utthanam*: raising; *śarīrasya*: of the body; *etat cihnam*: this sign; *jite*: vanquishes; *anile*: air.

Translation
Signs of the conquest of vāyu: At first [there is] excessive perspiration, then trembling, o esteemed Sage, and raising of the body, this sign vanquishes the air [element].

Commentary
This verse gives the signs, which can be recognised as the awakening of *prāṇa* and the mastery of *prāṇāyāma*. The first sign is excessive perspiration. Initially, prāṇāyāma purifies the nervous system and speeds up the metabolism. This causes the body to become heated and to perspire copiously, even in cool weather. The excess perspiration may be rubbed back into the body with a soft clean cloth, but a shower should not be taken at this time to wash it off. Prāṇāyāma purifies the body, so the perspiration that arises from the practice has no toxic substance or unpleasant odor. When this perspiration is reabsorbed, it helps to maintain the metabolic balance and tones the muscles and nerves.

The second sign is tremor, shaking or trembling of the muscles and nerves, especially in the spinal region, although this may also be experienced in the hands, feet, face, and various other parts. In this stage, the flow of prāṇa becomes intensified, causing the peripheral parts of the body to vibrate. Various impulses travel through the nervous system and cause itching, tingling or pulsating sensations. As prāṇa accumulates in different regions, it may cause sensations in the chest, abdomen, intestines or excretory organs. The third sign is levitation, when the body rises effortlessly on its own. These three signs indicate that the air element is purified and awakened.

Verses 44b to 51: Dawning of vairagya and removal of disease and sin

वायुजयेन रोगपापविनाश्वैराग्यपूर्विका ज्ञानोत्पत्तिः

एवमभ्यसतस्तस्य मूलरोगो विनश्यति ।।४४।।

भगन्धरं च नष्टं स्यात् सर्वरोगाश्च सांकृते ।

पातकानि विनश्यन्ति क्षुद्राणि च महान्ति च ।।४५।।

नष्टे पापे विशुद्धं स्याञ्चित्तदर्पणमद्भुतम् ।

पुनर्ब्रह्मादिभोगेभ्यो वैरग्यं जायते हृदि ।।४६।।

विरक्तस्य तु संसाराज्ज्ञानं कैवल्यसाधनम् ।

तेन पाशापहानिः स्यात् ज्ञात्वा देवं सदाशिवम् ।।४७।।

ज्ञानामृतरसो येन सकृदास्वादितो भवेत् ।

स सर्वकार्यमुत्सृज्य तत्रैव परिधावति ।।४८।।

ज्ञानस्वरूपमेवाहुर्जगदेतद्वि चक्षणाः ।

अर्थस्वरूपमज्ञानात् पश्यन्त्यन्ये कुद्धष्टयः ।।४९।।

आत्मस्वरूपविज्ञानादज्ञानस्य परिक्षयः ।

क्षीणे ऽज्ञाने महाप्राज्ञ रागादीनां परिक्षयः ।।५०।।

रागाद्यसंभवे प्राज्ञ पुण्यपापवि मर्शनम् ।

योर्नाशे शरीरेण न पुनः संप्रयुज्यते ।।५१।।

vāyujayena rogapāpavināśvairāgyapūrvikā jñānotpattiḥ
evamabhyasatastasya mūlarogo vinaśyati (44b)
bhagandharaṃ ca naṣṭaṃ syāt sarvarogāśca sāṃkṛte
pātakāni vinaśyanti kṣudrāṇi ca mahānti ca (45)
naṣṭe pāpe viśuddhaṃ syāñcittadarpaṇamadbhutam
punarbrahmādibhogebhyo vairagyaṃ jāyate hṛdi (46)
viraktasya tu saṃsārājjñānaṃ kaivalyasādhanam
tena pāśāpahāniḥ syāt jñātvā devaṃ sadāśivam (47)
jñānāmṛtaraso yena sakṛdāsvādito bhavet
sa sarvakāryamutsṛjya tatraiva paridhāvati (48)

jñānasvarūpamevāhrurjagadetadvi cakṣaṇāḥ
arthasvarūpamajñānāt paśyantyanye kuddhastayaḥ (49)
ātmasvarūpavijñānādajñānasya parikṣayaḥ
kṣīṇe 'jñāne mahāprājña rāgādīnāṃ parikṣayaḥ (50)
rāgādyasaṃbhave prājña puṇyapāpavi marśanam
tayornāśe śarīreṇa na punaḥ saṃprayujyate (51)

Anvay

vāyu-jayena: through the conquest of *vāyu*; *pūrvikā*: former; *utpattiḥ*: gives rise to; *jñāna*: knowledge; *vairagya*: non-attachment; *vināḥ*: removal of; *roga-pāpa*: disease and sins; *evam*: thus; *abhyasataḥ tasya*: with his constant practice; *mūla-rogaḥ*: root cause of disease; *vinaśyati*: is eradicated; *bhagandharam*: fistula; *syāt*: can be; *naṣṭam*: destroyed; *sarva-rogāḥ*: all diseases; *ca*: and; *pātakāni*: sins; *ca kṣudrāṇi*: both small; *ca mahānti*: and large; *vinaśyanti*: disappear; *sāṃkṛte*: o Sāmkṛti; *naṣṭe pāpe*: with the removal of sin; *citta*: mind; *syāt*: becomes; *viśuddham*: pure; *adbhutam*: wondrous; *darpanam*: mirror; *punaḥ*: then; *bhogebhyaḥ*: because of delight in; *brahma-ādi*: Brahma and other [gods]; *vairagyam*: *vairagya*; *jāyate*: is produced; *hṛdi*: in the heart; *viraktasya*: indifferent to; *saṃsārāt*: material world; *jñānam*: [this] knowledge; *sādhanam*: means for; *kaivalya*: liberation; *tena*: through it; *devam sadāśivam*: god Sadāśiva; *jñātvā*: now known; *pāśa*: snare; *apahāniḥ*: is removed; *yena*: thus; *sa bhavet āsvāditaḥ*: he who has tasted; *rasaḥ*: nectar; *jñāna-amṛta*: of immortality of *jñāna*; *sakṛt*: once; *utsṛjya*: having renounced; *sarva-kāryam*: all actions; *paridhāvati*: hastens; *eva tatra*: straight there; *ajñānāt*: because of ignorance of; *artha*: purpose of; *svarūpam*: their own true nature; *anye*: others; *paśyanti*: see; *kuddhastayaḥ*: with defective eyesight; *cakṣaṇāḥ*: appearances; *etat āhruḥ jagat*: of this crooked world; *vi*: not; *svarūpam jñāna*: true form of *jñāna*; *vijñānāt*: when there is realisation of; *svarūpa*: true nature; *ātma*: *ātman*; *parikṣayaḥ*: that is the end; *ajñānasya*: of ignorance; *ajñāne kṣīṇe*: [when] ignorance is eroded; *mahāprājña*: o Great Wise One;

parikṣayaḥ: that is the end; *rāga-ādīnāṃ*: of desires and other [afflictions]; *rāga-ādi-asaṃbhave*: [when] desires and other [afflictions] are absent; *prājña*: o Wise One; *vi marśanam*: [there is] no inquiring into; *puṇya-pāpa*: virtue [and] vice; *nāśe*: with the destruction; *tayoḥ*: of these; *na punaḥ*: no longer; *saṃprayujyate*: one is attached; *śarīreṇa*: to the body.

Translation

The conquest of *vāyu* gives rise to the knowledge of *vairagya*, non-attachment, and removal of disease and sins: Thus, with constant practice, the root cause of disease is eradicated. [Even] a fistula can be destroyed. All diseases and sins, both small and large, disappear, o Sāmkṛti. With the removal of sin, the mind becomes pure [and] wondrous [like] a mirror. Then, because of delight in Brahma and other [gods], vairagya is produced in the heart. Indifferent to the material world, [this] knowledge is the means for liberation. Through it, when one has known the god *Sadaśiva*, the snare is removed. Thus, he who has tasted the nectar of immortality, of *jñāna* once, having renounced all actions, hastens straight there. Because of ignorance of the purpose of their own true nature, others see with defective eyesight the appearances of this crooked world, not the true form of jñāna. When there is realisation of the true nature of the atman, that is the end of ignorance. When ignorance is eroded, great wise One, that is the end of desires and other [afflictions]. When desires and other [afflictions] are absent, o wise One, [there] is no inquiry into virtue and vice. With the destruction of these, one is no longer attached to the body.

Commentary

The practice of prāṇāyāma helps one to establish the state of equanimity, and leads to the awakening of prāṇa and the mastery of vāyu. The conquest of vāyu gives rise to the realisation of *vairagya*, non-attachment, and the removal of disease and sin. As long as there is attachment to the world and its relations and objects, there will be stress, anxiety and frustration. Interaction motivated by attraction causes a kind of pendulum effect, and leads one towards states of negativity, imbalance and disease. Hence, by regular and constant practice of prāṇāyāma, the root cause of disease is removed; even fistula can be eliminated. All disease and sin, whether large or small, are resolved.

With the removal of negativity and sin, the mind of the yogi becomes pure and reflective, like a mirror. In this state one takes great delight in worshipping and contemplating the gods, such as Brahma and others. This dedication to the divine leads to a kind of higher vairagya, which is experienced in the heart. With the dawning of this higher vairagya, the yogi becomes indifferent to the material world, which becomes the means to liberation. In this way, when the supreme Lord *Sadaśiva* is known, the worldly snare is totally removed. So, it is said that one who has tasted the nectar of immortality, of jñāna, even once, renounces all karma and hastens straight there.

Due to ignorance, or *avidya*, of one's true nature, most people see the appearances of this world with defective vision. They are unable to perceive the true form of knowledge. When there is realisation of the true nature of the *ātman*, or self, that is the end of ignorance. When ignorance is eroded, that is the end of desire and all other afflictions. When desire and affliction are absent, there is no further inquiry into good and bad, right and wrong. With the destruction of duality, one is no longer attached to the body.

इति षष्ठ: खण्डः

iti ṣaṣṭhaḥ khaṇḍaḥ

Thus [ends] the sixth section.

सप्तमः खण्डः

saptamaḥ khaṇḍaḥ

Seventh Section

Pratyāhāra

Verses 1 to 4a: Description of pratyāhāra

प्रत्याहारलक्षनं तद्भेदाश्च
अथातः संप्रवक्ष्यामि प्रत्याहारं महामुने ।
इन्द्रियाणां विचरतां विषयेषु स्वभावतः ॥१॥
बलादाहरणं तेषां प्रत्याहारः स उच्यते ।
यत्पश्यति तु तत्सर्वं ब्रह्म पश्यन्समाहितः ॥२॥
प्रत्याहारो भवेदेष ब्रह्मविद्भिः पुरोदितः ।
यद्यच्छुद्धमशुद्धं वा करोत्यामरणान्तिकम् ॥३॥
तत्सर्वं ब्रह्मणे कुर्यात् प्रत्याहारः स उच्यते ।४।

pratyāhāralakṣanaṃ tadbhedāśca
athātaḥ saṃpravakṣyāmi pratyāhāraṃ mahāmune
indriyāṇāṃ vicaratāṃ viṣayeṣu svabhāvataḥ (1)
balādāharaṇaṃ teṣāṃ pratyāhāraḥ sa ucyate
yatpaśyati tu tatsarvaṃ brahma paśyansamāhitaḥ (2)
pratyāhāro bhavedeṣa brahmavidbhiḥ puroditaḥ
yadyacchuddhamaśuddhaṃ vā karotyāmaraṇāntikam (3)
tatsarvaṃ brahmaṇe kuryāt pratyāhāraḥ sa ucyate (4a)

Anvay

pratyāhāra-lakṣanam: description of *pratyāhāra*; *ca*: and; *tat bhedāḥ*: its modifications; *athātaḥ*: now; *saṃpravakṣyāmi*: I will explain; *pratyāhāram*: sensory withdrawal; *mahāmune*:

o Great Sage; *indriyāṇām*: senses; *vicaratām*: move about; *svabhāvataḥ*: naturally; *viṣayeṣu*: in the sense organs; *balāt*: wilfully; *āharaṇam*: nourishing; *teṣām*: from them; *sa ucyate*: this is called; *pratyāhāraḥ*: sensory withdrawal; *paśyan*: seeing; *samāhitaḥ*: in this withdrawn state; *yat*: whatever; *paśyati*: one sees; *tat sarvam*: all that; *brahma*: creator, ultimate reality; *eṣa bhavet*: this is; *pura uditaḥ*: as formerly declared; *brahmavidbhiḥ*: by knowers of Brahma; *yadyat*: whatever; *karoti*: one does; *śuddham vā aśuddham*: pure or impure; *āmaraṇāntikam*: until the end of this life; *tatsarvam*: all this; *kuryāt*: one should do; *brahmane*: in Brahma; *sa ucyate*: this is called; *pratyāhāraḥ*: sensory withdrawal.

Translation

Description of *pratyāhāra* and its modifications: Now I will explain pratyāhāra, o great Sage. The senses move about naturally in the sense objects. Wilfully withdrawing [the senses] from them is called pratyāhāra. Seeing in this withdrawn state, whatever one sees, all that [is] Brahma. This is pratyāhāra, as formerly declared by knowers of Brahma. Whatever one does, [be it] pure or impure, until the end of this life, all this one should do in [the awareness of] Brahma; this is called pratyāhāra. Or one should perform regular and desired actions, knowing [that they are] homage to Brahma; this is called pratyāhāra.

Commentary

Here begins the description of the inner path of meditation. In the path of *aṣṭāṅga* yoga, the eightfold yoga, the first four limbs are known as *bahiraṅga*, or outer branches. The last four are called *antaraṅga*, the inner branches. Pratyāhāra is the fifth limb of aṣṭāṅga yoga, and the first limb on the inner path, which leads to the following levels of *dhāraṇa,* one pointed concentration, *dhyāna,* spontaneous meditation, and finally *samādhi*, transcendental consciousness.

Thus, pratyāhāra is the first stage of meditation, and it means 'sensory withdrawal'. The word *pratyāhāra* is comprised of two roots: *pratyaya,* which means 'inner or subtle impressions', and *āhāra,* meaning 'to nourish'. So, pratyāhāra means to wilfully withdraw the senses back inside the mind, allowing them to be nourished by the subtle impressions or mental patterns. Otherwise, the mind and awareness are drawn outside by the five senses, and are nourished by the outer impressions, formed and sustained by the sensory objects.

The five senses: eyes, ears, tongue, skin, and nose, are naturally attracted to those objects, which can be seen, heard, tasted, touched and smelled. Through the practice of yama, niyama, āsana and prāṇāyāma, the practitioner gradually learns to direct the awareness back towards his or her own behavior, discipline, bodily postures and breath. In this way, he or she prepares for the stage of pratyahara. By withdrawal of the senses from the external world, and focusing them within the mind, the inner journey towards the true self can unfold.

The verse states that whatever one sees in the withdrawn state of pratyāhāra is *Brahma*, the lord or the inner cause of creation. When the senses are withdrawn, along with the awareness, back inside the mind, one no longer perceives the external world. Rather, the thoughts, memories and stored impressions, which are the subtle cause of the external experiences of the world, are revealed. These mental patterns, being the causal factors, are referred to here as Brahma. So, all that is seen in the inner dimension of mind, in the state of pratyāhāra, is known as Brahma. These are the seeds of creation, or all that can be experienced, in the external world.

When the stage of pratyāhāra has been mastered through regular meditative practice, this inner awareness can also be experienced, even while carrying out one's daily activities in the world. Once the practitioner is fully established in the state of sensory withdrawal, then, whatever actions one may do throughout one's life, whether good or bad, all these can be done with full awareness of Brahma, the causal dimension, or mind. Or else, one should perform one's duties or actions as worship of or devotion to Brahma. This outer and inner awareness of mind and senses in action was also called pratyāhāra by the sages of old.

Verses 4b to 8: Pratyāhāra by focusing on prāṇa

अथवा वित्यकर्माणि ब्रह्माराधनबुद्धितः ।।४।।
काम्यानि च तथा कुर्यात् प्रत्याहारः स उच्यते ।
अथवा वायुमाकृष्य स्थानात् स्थानं निरोधयेत् ।।५।।
दन्तमूलात्तथा कण्ठादुरसि मारुतम् ।
उरोदेशात् समाकृष्य नाभिदेशे निरोधयेत् ।।६।।
नाभिदेशात् समाकृष्य कुण्डल्यां तु निरोधयेत् ।
कुण्डलीदेशतो विद्वान् मूलाधारे निरोधयेत् ।।७।।
अथापानात् कटिद्वन्द्वे तथोरौ च सुमध्यमे ।
तस्माज्जानुद्वये जङ्घे पादाङ्गुष्ठे निरोधयेत् ।।८।।

athavā nityakarmāṇi brahmārādhanabuddhitaḥ (4b)
kāmyāni ca tathā kuryāt pratyāhāraḥ sa ucyate
athavā vāyumākṛṣya sthānāt sthānaṃ nirodhayet (5)
dantamūlāttathā kaṇṭhe kaṇṭhādurasi mārutam
urodeśāt samākṛṣya nābhideśe nirodhayet (6)
nābhideśāt samākṛṣya kuṇḍalyāṃ tu nirodhayet
kuṇḍalīdeśato vidvān mūlādhāre nirodhayet (7)
athāpānāt kaṭidvandve tathorau ca sumadhyame
tasmājjānudvaye jaṅghe pādāṅguṣṭhe nirodhayet (8)

Anvay

athavā: or; *kuryāt*: one should perform; *nitya-karmāṇi*: regular actions; *ca*: and; *kāmyāni*: desired; *buddhitaḥ*: knowing; *brahma-ārādhana*: homage to Brahma; *sa ucyate*: this is called; *pratyāhāraḥ*: sensory withdrawal; *athavā*: or; *ākṛṣya*: having inhaled; *nirodhayet*: one should hold; *sthānāt sthānam*: from place to place; *tathā*: thus; *samākṛṣya*: having drawn in; *mārutam*: vital air; *nirodhayet*: one should retain; *dantamūlāt*: from the root of the teeth; *kaṇṭhe*: to the throat; *kaṇṭhāt*: from the throat; *urasi*: to the chest; *urodeśāt*: from the chest; *nābhideśe*: to the navel; *samākṛṣya*: drawing in;

nābhideśāt: from the navel; *vidvān*: wise one; *nirodhayet*: should retain; *kuṇḍalyām*: in the *kuṇḍalī*; *tu*: and; *kuṇḍalīdeśataḥ*: from the place of the *kuṇḍalī*; *mūlādhāre*: in the root center; *atha*: thereupon; *nirodhayet*: one should retain; *apānāt*: downward moving energy; *sumadhyame*: in the waist; *ca tathā*: and then; *kaṭidvandve*: in the hips; *ūrau*: in the thighs; *tasmāt*: from there; *jānudvaye*: in both knees; *jaṅghe*: in the lower legs; *pādāṅguṣṭhe*: in the toes.

Translation
One should perform daily actions and desired (actions) while knowing Brahma and (paying) homage to Brahma. This is called pratyāhāra. Or, having inhaled the *vāyu*, one should hold [it] from place to place. Thus, having drawn in the vital air, one should retain [it] from the root of the teeth to the throat, from the throat to the chest, [and] from the chest to the navel. Drawing [it] in from the navel, the wise one should retain [it] in the *kuṇḍalī,* from the place of the kuṇḍalī in *mūlādhāra.* Thereupon, one should retain the *apāna* in the waist, and then in the hips and thighs, from there in the knees, lower legs [and] toes.

Commentary
Pratyāhāra is the first stage of meditation, whereby one develops awareness of and mastery over the senses. The senses are what connect the mind with the world outside. Through regular practice of sensory withdrawal, one becomes aware of the mind, the inner world, and its multitude of patterns and expressions. After attaining a degree of mastery in this practice, one should then extend this practice of awareness into daily life and actions, be they actions performed out of duty or desire. In this way, one can live a meditative life, even while working through one's various roles in the world. The mind is the seed of all action, so, as the verse says, one can act in the world, even while knowing Brahma, the causal mind, the creator of the worlds,

and paying homage or respect to Brahma. This is called pratyāhāra.

Or, there is another way to practise pratyāhāra, withdrawal of the senses, which does not involve the mind. In this method, there is no need to observe the mental thoughts and patterns. This practice is performed by retention of *prāṇa* at the different centers in the body. This is a very different practice to the first one described in the previous verses and the technique is given as follows:

Technique
Sit quietly for a few moments and allow the breath to become slow and rhythmic. Next inhale deeply and retain the breath, while moving the awareness from place to place. First, hold the breath in the region between the root of the teeth and the throat (viśuddhi cakra) for a comfortable duration. Then exhale slowly.

Again inhale and draw the breath down to the region between the throat and the chest (anahata cakra). Hold the breath here for a comfortable duration, and then exhale slowly.

Next inhale and draw the breath down to the region between the chest and the navel (manipura cakra). Hold the breath here for a comfortable duration, and then exhale slowly.

Now, draw the breath inward from the navel and then downward to the mooladhara chakra, at the perineum. Retain the breath there, and merge it with the kundalini force. Then exhale slowly.

Next inhale and retain the breath in the region of *apāna*, the downward flowing energy, in between the waist and the pelvic floor. Following the same process, Inhale and focus the apana energy first at the waist, then the hips and thighs, and from there, the knees, calves, feet and toes.

This is an alternative method by which pratyāhāra can be achieved. In the first method pratyāhāra is to be practised by focusing the mind on the mind, and ultimately allowing this mental awareness to expand outside into one's daily life. In this method, however, pratyāhāra is attained by focusing the mind on the movement of energy, because breath and energy are closely aligned. When the mind is focused in the mind, the process may become difficult and tedious., because the thoughts and mental patterns seem to be never ending. Whereas, when the mind is focused on the movement of breath or energy, the process of awareness becomes fluid and effortless. The mind is subdued, so to speak, by the movement of breath and prana. In this way, pratyāhāra takes place very quickly and easily.

Verses 9 to 10a: Benefits of pratyāhāra

प्रत्याहारो ऽयमुक्तस्तु प्रत्याहारपरैः पुरा प्रत्याहारफलम् ।
एवमभ्यासयुक्तस्य पुरुषस्य महात्मनः ।।९।।
सर्वपापानि नश्यन्ति भवरोगश्च सुव्रत ।१०।

pratyāhāro 'yamuktastu pratyāhāraparaiḥ purā pratyāhāraphalam
evamabhyāsayuktasya puruṣasya mahātmanaḥ (9)
sarvapāpāni naśyanti bhavarogaśca suvrata (10a)

Anvay
ayam uktaḥ: this is said; *pratyāhāraparaiḥ*: by those accomplished in *pratyāhāra; purā*: in ancient times; *evam*: thus; *mahātmanaḥ puruṣasya*: great being; *yuktasya*: engaged in; *abhyāsa*: regular practice; *sarva-pāpāni*: all sins; *ca*: and; *bhavarogaḥ*: worldly disease; *naśyanti*: vanish; *suvrata*: o virtuous One.

Translation
This is said [to be] *pratyāhāra* by those accomplished in pratyāhāra in ancient times. Thus, [whenever] a great being [is] engaged in regular practice, all sins and worldly disease vanish, o virtuous One.

Commentary
Both of these methods described above were said to produce the state of *pratyāhāra* by those yogis of old, who had mastered meditation. Even today, in most meditative traditions, these two basic approaches to meditation are found: one focusing on the mind by the mind, as in *antar mouna* or mindfulness, and the other on the movement of the breath or prāṇa.

Pratyāhāra is the first stage of meditation, but its significance should never be underestimated or disregarded. In fact, for modern practitioners, it is probably the most difficult stage to master, due to the over-activation and stimulation of the mind, from an early age, in the world today. This stage may take years to master, while the higher stages of meditation that come afterwards, will be attained more easily and spontaneously. Thus, the mastery of pratyāhāra is an important attainment on the spiritual path for any aspirant.

The yogi, who has mastered pratyāhāra through regular practice, is considered to be a great being. Having attained mastery over the mind and senses, all of his or her sins, negative karmas, and diseases are resolved. This follows the yogic premise that all disease and negativity are ultimately stored in the subconscious mind of the individual. By witnessing the mental patterns and allowing the thoughts and memories to bubble up, the yogi is gradually able to eliminate them. In this way, he or she becomes free from the source of all guilt, negativity and disease.

Verses 10b to 12: Pratyāhāra by focusing on prāṇa (method 2)

वायुधारणात्मकप्रत्याहारः
नासाभ्याम् वायुमाकृष्य निश्चलः स्वस्तिकासनः ।।१०।।
पूरयेदनिलं विद्वानापादतलमस्तकम् ।
पश्चात पाददद्वये तद्वत् मूलाधारे तथैव च ।।११।।
नाभिकन्दे च हृद्मध्ये कण्ठमूले च तालुके ।
भ्रूवोर्मध्ये ललाटे च तथा मूर्धनि धारयेत् ।।१२।।

vāyudhāraṇātmakapratyāhāraḥ
nāsābhyāṃ vāyumākṛṣya niścalaḥ svastikāsanaḥ (10b)
pūrayedanilaṃ vidvānāpādatalamastakam
paścāt pādadvaye tadvat mūlādhāre tathaiva ca (11)
nābhikande ca hṛdmadhye kaṇṭhamūle ca tāluke
bhrūvormadhye lalāṭe ca tathā mūrdhani dhārayet (12)

Anvay
ākṛṣya: inhaling; *nāsābhyām*: through the nostrils; *niścalaḥ*: steady; *svastikāsanaḥ*: *svastikāsana*, auspicious pose; *vidvān*: wise one; *pūrayet*: should fill; *āpāda*: from; *tala*: soles of the feet; *mastakam*: to the top of the head; *paścāt*: next; *dhārayet*: it is held; *tadvat*: also; *pādadvaye*: in both legs; *ca tathā*: and then; *mūlādhāre*: at the root center; *nābhikande*: at the knot of the navel; *hṛdmadhye*: at the heart centre; *kaṇṭhamūle*: at the throat pit; *tāluke*: at the palate; *bhrūvormadhye*: at the eyebrow centre; *lalāṭe*: at the forehead; *ca tathā*: and then; *mūrdhani*: at the top of the head.

Translation
Pratyāhāra by holding the prāṇa within: Inhaling through the nostrils [while sitting] steadily in *svastikāsana*, the wise one should fill [the body] from the soles of the feet to the top of the head. Next it is held also in both legs, then at mūlādhāra,

at the knot of the navel, the heart centre, throat pit, palate, eyebrow centre, forehead and then the top of the head.

Commentary

These verses describe a variation of the pratyāhāra practice given previously. This method activates the cakra, *cakra kṣetrams*, or trigger-points, in the front of the body, and the regions surrounding them. The technique is explained below step by step in order to avoid confusion. Please bear in mind that this is an original technique, which modern techniques may have been drawn from, modified, and then given different names.

Technique

Sit in the position of svastikāsana, and allow the body to become steady and still. Begin to follow the movement of the breath with your awareness. Gradually feel the breath becoming slow and rhythmic.

Inhale slowly and evenly through both nostrils, and feel the awareness and breath flowing upward, filling the entire body with prana or energy from the soles of the feet to the top of the head. Retain the breath inside for a comfortable duration, feeling the prāṇa within the entire body, and then exhale slowly.

Next, inhaling slowly through both nostrils, fill the region within both legs, from the hips to the toes, with energy or prāṇa. Hold the breath for a comfortable duration, feeling the prāṇa in this region, and then exhale slowly.

Inhaling slowly with awareness through both nostrils, fill the region of mūlādhāra cakra, at the pelvic floor, with energy. Retain the breath for a comfortable duration, and feel the prāṇa expanding into the entire pelvic region. Exhale slowly.

Inhale slowly with awareness through both nostrils, and fill the region of the maṇipura cakra trigger-point, at the navel, with energy. Retain the breath for a comfortable duration, and feel the prāṇa expanding into the entire abdominal region. Exhale slowly.

Inhale slowly with awareness through both nostrils, and fill the region of anāhata cakra, the heart center, with energy. Retain the breath for a comfortable duration, and feel the prāṇa expanding into the entire region of the chest. Exhale slowly.

Inhale slowly with awareness through both nostrils, and fill the region of viśuddhi cakra triggerpoint, at the throat pit, with energy. Retain the breath for a comfortable duration, and feel the prāṇa expanding into the entire region of the throat. Exhale slowly.

Inhale slowly with awareness through both nostrils, and fill the region of *lalanā cakra*, at back of the throat, where it meets the palate, with energy. Retain the breath for a comfortable duration, and feel the prāṇa expanding into the entire region at the back of the throat. Exhale slowly.

Inhale slowly with awareness through both nostrils, and fill the region of the ājñā cakra triggerpoint, at the eyebrow center, with energy. Retain the breath for a comfortable duration, and feel the prāṇa expanding into the mid region of the brain. Exhale slowly.

Inhale slowly with awareness through both nostrils, and fill the region of bindu cakra triggerpoint, at the forehead, with energy. Retain the breath for a comfortable duration, and feel the prāṇa expanding into the entire frontal brain region. Exhale slowly.

Inhale slowly with awareness through both nostrils, and fill the region of *sahasrāra cakra*, at the crown of the head, with energy. Retain the breath for a comfortable duration, and feel the prāṇa expanding in all directions from sahasrara. Exhale slowly.

Sit quietly for a few moments and experience the effects of this practice. Slowly begin to externalise your awareness. Become aware of the physical body, of the posture, and of stillness. Gradually, begin to follow the external sounds, the external breath. Then slowly release the posture and open the eyes.

Verses 13 and 14: Pratyāhāra according to vedānta

वेदान्तसंमतप्रत्याहारः

देहे त्स्वात्मभुतिं विद्वान् समाकृष्य समाहितः ।

आत्मनात्मनि निर्द्वन्द्वे निर्विकल्पे निरोधयेत् ।।१३।।

प्रत्याहारः समाख्यातः साक्षाद्वेदान्तवेदिभिः ।

एवमभ्यसतस्तस्य न किंचिदपि दुर्लभम् ।।१४।।

vedāntasaṃmatapratyāhāraḥ
dehe svātmabhutiṃ vidvān samākṛṣya samāhitaḥ
ātmanātmani nirdvandve nirvikalpe nirodhayet (13)
pratyāhāraḥ samākhyātaḥ sākṣādvedāntavedibhiḥ
evamabhyasatastasya na kiṃcidapi durlabham (14)

Anvay
saṃmata: according to; *vedānta*: end of the Vedas; *samākṛṣya*: withdrawing; *dehe sva ātmabhutim*: attachment to his body; *vidvān*: wise one; *nirodhayet*: is withdrawn; *ātmanātmani*: true self; *nirdvandve*: non-dual; *nirvikalpe*: thoughtless; *sākṣāt*: clearly; *samākhyātaḥ*: called; *vedāntavedibhiḥ*: by knowers of vedānta; *tasya abhyasataḥ*: for one who practises; *evam*: thus; *na kiṃcidapi*: nothing; *durlabham*: difficult to attain.

Translation
Pratyāhāra, according to vedānta: Withdrawing the attachment to his body, the wise one is withdrawn into the true self, non-dual [and] thoughtless. [This is] clearly called pratyāhāra by knowers of vedānta. For one who practises thus, nothing [is] difficult to attain.

Commentary
According to vedānta, there is only the one reality, one truth, which is non-dual and the core of all existence. The world, and all of our experiences relating with it, are part of the relative reality, which is dualistic. The practice of pratyāhāra

enables one to withdraw the senses and awareness from the world, and identify with that one reality, which is beyond thought, instead of with the body and mind. Thus, it is said here that, nothing is difficult to attain for one who practices pratyāhāra.

इति सप्तमः खण्डः

iti saptamaḥ khaṇḍaḥ

Thus [ends] the seventh section.

अष्टमः खण्डः

aṣṭamaḥ khaṇḍaḥ

Eighth Section

Dhāraṇā

Verses 1 to 6: Pañca bhūta dhāraṇā, concentration on the five elements

पञ्चभूतेषु धारणा
अथातः संप्रवक्ष्यामि धारणाः पञ्च सुव्रत ।
देहमध्यगते व्योम्नि बाह्याकाशं तु धारयेत् ।।१।।
प्राणे बाह्यानिलं तद्वत् ज्वलने चाग्निमौदरे ।
तोयं तोयम्शके भूमिं भूमिभागे महामुने ।।२।।
हयरावलकाराख्यं मन्त्रमुञ्चारयेत् क्रमात् ।
धारणैषा परा प्रोक्ता सर्वपापविशोधिनी ।।३।।
जान्वन्तं पृथिवी ह्यंशो हयपां पात्वन्तमुच्यते ।
हृदयांशस्तथाग्न्यंशो भ्रूमध्यान्तो ऽनिलांशकः ।।४।।
आकाशाम्शस्तथा प्राज्ञ मुर्धांशः परिकीर्तितः ।
ब्रह्माणं पृथिवीभागे विष्णुं तोयंशके तथा ।।५।।
अग्न्यंशे च महेशानमीश्वरं चानिलांशके ।
आकाशांशे महाप्राज्ञ धारयेतु सदाशिवम् ।।६।।

pañcabhūteṣu dhāraṇā
athātaḥ saṃpravakṣyāmi dhāraṇāḥ pañca suvrata
dehamadhyagate vyomni bāhyākāśaṃ tu dhārayet (1)
prāṇe bāhyānilaṃ tadvat jvalane cāgnimaudare
toyaṃ toyamśake bhūmiṃ bhūmibhāge mahāmune (2)
hayaravalakārākhyaṃ mantramuñcārayet kramāt

dhāraṇaiṣā parā proktā sarvapāpaviśodhinī (3)
jānvantaṃ pṛthivī hyaṃśo hyapāṃ pātvantamucyate
hṛdayāṃśastathāgnyaṃśo bhrūmadhyānto 'nilāṃśakaḥ (4)
ākāśāmśastathā prājña murdhośaḥ parikīrtitaḥ
brahmāṇaṃ pṛthivībhāge viṣṇuṃ toyaṃśake tathā (5)
agnyaṃśe ca maheśānamīśvaraṃ cānilāṃśake
ākāśāmśe mahāprājña dhārayettu sadāśivam (6)

Anvay

dhāraṇā: concentration; *pañca-bhūteṣu*: on the five elements; *athātaḥ*: thus; *saṃpravakṣyāmi*: I shall describe; *pañca*: five; *dhāraṇāḥ*: concentrations; *suvrata*: o Virtuous One; *tu*: now; *dhārayet*: one should concentrate on; *bāhya-ākāśam*: external ether; *vyomni*: in the atmosphere; *gate*: contained in; *dehamadhya*: centre of the body; *tadvat*: also; *bāhya-ānilam*; external air; *prāṇe*: in the *prāṇa*; *ca*: and; *agnim*: fire; *jvalane*: burning; *audare*: in the belly; *toyam*: water; *toyamśake*: in the watery part; *bhūmim*: earth; *bhūmi-bhāge*: in the earthy place; *mahāmune*: o Great Sage; *muñcārayet*: one should utter; *kramāt*: in sequence; *kāra*: sounds; *ākhyam*; names; *eṣā*: this; *proktā*: declared; *parā dhāraṇā*: supreme concentration; *viśodhinī*: purifying; *sarva pāpa*: all sins; *hi*: for; *ucyate*: it is said; *pṛthivī aṃśaḥ*: earth section; *pātvantam*: down from; *jānvantam*: knees; *apām*: water; *tathā*: then; *agni-aṃśaḥ*: fire section; *hṛdaya-aṃśaḥ*: heart centre; *anila-aṃśakaḥ*: air section; *bhrūmadhyāntaḥ*: eyebrow centre; *ākāśa-aṃśaḥ*: ether section; *murdhośaḥ*: at the top of the head; *tathā*: thus; *parikīrtitaḥ*: it is proclaimed; *prājña*: o Wise One; *tathā*: then; *dhārayet*: one should concentrate on; *brahmāṇam*: Brahma; *pṛthivī-bhāge*: in the earth place; *viṣṇum*: Viṣṇu; *toyaṃ-śake*: in the water area; *maheśānam*: Maheśa; *agni-aṃśe*: in the fire section; *īśvaram*: Īśvara; *anilāṃ-śake*: in the air portion; *ca*: and; *sadāśivam*: Sadāśiva; *ākāśa-aṃśe*: ether section; *mahāprājña*: o Great Wise One.

Translation

Dhāraṇā, or concentration, on the five elements: Thus I shall describe the five forms of concentration, o virtuous One. Now, one should concentrate on the external ether in the atmosphere, contained in the centre of the body; also on the external air in the *prāṇa*, and on the fire burning in the belly, water in the watery part [and] earth in the earthy place, o great Sage. One should utter in sequence the sounds [of the] names [of the] mantras: *Ham*, *Yam*, *Ram*, *Vam*, *Lam*. This [is] declared the supreme concentration, purifying all sins. For it is said the earth section is down from the knees, water [is up from the knees], then fire section in the area the heart centre, air section at the eyebrow centre [and] ether section is at the top of the head; thus it is proclaimed, o wise One. Then one should concentrate on Brahma in the earth place, Viṣṇu in the water area, Maheśa in the fire section, Īśvara in the air portion and Sadāśiva in the ether section, o great wise One.

Commentary

Dhāraṇā is the second stage of *antaraṅga*, the inner practices of rāja yoga.The word *dhāraṇā* means 'one pointed focus' or 'concentration'. The ability to focus the mind and hold the focus at will is difficult for most people to achieve without prior mastery of pratyāhāra, which was described in the previous section. These verses describe the practice of *pañcabhūta dhāraṇā*, the five forms of concentration on the elements, which were the traditional form of dharana in the upanishadic times. The word *pañca* means 'five' and *bhūta* means 'elements'.

The five elements are the same components in all beings, whether sentient or insentient, in this world. The only difference between one being and another, or one species and another, is the proportion of the elemental composition in their makeup. In astrology, for example, we can see how the different elements are influenced in various individuals, making each person unique, and also creating opportunities and obstructions at different times.

Therefore, concentration on the elements is also a way to connect with the basic elemental energies within oneself and in all beings of creation. The five elements are: ether, air, fire, water, and earth. The method for this practice of concentration is described below:

Technique
Sit quietly in a steady meditative posture and close the eyes. Relax the whole body systematically, from head to toe. Develop the feeling of stillness within. Become aware of the natural rhythm of the breath. Focus the awareness at the nose-tip, and feel each inhalation and exhalation flowing in and out through the nostrils.

Now, leave the awareness of the breath and become aware of the element of space or ether, which surrounds you in all directions. Space is all pervasive. Feel that your entire body is also pervaded by space. The quality of space is stillness. See space wherever you look; inside of you and outside of you, there is nothing but space. Everything in creation exists in this same space. Draw your awareness deep within and focus on the space contained at the center, or core, of your being.

Allow this perception of space to fade, and become aware of the element of air. While space is all pervasive and still, air is a gaseous substance in constant movement. Air moves all through the space and fills it with kinetic energy, like the movement of the wind or prāṇa. We can feel the movement of air on our skin and in the flow of our breath. Air is the breath of life, and it travels all through us, enlivening every cell, organ and part. Our whole body breathes in the air from the atmosphere, and expels the air, which has been utilised by the cellular structures, from moment to moment. Focus on the element of air.

The movement of air produces friction, and heat or fire is produced. Fire has two qualities, heat and light. Become aware of the fire burning in your belly. Fire is a dynamic force, which has form and is visible. The heat produced by fire is responsible for the digestive and metabolic processes. The light enables us to see and thus to differentiate myself from another. Become aware of the fire burning within you.

When the heat of fire cools, water is produced. Water has the quality of fluidity and movement. Our bodies are more than 75% water, and the water is in constant flow and movement. Fluids are continually flowing to and from every cell, organ and part. Focus on the element of water, below the navel, in the pelvic region.

When water ceases its movement, it becomes still and solidifies into earth. Become aware of the earth element, which is dense, heavy and unmoving. Feel the quality of earth within you and all around you. Feel the weight of the body, the bones, the muscle, the skin, the hair, the teeth, the nails. The body is supported by earth, nourished by earth, walks upon earth. Focus on the earth element at the pelvic floor. Feel the connection between the pelvic floor and the earth beneath you.

Concentration on the five sound forms of the elements: Now, leave the awareness of the earth element. Bring your attention back up to the region between the crown of the head and the eyebrows. Become aware of the space element in this region and repeat the sound *Ham* 12 times. Next, move the awareness to the region between the eyebrows and the heart. Become aware of the air element in this space. Repeat the sound *Yam* 12 times. Move the awareness to the region between the heart and the navel. Become aware of the fire element in this space. Repeat the sound *Ram* 12 times. Bring the awareness to the region between the navel and the knees. Become aware of the water element in this space. Repeat the mantra *Vam* 12 times. Bring the awareness to the region between the knees and the toes. Become aware of the earth element in this space. Repeat the sound *Lam* 12 times.

Concentration on the deities of the five elements: one should concentrate on the form of Brahma, the creator, in the earth region, between the toes and the knees. Then focus on Viṣṇu, the sustainer, in the region of water, between the knees and the navel. Next, see Maheśa in the region of fire, between the navel and the heart. Concentrate on Īśvara in the region of air, between the heart and the eyebrows. Finally, forcus on Sadāśiva in the region of space, between the eyebrows and the crown of the head.

Ending the practice: Now, leave the awareness of the deities and the elements. Bring your attention back to the body. Become aware of the position of the body, the weight of the body. Be aware of the breath. Listen to the sounds that you can hear from outside. Slowly release the body posture and open the eyes.

This is the original practice of pañcabhūta dhāraṇā, concentration on the five elements, and it is very powerful. Regular practice purifies and rebalances the elemental energies within the body, and helps to bring about a deep state of meditation. It should ideally be practiced in the early morning at dawn, or in the early evening at dusk. Even today, pañcabhūta dhāraṇā is still practised in similar and modified versions, for example, in the practice of *tattva śuddhi,* purification of the tattwas. The words tattwa and bhūta have the same meaning. Although the five elements and their related sounds, ie. *Lam*, *Vam*, *Ram*, and so on, are also found within the symbols of the cakras, it is important to note that the tattwa system of meditation, and the location of the tattwas, is completely separate from the cakra system.

The Rishi of this upaniṣad declared this practice of pañcabhūta dhāraṇā to be the supreme or highest form of concentration, which will purify and remove the effects of all sins and negativity, that obstruct the practitioner in life and on the spiritual path.

Verses 7 to 9: Dhāraṇā on the Self

आत्मनि धारणा

अथ वा तव वक्षामि धारणां मुनिपुङ्गव ।

पुरुषे सर्वशास्तारं बोधानन्दमयं शिवम् ।।७।।

धारयेद्बुद्धिमान् नित्यं सर्वपापविशुद्धये ।

ब्रह्मादिकर्यरूपाणि स्वेस्वे संहृत्य कारणे ।।८।।

र्वकारणमव्यक्तमनिरूप्यमचेतनम् ।

साक्षादात्मनि संपूर्णे धारयेत् प्रणवे मनः ।

इन्द्रियाणि समहृत्य मनसात्मनि योजयेत् ।।९।।

ātmani dhāraṇā
atha vā tava vakśyāmi dhāraṇāṃ munipuṅgava
puruṣe sarvaśāstāraṃ bodhānandamayaṃ śivaṃ (7)
dhārayedbuddhimān nityaṃ sarvapāpaviśuddhaye
brahmādikāryarūpāṇi svesve saṃhṛtya kāraṇe (8)
sarvakāraṇamavyaktamanirūpyamacetanam
sākṣādātmani saṃpūrṇe dhārayet praṇave manaḥ
indriyāṇi samāhṛtya manasātmani yojayet (9)

Anvay

dhāraṇā: concentration; *ātmani*: on the self; *atha*: now; *vakśyāmi*: shall I describe; *vā*: *interrogative*; *tava*: to you; *dhāraṇām*: concentration; *munipuṅgava*: o esteemed Sage; *ayam*: this; *puruṣe*: in the *puruṣa*, soul; *śivam*: Śiva; *sarva-śāstāram*: ruler of all; *ānandam*: blissful; *bodha*: all-knowing; *buddhimān*: wise one; *viśuddhaye*: for the purification of; *sarva-pāpa*: all sins; *dhārayet*: should concentrate on; *nityam*: always; *rūpāṇi*: forms; *kārya*: deeds; *brahma-ādi*: Brahma and other [gods]; *saṃhṛtya*: absorbing; *svesve kāraṇe*: into one's own cause; *avyaktaman*: unmanifest; *nirūpyam*: without form; *acetanam*: indefinable; *kāraṇa*: cause of; *sarva*: everything; *dhārayet*: one should fix; *manaḥ*: mind; *sākṣāt*: clearly; *saṃpūrṇe*: completely;

praṇave: on the *praṇava*, Aum; *ātmani*: in the *ātman*, self; *samāhṛtya*: having withdrawn; *indriyāṇi*: senses; *yojayet*: one should merge; *manas-ātmani*: mind with the self.

Translation

Concentration on the self: Now shall I describe to you [this] concentration, o esteemed Sage? This [is] in the *puruṣa*, (who is) Śiva, the ruler of all, blissful [and] all-knowing. The wise one, for the purification of all sins, should always concentrate on the forms [and] deeds of Brahma and other [gods], absorbing [them] into one's own cause, [concentrating on] the unmanifest, without form [and] indefinable [which is] the cause of everything. One should fix the mind clearly [and] completely on the *praṇava* in the *ātman*; having withdrawn the senses, one should merge the mind with the self.

Commentary

Concentration on the self is considered to be the highest dhāraṇā, and also the most difficult, because the self has no form or material existence. The self is known by different terms, such as atman, spirit or soul. We are familiar with these words, but we do not know or understand what is the self, where does it come from, and how does it live within us. This is the great difficulty of this meditation. There is no visible or manifest form that we can hold onto, identify with or relate with, as we are used to doing in the world around us. Perhaps, this is why the Rishi has asked, shall I describe this concentration to you now, or not?

The Rishi continues to explain that this meditation takes place in the *puruṣa*, the soul, who is the pure self, the pure consciousness. The puruṣa is also known as Śiva, the ruler of all, who is ever blissful and all knowing. In order to prepare oneself for this meditation, the wise aspirant should begin by studying or listening to the scriptures and stories about Brahma and the other gods, gradually absorbing them into his or her mind and consciousness. With this understanding, the aspirant may then practice concentration on the forms and deeds of the gods, for the purification of all accumulated sins and negative karmas.

Finally, the aspirant should concentrate on the unmanifest, the essence of all being, which is formless and indefinable, and the cause of everything that exists. While practising this concentration, which is beyond thought, one should focus the mind clearly and completely on the *praṇava,* the pure sound of *Aum.* The *Aum* sound is the first resonance or vibration of creation, and it is heard within the depths of the pure consciousness, the atman or the soul. In this way, having withdrawn the senses back into the mind, one should merge the mind with the Self, even while living in this world. This is the highest attainment of yoga.

इत्यष्टमः खण्डः

iti aṣṭamaḥ khaṇḍaḥ

Thus [ends] the eighth section.

नवमः खण्डः

navamaḥ khaṇḍaḥ

Ninth Section

Dhyāna

Verses 1 and 2: Meditation on Brahma with attributes

सविशेषब्रह्मध्यानम्

अथातः संप्रवक्ष्यामि ध्यानं संसारनाशनम् ।

ऋतं सत्यं परं ब्रह्म सर्वसंसारभेषजम् ।।१।।

ऊर्ध्वरेतं विरूपाक्षं विश्वरूपं महेश्वरम् ।

सो ऽहमित्यादरेणैव ध्यायेद्योगीश्वरेश्वरम् ।।२।।

saviśeṣabrahmadhyānam
athātaḥ saṃpravakṣyāmi dhyānaṃ saṃsāranāśanam
ṛtaṃ satyaṃ paraṃ brahma sarvasaṃsārabheṣajam (1)
ūrdhvaretaṃ virūpākṣaṃ viśvarūpaṃ maheśvaram
so 'hamityādareṇaiva dhyāyedyogīśvareśvaram (2)

Anvay

dhyānam: meditation; *saviśeṣa brahma*: attributes of Brahma; *thātaḥ*: now; *saṃpravakṣyāmi*: I shall describe; *nāśanam*: destroys; *saṃsāra*: illusory world; *ṛtam*: divine harmony; *satyam*: truth; *param brahma*: supreme Brahma; *bheṣajam*: remedy for; *sarva saṃsāra*: all delusions; *iti*: saying; *ādareṇa*: reverently; *soham*: I am that; *yogī*: *yogin*; *dhyāyet*: should meditate on; *īśvara-īśvaram*: Lord of Lords; *ūrdhvaretam*: [whose] seed [is] contained; *virūpākṣam*: Śiva, many forms; *viśvarūpam*: cosmic form; *maheśvaram*: Maheśvara, highest reality.

Translation

Meditation on the attributes of Brahma: Now I shall describe *dhyāna*, [which] destroys the illusory world, [which is] divine harmony, truth, the supreme Brahma, the remedy for all delusions. Saying reverently 'I Am That', the yogin should meditate on the Lord of Lords, [whose] seed [is] contained, [who is] Śiva of many forms, of the cosmic form, [and] Maheśvara, the highest reality.

Commentary

Dhyāna is the third limb of *antaraṅga* in rāja yoga. *Pratyāhāra* and *dhāraṇā*, the first and second limbs, require regular and vigilant practice. Dhyāna is the outcome of their mastery, when the awareness flows steadily upon one object or ideal, without any dissipation or break, just as oil is poured from one container into another in one steady stream. From the stage of dhyāna onward, meditation takes place spontaneously and effortlessly. It is no longer considered to be a practice, which needs constant application of will and direction.

In pratyāhāra, the awareness is focused within the conscious and subconscious mind on the immediate and latent mental impressions and patterns. In dhāraṇā, the awareness is focused on one object or ideal within the conscious and subconscious mind, but there are breaks. The mind wanders and the practitioner brings it back again and again to the object of focus. In dhyāna, the awareness flows smoothly and steadily towards the object or ideal in the deep levels of the subconscious mind, without any break.

In the above verses, the Rishi describes dhyāna on the attributes of Brahma. The state of dhyāna is one of divine harmony. In this state the absolute truth, which is the remedy for all delusions, relating with time, space and object, is known. The yogi who becomes established in dhyāna has the direct experience of the supreme Brahma, the Lord of creation, and is no longer affected by the illusory appearances and experiences of the external world.

Repeating the mantra *Soham,* 'I am That', with faith and reverence, the yogi should meditate on Īśvara, the Lord of all the worlds. Being the universal Lord of Lords, he has no desire or inclination to procreate further, so his seed or creative potential is contained. He is Śiva in his cosmic form, and also in his many manifest forms. He is Maheśvara, the great Īśvara, the highest reality.

Verses 3 to 5: Meditation on Brahma without attributes

निर्विशेषब्रह्मध्यानम्

अथ वा सत्रमीशानं ज्ञानमानन्दमद्वयम् ।

अत्यर्थम् अमलं नित्यमादिमध्यान्तवर्जितम् ।।३।।

तथास्थूलमनाकाशमसंस्पृश्यमचाक्षुषम् ।

न रसं न च गन्धाख्यमप्रमेयमनुपमम् ।।४।।

आत्मानं सञ्चिदानन्दमनन्तं ब्रह्म सुव्रत ।

अहमस्मीत्यभिध्यायेद्देहातीतं विमुक्तये ।।५।।

nirviśeṣabrahmadhyānam
atha vā satyamīśānaṃ jñānamānandamadvayam
atyarthamamalaṃ nityamādimadhyāntavarjitam (3)
tathāsthūlamanākāśamasaṃspṛśyamacākṣuṣam
na rasaṃ na ca gandhākhyamaprameyamanupamam (4)
ātmānaṃ sañcidānandamanantaṃ brahma suvrata
ahamasmītyabhidhyāyeddehātītaṃ vimuktaye (5)

Anvay
dhyānam: meditation; *nirviśeṣa brahma*: Brahma without attributes; *atha*: now; *īśānam satyam*: Śiva, possessor of truth; *jñāna*: knowledge; *ānanda*: bliss; *advayam*: non-dual; *ati-artham*: beyond meaning; *amalam*: pure; *nityam*: eternal; *varjitam*: without; *ādi madhya anta*: beginning, middle, end; *tathā*: thus; *asthūlam*: without matter; *anākāśam*: without space; *asaṃspṛśyam*: without touch; *acākṣuṣam*: without sight; *na rasam*: without taste; *ca*: and; *na gandha-ākhyam*: without any smell; *aprameyam*: immeasurable; *anupamam*: incomparable; *ātmānam*: soul; *anantam*: infinite; *sat-cit-ānandam*: existence-consciousness-bliss; *suvrata*: o virtuous One; *abhidhyāyet*: being absorbed in; *iti aham asmi*: Thus I Am; *dehātītam*: one transcends the body; *vimuktaye*: is liberated.

Translation

Meditation on Brahma without attributes: Now [this is] Śiva, the possessor of truth, [whose] knowledge [and] bliss [are] non-dual, [who is] beyond meaning, pure, eternal, without beginning, middle [and] end. Thus, [being] without matter, space, touch, sight, taste and smell, [he is] immeasurable [and] incomparable. Brahma [is] the soul, infinite existence-consciousness-bliss, o Virtuous One. Being absorbed in the mantra *iti aham asmi,* 'Thus I Am', one transcends the body [and] is liberated.

Commentary

There are basically two kinds of meditation, one with form and the other without form. The previous verses described meditation with form, and now a brief description of meditation without form is given. Meditation on a form provides the mind with a base, upon which it can steady itself, and always know where it is in the vast domains of consciousness. Meditation without any form is more difficult in the sense that the mind has nothing to hold onto and may drift in the abstract space of consciousness, which is beyond time and object. Down through the ages, these two kinds of meditation have been debated, as to which one is superior or inferior. Ultimately, it comes down to the personal preference of the meditator.

Meditation is a journey through the inner dimensions of consciousness. Śiva, the primordial yogi, is also a symbol of this journey, as he is usually depicted sitting in *padmāsana*, deep in meditation. So, Śiva also represents the state of absolute consciousness, wherein there are no boundaries or limitations. Therefore, Śiva is described here as that state of consciousness, where truth, knowledge and bliss exist throughout in the non-dual state. In the world we have the experience of duality: relative truth, relative knowledge, and relative happiness. Everything we experience is always related with I and another, and this is called duality. Whereas, Śiva represents the experience of consciousness in the non-dual state, the state of oneness.

Śiva represents the state of consciousness, which is beyond mind and any kind of meaning. This state is absolutely pure, permanent and eternal. As such, it has no beginning, middle or end. Thus, having transcended the world of matter and the sensorial impressions, ie: sound, touch, sight, taste and smell, he is immeasurable and incomparable. As Śiva represents the absolute consciousness, Brahma represents the soul, the *ātman*, the self of the consciousness, and is experienced as infinite *sat-cit-ānandam,* truth, existence and bliss. This state is said to be attained by total absorption into the mantra: *iti aham asmi,* Thus I am. In this way, the yogi transcends the body and mind, and is liberated.

Verse 6: Fruits of meditation

ध्यानफलम्

एवमभ्यासयुक्तस्य पुरुषस्य महात्मनः ।

क्रमाद्वेदान्तविज्ञानं विजायेत न संशयः ॥६॥

dhyānaphalam
evamabhyāsayuktasya puruṣasya mahātmanaḥ
kramādvedāntavijñānaṃ vijāyeta na saṃśayaḥ (6)

Anvay
dhyāna-phalam: fruits of dhyāna; *na saṃśayaḥ*: without doubt; *kramāt*: gradually; *vijāyeta*: there should bring forth; *mahātmanaḥ puruṣasya*: in a great soul; *abhyāsa*: [who] engages; *evam*: thus; *abhyāsa*: in regular practice; *vedānta-vijñānam*: knowledge of *vedānta.*

Translation
Fruits of dhyāna: Without doubt there should gradually bring forth in a great soul, [who] engages thus in regular practice, knowledge of *vedānta.*

Commentary
Vedānta is the philosophy, which was given at the end of the vedas, concerning the pure consciousness and the oneness of being. This knowledge was attained through the direct experience of yogis and rishis, who had meditated deeply and discovered the entire field of consciousness for themselves. This verse states that the great person, who practises dhyāna regularly, will undoubtedly attain the knowledge of vedānta. This also attests to the fact that rāja yoga leads to vedānta, and that the two systems ultimately bring the aspirant to the same point.

इति नवमः खण्डः
iti navamaḥ khaṇḍaḥ

Thus [ends] the ninth section.

दशमः खण्डः

daśamaḥ khaṇḍaḥ

Tenth Section

Samādhi

Verses 1 to 5: Nature of samādhi

समाधस्वरूपम्

अथातः संप्रवक्ष्यामि समाधिं भवनाशनम् ।
समाधिः संविदुत्पत्तिः परजीवैकतां प्रति ॥१॥
नित्यः सर्वगतो ह्यात्मा कूटस्थो दोषवर्जितः ।
एकः सन् भिद्यते भ्रान्त्या मायया न स्वरूपतः ॥२॥
तस्माददद्वैतमेवास्ति न प्रपञ्चे न संसृतिः ।
यथा ऽकाशो घटाकाशो मठाकाश इतीरितः ॥३॥
तथा भ्रान्तैर्द्विधा प्रोतो ह्यात्मा जीवेश्वरात्मना ।
नाहं देहो न च प्राणो नेन्द्रियाणि मनो न हि ॥४॥
सदा साक्षिस्वरूपत्वाच्छिव एवास्मि केवलः ।
इति धीर्या मुनिश्रेष्ठ सा समाधिरिहोच्यते ॥५॥

samādhisvarūpam
athātaḥ saṃpravakṣyāmi samādhiṃ bhavanāśanam
samādhiḥ saṃvidutpattiḥ parajīvaikatāṃ prati (1)
nityaḥ sarvagato hyātmā kūṭastho doṣavarjitaḥ
ekaḥ san bhidyate bhrāntyā māyayā na svarūpataḥ (2)
tasmādadvaitamevāsti na prapañce na saṃsṛtiḥ
yathā 'kāśo ghaṭākāśo maṭhākāśa itīritaḥ (3)
tathā bhrāntairdvidhā prokto hyātmā jīveśvarātmanā

nāhaṃ deho na ca prāṇo nendriyāṇi mano na hi (4)
sadā sākṣisvarūpatvācchiva evāsmi kevalaḥ
iti dhīryā muniśreṣṭha sā samādhirihocyate (5)

Anvay

svarūpa: nature; *athātaḥ*: now; *saṃpravakṣyāmi*: I shall describe; *nāśanam*: destroyer; *bhava*: worldly existence; *utpattiḥ*: gives rise to; *samvid*: knowledge; *prati*: hence; *ekatām*: oneness; *parajīva*: other beings; *ātmā*: self; *hi*: for sure; *nityaḥ*: eternal; *sarvagataḥ*: everywhere; *kūṭasthaḥ*: unchangeable; *doṣavarjitaḥ*: devoid of faults; *san*: being; *ekaḥ*: one; *bhidyate*: it differs; *bhrāntyā māyayā*: from the mistaken illusion; *na svarūpataḥ*: not in its own form; *tasmāt*: therefore; *asti*: there is; *evam*: really; *advaitam*: no duality; *na prapañce*: no phenomenal world; *na saṃsṛtiḥ*: no transmigration; *yathā*: just as; *iti*: it is said; *ghaṭa-ākāśaḥ*: space in a pot; *maṭha-ākāśaḥ*: space in a hermitage; *īritaḥ*: is obtained from; *ākāśaḥ*: ether element; *tathā*: so; *bhrāntaiḥ*: because of false notions; *dvidhā*: duality; *proktaḥ*: is called; *jīva*: individual consciousness; *īśvara*: *Īśvara*, higher consciousness; *hi*: indeed; *na aham*: I am not; *dehaḥ*: body; *na*: nor; *prāṇaḥ*: vital energy; *indriyāṇi*: senses; *manaḥ*: mind; *asmi*: I am; *śivaḥ*: Śiva; *kevalaḥ*: alone; *sadā*: ever; *sākṣi*: witness; *svarūpa*: true form; *sā dhīryā*: this wisdom; *ucyate*: is said; *iha*: in this life; *muniśreṣṭha*: o excellent Sage.

Translation

Nature of samādhi: Now I shall describe *samādhi*, the destroyer of worldly existence. Samādhi gives rise to knowledge [and] hence oneness with other beings. The ātman is, for sure, eternal, everywhere, unchangeable [and] devoid of faults. Being one, it differs from the mistaken illusion, [but] not in its own form. Therefore, there is really no duality, no phenomenal world, no transmigration, just as, it is said, the space in a pot or hermitage is obtained from the ether element. So, because of false notions [of] duality, the ātman is called *jīva* [and] *Īśvara*. Indeed I am not the body, nor the prāṇa, nor the senses, nor the mind. I am Śiva alone, ever the witness [of my] true form. This wisdom is said [to be] samādhi in this life, o excellent Sage.

Commentary
Here the Rishi explains the nature of *samādhi*, the eighth limb of rāja yoga. Samādhi is not a practice or even the outcome of any practice. It is the transcendental state of consciousness, in which all barriers and limitations of the conscious, subconscious, and unconscious are removed. In samādhi the consciousness is one indivisible field, total and complete. Within this totality of consciousness, all knowledge exists; so the Rishi says that samādhi gives rise to knowledge. And because this state of consciousness is complete within itself, it is therefore the same everywhere and in all beings. Hence, there is the experience of oneness with all beings.

The Sanskrit term for this totality of consciousness in the individual is *ātman*, the soul or the self. The Rishi describes the ātman as eternal, which means it is the one permanent reality, unaffected by change, by time and space, or by birth and death. This ātman, this pure consciousness, within each individual, is the same as the pure consciousness everywhere, on all the planes of existence, whether manifest or unmanifest. Being the basis or the substratum of all beings and all existence, the ātman is in itself unchangeable and devoid of any faults or imperfections.

Being the state of perfect oneness, the ātman differs from the limited states of consciousness, by which the relative worlds of duality, dreams and illusions are perceived. But there is no differentiation within its own transcendental state. Therefore, samādhi is the complete union of the mind and psyche, which are capable of differentiation, with the ātman, the pure individual consciousness, which is undifferentiated. In samādhi there is no experience of duality, no experience of the mind and senses or the phenomenal world, no further experience of transmigration, or birth and death.

In the scriptures, we find the analogy of the space in the pot or the space in the dwelling, being the same space as that which exists all around the pot, or all around the dwelling. Although, our mind perceives the space in the pot or in the dwelling as different from the space all around. This is an example of the false notion of duality. Similarly, due to this same false notion, the ātman, the unlimited, unborn reality, is called *jīva,* the consciousness that is born and lives in the body, and is considered to be limited in this sense, like the space that exists inside the pot, or the dwelling. And again, in the universal sense, the pure cosmic consciousness, which sustains the manifest order of existence, is called *Īśvara*.

So, the Rishi, who has established his awareness in samādhi says to his disciples: Indeed I am not the body, nor am I the prāṇa, nor am I the senses, nor am I the mind. I am Śiva, pure consciousness alone, ever the witness of my true self. This wisdom is said to be samādhi in this life.

Verses 6 to 12: Only Brahma remains

ब्रह्मात्रावशेषः

सो ऽहं ब्रह्म न संसारी न मत्तो ऽन्यः कदाचन ।
यथा फेनतरङ्गादि समुद्रादुत्थितं पुनः ।।६।।
समुद्रे लीयते तद्वत् जगन्मय्यनुलीयते ।
तस्मान्मनः पृथङ् नास्ति जगन्माया च नास्ति हि ।।७।।
यस्यैवं परमात्मायं प्रत्यग्भूतः प्रकाशितः ।
स तु याति च पुंभावं स्वयं साक्षात् परामृतम् ।।८।।
यदा मनसि चैतन्यं भाति सर्वत्रगं सदा ।
योगिनो ऽव्यवधानेन तदा सम्पद्यते स्वयम् ।।९।।
यदा सर्वाणि भूतानि स्वात्मन्येव हि पश्यति ।
सर्वभूतेषु चात्मानं ब्रह्म संपद्यते तदा ।।१०।।
यदा सर्वाणि भूतानि समाधिस्थो न पश्यति ।
एकीभूतः परेणासौ तदा भवति केवलः ।।११।।
यदा पश्यति चात्मानं केवलं परमार्थतः ।
मायामात्रं जगत् कृत्स्नं तदा भवति निर्वृतिः ।।१२।।

brahmātrāvaśeṣaḥ

so 'haṃ brahma na saṃsārī na matto 'nyaḥ kadācana
yathā phenataraṅgādi samudrādutthitaṃ punaḥ (6)
samudre līyate tadvat jaganmayyanulīyate
tasmānmanaḥ pṛthaṅ nāsti jaganmāyā ca nāsti hi (7)
yasyaivaṃ paramātmāyaṃ pratyagbhūtaḥ prakāśitaḥ
sa tu yāti ca puṃbhāvaṃ svayaṃ sākṣāt parāmṛtam (8)
yadā manasi caitanyaṃ bhāti sarvatragaṃ sadā
yogino 'vyavadhānena tadā sampadyate svayam (9)
yadā sarvāṇi bhūtāni svātmanyeva hi paśyati
sarvabhūteṣu cātmānaṃ brahma saṃpadyate tadā (10)
yadā sarvāṇi bhūtāni samādhistho na paśyati
ekībhūtaḥ pareṇāsau tadā bhavati kevalaḥ (11)

yadā paśyati cātmānaṃ kevalaṃ paramārthataḥ
māyāmātraṃ jagat kṛtsnaṃ tadā bhavati nirvṛtiḥ (12)

Anvay

atra: here; *avaśeṣaḥ*: remains; *aham*: I am; *saḥ brahma*: this Brahma; *na*: not; *saṃsārī*: worldly being; *na kadācana*: nothing; *anyaḥ*: other; *mattaḥ*: than me; *yathā*: just as; *phena*: foam; *taraṅga*: waves; *utthitam*: arising; *samudrāt*: from the ocean; *līyate*: is absorbed; *punaḥ*: back; *samudre*: into the ocean; *tadvat*: in the same way; *jagat*: world; *anulīyate*: is absorbed; *mayi*: in me; *tasmāt*: thus; *manaḥ*: mind; *na asti*: is not; *pṛthaṅ*: separate; *na asti*: nor is; *jaganmāyā*: material world; *sa*: he; *yasya*: whose; *paramātmā*: supreme self; *bhūtaḥ*: has been purified; *pratyak*: within; *prakāśitaḥ*: illumined; *sākṣāt*: immediately; *yāti*: reaches; *puṃbhāvam*: maturity; *ca*: and; *svayam*: his own; *parāmṛtam*: immortality; *yadā*: when; *sarvatragam*: all-pervading; *caitanyam*: consciousness; *bhāti*: shines; *sadā*: continually; *avyadhānena*: without interruption; *manasi*: in the mind; *tadā*: then; *yoginaḥ*: *yogin*; *sampadyate*: becomes absorbed in; *svayam*: himself; *yadā eva hi*: when indeed; *paśyati*: he sees; *sarvāṇi bhūtāni*: all creatures; *svātmani*: in himself; *ca*: and; *ātmānam*: himself; *sarvabhūteṣu*: in all creatures; *tadā*: then; *brahma sampadyate*: he merges with Brahma; *yadā*: when; *samādhisthaḥ*: absorbed in *samādhi*; *na paśyati*: he does not see; *sarvāṇi bhūtāni*: all creatures; *pareṇa*: but; *ekībhūtaḥ*: as one; *tadā*: then; *asau kevalaḥ*: that pure consciousness; *bhavati*: is attained; *ca*: and; *yadā*: when; *paśyati*: he sees; *ātmānaṃ kevalam*: self alone; *paramārthataḥ*: true reality; *tadā*: then; *bhavati*: he is; *nirvṛtiḥ*: set free from; *kṛtsnam jagat*: whole world; *mātram*: merely; *māyā*: illusion.

Translation

Here Brahma Remains: I am this Brahma, not the worldly being. [There is] nothing other than me. Just as the foam [of the] waves, arising from the ocean, is absorbed back into the ocean, in the same way the world is absorbed in me. Thus, the mind is not separate, nor is the material world. He, whose supreme self has been purified within [and] illumined, immediately reaches maturity and his own immortality. When the all-pervading consciousness shines continually [and] without interruption in the mind, then the yogin becomes absorbed in himself. When indeed he sees all creatures in himself and himself in all creatures, then he merges with Brahma. When, absorbed in samādhi, he does not see all creatures [as many], but [as] one, then that pure consciousness is attained. And when he sees the self alone [as] the true reality, then he is set free from the whole world, [which is] merely an illusion.

Commentary

In samādhi, only Brahma remains. In this sense, we can equate Brahma with the super-conscious state, from which all existence is born and to which all returns. In this state, therefore, 'I am Brahma'; I am the absolute, and there is nothing other than me. I am not this limited physical being with name and form, who dwells in a place, works at a profession, and is part of a family with a circle of friends. There is no other reality in this state, except Brahma, the super-conscious field, which is ever luminous, vast and expansive.

Just as the foam, riding on the waves, which arise from the ocean, is absorbed back into the ocean, similarly, the entire perception of myself in the world is absorbed back into me. Thus, the mind is not separate from me, nor is the world, because, like the foam on the waves, they too have merged back into the infinite sea of consciousness. The yogi, who has purified the karmas and samskaras that reside in the individual consciousness, and illumined the supreme self within, attains the goal of spiritual evolution. With this attainment, the self immediately reaches the state of fullness, or maturity, and realises its own immortality. When the yogi remains absorbed in this state, the all-pervading, ever effusive, consciousness shines continually, without interruption, in the mind.

When the consciousness of the yogi, who has established the awareness in the superconscious state, returns once again to the external world, he sees life and all beings within himself, and himself in all beings. There is no separation or differentiation. The experience of 'I am in you', and 'You are in me' arises wherever and with whomever he may be. This is the quality of oneness, which expresses itself outside as pure love. We may also call it the love of God, that sees and knows all beings as one and the same. In this state of love and oneness with all existence, the yogi merges with Brahma, the superconsciousness, even in the external world.

Hence, absorbed in samādhi in every situation, with the mind ever directed towards the self, he does not see all beings as diverse or many, but as one continuum of creation, ever unfolding from and returning back to the source of Brahma. In this way, pure consciousness is attained, which is unaffected or dissipated by any worldly relations or situations. When the yogi sees the self alone as the one true reality, then he is liberated from the entire world, which after all, is merely an illusion.

Verse 13: Epilogue

उपसंहारः

एवमुक्त्वा स भगवान् दत्तात्रेयो महामुनिः ।

सांकृतिः स्वस्वरूपेण सुखमास्थ तिनिर्भयः ।।१३।।

upasaṃhāraḥ

evamuktvā sa bhagavān dattātreyo mahāmuniḥ

sāṃkṛtiḥ svasvarūpeṇa sukhamāstha 'tinirbhayaḥ (13)

Anvay

upasaṃhāraḥ: epilogue; *mahāmuniḥ*: great sage; *bhagavān*: Lord; *Dattātreyaḥ*: Dattātreya; *uktvā*: having spoken; *evam*: thus; *sāṃkṛtiḥ*: Sāṃkṛti; *sukham*: joyfully; *atinirbhayaḥ*: fearlessly; *āsthaḥ*: established; *svasvarūpeṇa*: in his own true nature.

Translation

Epilogue: The great sage Lord Dattātreya having spoken thus, Sāṃkṛti [is] joyfully [and] fearlessly established in his own true nature.

Commentary

Thus ends the original teaching on *aṣṭaṅga yoga*, the eightfold path of yoga, given by the great yogi and *avatāra*, or divine incarnation, Dattātreya to his worthy disciple, Sāṃkṛti. From this text and the nature of the teaching, we can see how the ancient masters passed on their knowledge and experience, with great diligence, patience and skill. The teachings were not expounded in large assemblies or practice halls, but rather passed down from master to student in a very close, symbiotic relationship.

As the student mastered one level or area of practice, the master would then carefully introduce him to the next. The eightfold path of yoga, which is also known as *rāja yoga*, was originally a step by step path which led the worthy aspirant from a life of worldly perception and involvement to the fullness of enlightenment. We can further assume that in such a profound relationship as this, there would have been a high degree of transmission, between the fully illumined master and the disciple, who must have been purified, receptive and fully prepared to imbibe this higher teaching on yoga. Hence, under the watchful eye of the master, the disciple gradually attained mastery of yoga and was joyfully and fearlessly established in his own true nature.

इति दशमः खण्डः
iti daśamaḥ khaṇḍaḥ

Thus [ends] the Tenth Section

Appendices

1. Sanskrit text

आप्यायन्तु । इति शान्तिः

प्रथमः खण्डः

जीवन्मुक्तिसाधनं अष्टाङ्गयोगः

दत्तात्रेयो महायोगी भगवान्भूतभावनः ।
चतुर्भुजो महाविष्णुर्योगसाम्राज्यदीक्षितिः ॥१॥

तस्य शिष्यो मुनिवरः सांकृतिर्नाम भक्तिमान् ।
पप्रच्छ गुरुमेकान्ते प्राञ्जलिर्विनयान्वितः ॥२॥

भगवन्ब्रूहि मे योगं साष्टाङ्गं सप्रपञ्चकम् ।
येन विज्ञानमात्रेण जीवन्मुक्तो भवाम्यहम् ॥३॥

सांकृते शृणु वक्ष्यामि योगं साष्टाङ्गदर्शनम् ।

अष्टङ्गोद्देशः

यमश्च नियमश्चैव तथैवासनमेव च ॥४॥
प्राणायामस्तथा ब्रह्मन्प्रत्याहारस्ततः ।
धारणा च तथा ध्यानं समाधिश्चाष्टमं मुने ॥५॥

दशविद्यमः

अहिंसा सत्यमस्तेयं ब्रह्मचर्यं दयार्जवम् ।
क्षमा धृतिर्मिताहारः शौचं वेति यमा दश ॥६॥

अहिंसा

वेदोक्तेन प्रकारेण विना सत्यं तपोधन ।
कायेन मनसा वाचा हिंसा हिंसा न चान्यथा ॥७॥
आत्मा सर्वगतोऽच्छेद्यो न ग्राह्य इति या मतिः ।
मा चाहिंसा वरा प्रोक्ता मुने वेदान्तवेदिभिः ॥८॥

सत्यम्

चक्षुरादीन्द्रियैर्दृष्टं श्रुतं घ्रातं मुनीश्वर ।
तस्यैवोक्तिर्भवेत्सत्यं विप्र तन्नान्यथा भवेत् ॥९॥
सर्वं सत्यं परं ब्रह्म न चान्यदिति या मतिः ।
तञ्च सत्यं परं प्रोक्तं वेदान्तज्ञानपारगैः ॥१०॥

अस्तेयम्

अन्यदीये तृणे रत्ने कानञ्चने मौक्तिके ऽपि च ।
मनसा विनिवृत्तिर्या तदस्तेयं विदुर्बुधाः ॥११॥
आत्मन्यनात्मभावेन व्यवहारविवर्जितम् ।
यत्तदस्तेयमित्युक्तमात्मविद्भिर्महा मुने ॥१२॥

ब्रह्मचर्यम्

कायेन वाचा मनसा स्त्रीणं परिविवर्जनम् ।
ऋतौ भार्यां तदा स्वस्य ब्रह्मचर्यं तदुच्यते ॥१३॥
ब्रह्मभावे मनश्चागं ब्रह्मचर्यं परंतप ।१४।

दया

स्वात्मवत्सर्वभूतेषु कायेन मनसा गिरा ॥१४॥
अनुज्ञा या दया सैव प्रोक्ता वेदान्तवेदिभिः ।१५।

आर्जवम्

पुत्रे मित्रे कलत्रे च रिपौ स्वात्मनि संततम् ॥१५॥
एकरूपं मुने यत्तदार्जवं प्रोच्यते मया ।१६।

क्षमा

कायेन मनसा वाचा शत्रुभिः परिपीडिते ।।१६।।
बुद्धिक्षोभनिवृत्तिर्या क्षमा सा मुनिपुङ्गव ।१७।

धृतिः

वेदादेव विनिर्मोक्षः संसारस्य न चान्यथा ।।१७।।
इति विज्ञाननिष्पत्तिर्धृतिः प्रोकता हि वैदिकैः ।
अहमात्मा न चान्यो ऽमीत्येवमप्रच्युता मतिः ।।१८।।

मिताहारः

अल्पभृष्टाशनाभ्यां च चतुर्थांशा वशेषकम् ।
तस्माद्योगानुगुण्येन भोजनं मितभोजनम् ।।१९।।

शौचम्

स्वदेहमलनिर्मोक्षो मृज्जलाभ्यां महामुने ।
यत्तच्छौचं भवेद्बाह्यं मानसं मननं विदुः ।।२०।।
अहं शुद्ध इति ज्ञानं शौचबाहुर्मनीषिणः ।
अत्यन्तमलिनो देहो देही चात्यन्तनिर्मलः ।।२१।।
उभयोरन्तरं ज्ञात्वा कस्य शौचं विधीयते ।
ज्ञानशौचं परित्यज्य बाह्ये यो रमते नारः ।।२२।।
स मुढः काञ्चनं त्यक्त्वा लोष्टं गृह्णाति सुव्रत ।२३।

ब्रह्मात्मवेदनविधिः

ज्ञानामृतेन तृप्तस्य कृतकृत्यस्य योगिनः ।।२३।।
न चास्ति किंचित्कर्तव्यमस्ति चेन्न स तत्त्ववित् ।
लोकत्रये ऽपि कर्तव्यं किंचिन्नास्त्यात्मवेदिनाम् ।।२४।।
तस्मात्सर्वप्रयत्नेन मुने ऽहिंसादिसाधनैः ।
आत्मानमक्षरं ब्रह्म विद्धि ज्ञानात्तु वेदनात् ।।२५।।

द्वितीयः खण्ड:

दशविधनियमः

तप: सन्तोषमास्तिक्यं दानमीश्वरपूजनम् ।
सिद्धान्तश्रवणं चैव ह्रीर्मतिश्च जपो व्रतम् ।।१।।
एते च नियमाः प्रोक्तास्तान्वक्ष्यामि क्रमाच्छृणु ।२।

तपः

वेदोक्तेन प्रकारेण कृच्छ्रचान्द्रायणादिभिः ।।२।।
शरिरशोषणं यत्तत्तप इत्युच्यते बुधैः ।
को वा मोक्षः कथं केन संसारं प्रतिपन्नवान् ।।३।।
इत्यालोचनमर्थज्ञास्तपः शंसन्ति पण्डिताः ।४।

सन्तोष:

यदिच्छालाभतो नित्यं प्रीतिर्या जायते नृणाम् ।।४।।
तत्सन्तोषं विदुः प्राजज्ञाः परिज्ञानैकतत्परा: ।
ब्रह्मावलोकपर्यन्ताद्विरक्त्या यल्लभेत्प्रियम् ।।५।।
सर्वत्र विगतस्नेह: सन्तोषं परं विदुः ।६।

आस्तिक्यम्

श्रौते स्मार्ते च विश्वासो यत्तदास्तिक्यमुच्यते ।।६।।

दानम्

न्यायार्जितधनं श्रान्ते श्रद्धया वैदिके जने ।
अन्यद्वा यत्प्रदीयते तद्दानं प्रोच्यते मया ।।७।।

ईश्वरपूजनम्

रागाद्यपेतं हृदयं वागदुष्टा ऽनृतादिना ।
हिंसादिरहितं कर्म यत्तदीश्वरपूजनम् ।।८।।

सिद्धन्तश्रवणम्

सत्यं ज्ञानमनन्तं च परानन्दं परं ध्रुवम् ।
प्रत्यगित्यवगन्तव्यं वेदान्तश्रवणं बुधः ।।९।।

ह्री:

देवलौकिकमार्गेषु कुत्सितं कर्म यद्भवेत् ।
तस्मिन्भवति या लज्जा ह्री: सैवेति प्रकीर्तिता ।।१०।।

मतिः

वैदिकेषु च सर्वेषु श्रद्धा या सा मतिर्भवेत् ।
गुरुणा चोपदिष्तो ऽपि तन्त्र संबन्धवर्जितः ।।११।।

जपः

वेदोक्तेनैव मार्गेण मन्त्राभ्यासो जपः स्मृतः ।
कल्पसूत्रे यथा वेदे धर्मशास्त्रे पुराणके ।।१२।।
इतिहासे च वृत्तिर्या स जपः प्रोच्यते मया ।
जपस्तु द्विविधः प्रोक्तो वाचिको मानसस्तथा ।।१३।।
वाचिकोपांशुरुच्चैश्च द्विविधः परिकीर्तितः ।
मानसो मननध्यानभेदाद्द्वैविध्यमाश्रितः ।।१४।।
उच्चैर्जपादुपांशुश्च सहस्रगुणमुच्यते ।
मानसश्च तथोपांशोः सहस्रगुणमुच्यते ।।१५।।
उच्चैर्जपश्च सर्वेषां यथोक्तफलदो भवेत् ।
निचैः श्रोत्रेण चेन्मन्त्रः श्रुतश्चेन्निष्फलं भवेत् ।।१६।।

तृतीयः खण्डः

आसनानि नव

स्वास्तिकं गोमुखं पद्मं वीरसिंहासने तथा ।
भद्रं मुक्तासनं चैव मयूरासनमेव च ।।१।।
सुखाससनाख्यं च नवमं मुनिपुङ्गव ।२।

स्वस्तिकम्

जानूर्वोरन्तरे कृत्वा सम्यक् पादतले उभे ।।२।।
समग्रीवशिरः कायः स्वस्तिकं नित्यमभ्यसेत् ।३।

गोमुखम्

सव्ये दक्षिणगुल्फं तु पृष्ठपश्चा नियोजयेत् ।।३।।
दक्षिणे ऽपि तथा सव्यं गोमुखं तत्प्रचक्षते ।४।

वीरासनम्

दक्षिणेतरपादं तु दक्षिणोरुणि विन्यसेत् ।
ऋजुकायः समासीनो वीरासनमुदाहृतम् ।।६।।

सिंहासनम्

गुल्फौ च वृषणस्याधः सीविन्यः पार्श्वयोः क्षिपेत् ।
दक्षिणं सव्यगुल्फेन दक्षिणेन तथेतरत् ।।६-१।।
हस्तौ जानौ समास्थाप्य स्वाङ्गुलींरिप्रसर्य च ।
व्यक्तवक्त्रो निरीक्षेत नासाग्रं सुसमाहितः ।।६-२।।
सिंहासनं भवेदेतत् पूजितं योगिभिः सदा ।।६-३।।

भद्रासनम्

गुल्फौ तु वृषणस्याधः सीविन्याः पार्श्वयोः क्षिपेत् ।
पार्श्वपादौ च पाणिभ्यां दृधं बद्धवा सुनिर्लिम् ।।७।।
भद्रासनं भवेदेतद्विषरोगविनाशनम् ।८।

मुक्तासनम्

निपीड्य सीविनीं मूक्ष्मा दक्षिणेतरगुल्फतः ।।८।।
वामं याम्येन गुल्फेन मुक्तासनमिदं भवेत् ।

मेढ्रादुपरि मिक्षिप्य सव्यं गुल्फं ततोपरि ।।९।।
गुल्फान्तरं च संक्षिप्य मुक्तासनमिदं मुने ।१०।

मयूरासनम्

कूर्परागे मुनिश्रेष्ठ निक्षिपेन्नाभिपार्श्वयोः ।।१०।।
भूम्यां पाणितलद्वन्द्वं निक्षिप्यैकाग्रमानसः ।
समुन्नतशिरःपादो दण्डवत् व्योम्नि संस्थितः ।।११।।
मयूरासनमेतत् स्यात् सर्वपापप्रणाशनम् ।१२।

सुखासनम्

येन केन प्रकारेण सुखं धैर्यं च जायते ।।१२।।
तत् सुखासनमित्युक्तमशक्तस्तत् समाश्रयेत् ।१३।

आसनजयफलम्

आसनं विजितं येन जितं तेन जगत्त्रयं ।।१३।।
अनेन विधिना युक्तः प्राणायामं सदा कुरु ।।१४।।

चतुर्थः खण्डः

देहप्रमाणम्

शरीरं तावदेव स्यात् षण्णवत्यङ्गुलात्मकम् ।
देहमध्ये शिखिस्थानं तप्तजाम्बूनदप्रभम् ।।१।।
त्रिकोणं मनुजानां तु सत्यमुक्तं हि सांकृते ।
गुदात्तु द्व्यङ्गुलादूर्ध्वं मेढ्रात्तु द्व्यङ्गुलादधः ।।२।।

देहमध्यं विजानीहि मानुजानां तु सांकृते ।
कन्दस्थानं मुनिश्रेष्ठ मूलाधारान्नवाङ्गुलम् ।।३।।

चतुरङ्गुलमायामविस्तारं मुनिपुङ्गव ।
कुक्कुटाङ्डवदाकारं भूषितं तु त्वगादिभिः ।।४।।
तन्मध्ये नाभिरित्युक्तं योगज्ञैर्मुनिपुङ्गव ।५।

नाडीपरिगणनम्

कन्दमध्यस्थिता नाडी सुषुम्नेति प्रकीर्तिता ।।५।।
तिष्ठन्ति परितस्तस्य नाडयो मुनिपुङ्गव ।
द्विसप्ततिसहस्राडि तासां मुख्याश्चतुर्दश ।।६।।
सुषुम्ना पिङ्गला तद्वदिडा चैव सरस्वती ।
पूषा च वरुणा चैव हस्तिजिह्वा यशस्विनी ।।७।।
अलम्बुसा कुहूश्चैव विश्वोदारा पयस्विनी ।
शन्खिनी चैव गान्धारा इति मुख्याश्चतुर्दश ।।८।।

आसां मुख्यतमास्तिस्रस्तिसृष्वेकोत्तमोत्तमा ।
ब्रह्मनाडीति सा प्रोक्ता मुने वेदान्तवेदिभिः ।।९।।
पृष्ठमध्यस्थितेनास्था वीणादण्डेन सुव्रत ।
सह मस्तकपर्यन्तं सुषुम्ना सुप्रतिष्थिता ।।१०।।

कुण्डल्याः स्थानं स्वरूपं च

नाभिकन्दादधः स्थानं कुण्डल्या द्व्यङ्गुलं मुने ।
अष्टप्रकृतिरूपा सा कुण्डली मुनिसत्तम ।।११।।
यथावद्वायुचेष्टां च जलन्नादिनि नित्यशः ।
परितः कन्दपार्श्वेषु निरुध्यैव सदा स्थिता ।।१२।।
स्वमुखेन संवेष्टय ब्रह्मरन्ध्र मुखं मुने ।१३।

नाडीस्थानानि

सुषुम्नाया इडा सव्ये दक्षिणे पिङ्गला स्थिता ।।१३।।

सरस्वती कुहूश्चैव सुषुम्नापार्श्वयोः स्थिते ।
गान्धारा हस्तिजिह्वा च इडायाः पृष्ठपूर्वयोः ।।१४।।
पूषा यशस्विनी चैव पिङ्गलापृष्ठपूर्वयोः ।
कुहाश्च हस्तिजिह्वाया मध्ये विश्वोदरा स्थिता ।।१५।।
यशस्विन्याः कुहार्मध्ये वरुणा सुप्रतिष्ठिता ।
पूषायाश्च सरस्वत्या मध्ये प्रोक्ता यशस्विनी ।।१६।।
गान्धारायाः सरस्वत्या मध्ये प्रोक्ता च शङ्खिनी ।
अलम्बुसा स्थिता पायुपर्यन्तं कन्दमध्यगा ।।१७।।

पूर्वभागे सुषुम्नाया राकायाः संस्थिताः कुहूः ।
अधश्चोर्ध्वं स्थिता नाडी याम्यनासान्तमिष्यते ।।१८।।
इडा तु सव्यनासान्तं संस्थिता मुनिपुङ्गव ।
यशस्विनी च वामस्य पादाङ्गुष्ठान्तमिष्यते ।।१९।।
पूषा वामाक्षिपर्यन्ता पिङ्गलायास्तु पृष्ठतः ।
पयस्विनी च याम्यस्य कर्णान्तं प्रोच्यते बुधैः ।।२०।।
सरस्वती तथा चोर्ध्वं गता जिह्वा तथा मुने ।
हस्तिजिह्वा तथा सव्यपादाङ्गुष्ठान्तमिष्यते ।।२१।।
शङ्खिनी नाम या नाडी सव्यकर्णान्तमिष्यते ।
गान्धारा सव्यनेत्रान्ता प्रोक्ता वेदान्तवेदिभिः ।।२२।।
विष्वोदराभिधा नाडी कन्दमध्ये व्यवस्थिता ।२३।

नाडीषु वायुसञ्चरः

प्राणो ऽपानस्तथा व्यानः समानोदान एव च ।।२३।।
नागः कूर्मश्च कृकरो देवदत्तो धनंजयः ।
एते नाडीषु सर्वासु चरन्ति दश वायवः ।।२४।।
तेषु प्राणादयः पञ्च मुख्याः पञ्चसु सुव्रत ।
प्राणसंज्ञस्तथा ऽपानः पूज्यः प्राणस्तयोर्मुने ।।२५।।
आस्यनासिकयोर्मध्ये नाभिमध्ये तथा हृदि ।
प्राणसंज्ञो ऽनिलो नित्यं वर्तते मुनिसत्तम ।।२६।।

अपानो वर्तते नित्यं गुदमध्योरुजानुषु ।
उदरे सकले कट्यां नाभौ जङ्घे च सुव्रत ।।२७।।
व्यानः श्रोत्राक्षिमध्ये च कुकुद्भ्यां गुल्फयोरपि ।
प्राणस्थाने गले चैव वर्तते मुनिपुङ्गव ।।२८।।
उदानसंज्ञो विज्ञेयः पादयोर्हस्तयोरपि ।
समानः सर्वदेहेषु व्याप्य तिष्ठत्यसंशयः ।।२९।।
नागादिवायवः पञ्च त्वगस्थ्यादिषु संस्थिताः ।३०।

वायुव्यापाराः

निःश्वासोच्छ्वासकासाश्च प्राणक्रम हि सांकृते ।।३०।।
अपानाख्यस्य वायोस्तु विण्मूत्रादिविसर्जनम् ।
समानः सर्वसामीप्यं करोति मुनिपुङ्गव ।।३१।।
उदान ऊर्ध्वगमनं करोत्येव न संशयः ।
व्यानो विवादकृत् प्रोक्तो मुने वेदान्तवेदिभिः ।।३२।।
उद्गारादिगुणः प्रोक्तो नागाख्यस्य महामुने ।
धनंजयस्य शोभादि कर्म प्रोक्तं हि सांकृते ।।३३।।
निमीलनादि कूर्मस्य क्षुधा तु कृकरस्य च ।
देवदत्तस्य विप्रेन्द्र तन्द्रीकर्म प्रकीर्तितम् ।।३४।।

नाडीदेवताः

सुषुम्नायाः शिवो देव इडाया देवताहरिः ।
पिङ्गलाया विरिञ्चः स्यात् सरस्वत्या विराण्मुने ।।३५।।
पूषा ऽधिदेवता प्रोक्तो वरुणा वायुदेवता ।
हस्तिजिह्वाभिधायास्तु वरुणो देवता भवेत् ।।३६।।
यशस्विन्या मुनिश्रेष्ठ भगवान् भास्करस्तथा ।
अलम्बुसाया अबात्मा वरुणः परिकीर्तितः ।।३७।।
कुहोः क्षुद्देवता प्रोक्ता गान्धारी चन्द्रदेवता ।
शङ्खिन्याश्चन्द्रमास्तद्वत् पयस्विन्याः प्रजापतिः ।।३८।।
विश्वोदराभिधायास्तु भगवान् पावकः पतिः ।३९।

नाडीषु चन्द्रसुर्यसञ्चारः

इडायां चन्द्रमा नित्यं चरत्येव महामुने ।।३९।।
पिङ्गलायां रविस्तद्वन्मुने वेदविदां वर ।४०।

नाडीषु संवत्सरात्मकप्राणसूर्यसञ्चारः

पिङ्गलाया इडायां तु वायोः संक्रमणं तु यत् ।।४०।।
तदुत्तरायणं प्रोक्तं मुने वेदान्तवेदिभिः ।
इडायाः पिङ्गलायां तु प्राणसंक्रमणं मुने ।।४१।।
दक्षिणायनमित्युक्तं पिङ्गलायामिति श्रुतिः ।
इडापिङ्गलयोः संधि यदा प्राणः समागतः ।।४२।।
अमावास्या तदा प्रोक्ता देहे देहभृतां वर ।४३।

मूलाधारं यदा प्राणः प्रविष्ट: पण्डितोत्तम ।।४३।।
तदाद्यं विषुवं प्रोक्तं तापसैस्तापसोत्तम ।
प्राणासंज्ञो मुनिश्रेष्थ मूर्धानं प्राविशेद्यदा ।।४४।।
तदन्त्यं विषुवं प्रोक्तं तापसैस्तत्त्वचिन्तकैः ।
निःश्वासोच्छ्वासनं सर्वं मासानां संक्रमो भवेत् ।।४५।।
इडया कुण्डलीस्थानं यदा प्राणः समागतः ।
सोमग्रहणमित्युक्तं तदा तत्त्वविदां वर ।।४६।।
यदा पिङ्गलया प्राणः कुण्डलीस्थानमागतः ।
तदातदा भवेत् सूर्यग्रहणं मुनिपुण्गव ।।४७।।

अन्तस्तीर्थप्राशस्त्यम्

श्रीपर्वतं शिरःस्थाने केदारं तु ललाटके ।
वाराणसीं महाप्राज्ञ भ्रुवोर्घ्राणस्य मध्यमे ।।४८।।
कुरुक्षेत्रं कुचस्थाने प्रयागं हृत्सरोरुहे ।
चिदम्बरं तु हृन्मध्ये आधारे कमलालयम् ।।४९।।
आत्मतीर्थंसमुत्सृज्य बहिस्तीर्थानि यो व्रजेत् ।
करस्थं स महारत्नं त्यक्त्वा काचं विमार्गते ।।५०।।

भावतीर्थं परं तीर्थं प्रमाणं सर्वकर्मसु ।
अन्यथा ऽलिङ्ग्यते कान्ता अन्यथा ऽलिङ्ग्यते सुता ।।५१।।
तीर्थानि तोयपूर्णानि देवान् काष्ठादिनिर्मितान् ।
योगिनो न प्रपद्यन्ते स्वात्मप्रत्ययकारणात् ।।५२।।
बहिस्तीर्थात् परं तीर्थमन्तस्तीर्थं महामुने ।
आत्मतीर्थं महातीर्थमन्यत्तीर्थं निरर्थकम् ।।५३।।
चित्तमन्तर्गतं दुष्टं तीर्थस्नानैर्न शुध्यति ।
शतशो ऽपि जलैर्धौतं सुराभाण्डमिवाशुचि ।।५४।।
विशुवायनकालेषु ग्रहणे चान्तरे सदा ।
वाराणस्यादिके स्थाने स्नात्वा शुद्ध भवेन्नरः ।।५५।।
ज्ञानयोगपराणां तु पादप्रक्षालितं जलम् ।
भवशुद्ध्यर्थ मज्ञानां तत्तीर्थं मुनिपुङ्गव ।।५६।।

आत्मनि शिवदृष्टिः

तीर्थे दाने जपे यज्ञे काष्ठे पाषाणके सदा ।
शिवं पश्यति मूढात्मा शिवे देहे प्रतिष्ठिते ।।५७।।
अन्तःस्थं मां परित्यज्य बहिष्ठं यस्तु सेवते ।
हस्तस्थं पिण्डमुत्सृज्य लिहेत् कूर्परमात्मनः ।।५८।।
शिवमात्मनि पश्यन्ति प्रतिमासु न योगिनः ।
अज्ञानां भावनार्थाय प्रतिमाः परिकल्पिताः ।।५९।।

ब्रह्मदर्शनेन ब्रह्मभावः

अपूर्वमपरं ब्रह्म स्वात्मानं सत्यमद्वयम् ।
प्रज्ञानघनमानन्दं यः पश्यति स पश्यति ।।६०।।
नाडीपुञ्जं सदासारं नरभावं महामुने ।
समुत्सृज्यात्मनात्मानमहमित्यवधारय ।।६१।।
अशरीरं शरीरेषु महान्तं विभुमीश्वरम् ।
आनन्दमक्षरं साक्षान्मत्वा धीरो न शोचति ।।६२।।
विभेदजनके ज्ञाने नष्टे ज्ञानबलान्मुने ।

आत्मनो ब्रह्मणो भेदमसन्तं किं करिष्यति ।।६३।।

पञ्चमः खण्डः

नाडीशोधनम्

सम्यक्कथय मे ब्रह्मन् नाडीशुद्धिं समासतः ।
यया शुद्धया सदा ध्यायन् जीवन्मुक्तो भवाम्यहम् ।।१।।
साम्कृते शृणु वक्ष्यामि नाडीशुद्धिं समासतः ।
विध्युक्तकर्मसंयुक्तः कामसंकल्पवर्जितः ।।२।।
यमाद्यष्टाङ्गसंयुक्तः शान्तः सत्यपरायणः ।
स्वात्मन्यवस्थितः सम्यक् ज्ञानिभिश्च सुशिक्षितः ।।३।।
पर्वताग्रे नदीतीरे बिल्वमूले वने ऽथवा ।
मनोरमे शुचौ देशे मठं कृत्वा समाहितः ।।४।।

आरभ्य चासनं पश्चात् प्राङ्मुखोदङ्मुखो ऽपि वा ।
समग्रीवशिरःकायः संवृतास्यः सुनिश्चलः ।।५।।
नासाग्रे शशभृद्बिम्बे बिन्दुमध्ये तुरीयकम् ।
स्रवन्तममृतं पश्येन्नेत्राभ्यां सुसमाहितः ।।६।।
इडया प्राणमाकृष्य पूरयित्वोदरस्थितम् ।
ततो ऽग्निं देहमध्यस्थं ध्यायन् ज्वालावलीयुतम् ।।७।।
बिन्दुनादसमायुक्तमग्निबीजं विचिन्तयेत् ।
पश्चाद्विरेचयेत् सम्यक् प्राणं पिङ्गलया बुधः ।।८।।
पुनः पिङ्गलया ऽपूर्य वह्निबीजमनुस्मरेत् ।
पुनर्विरेचयेद्धीमानिडयैव शनैः शनैः ।।९।।
त्रिचतुर्वासरं वा ऽथ त्रिचतुर्वारमेव च ।
षट्कृत्वो विचरेन्नित्यं रहस्येवं त्रिसंधिषु ।।१०।।

नाडीशुद्धिचिह्नानि

नाडीशुद्धिमवाप्नोति पृथक्चिह्नोपलक्षितः ।

शरिरलघुता दीप्तिर्वह्नेर्जाठरवर्तिनः ॥११॥
नादाभिव्यक्तिरित्येतच्चिह्नं तत्सिद्धिसूचकम् ।
यावदेतानि सम्पश्येत्तावदेवं समाचरेत् ॥१२॥

स्वात्मशुद्धिः

अथवैतत् परित्यज्य स्वात्मशुद्धिं समाचरेत् ।
आत्मा शुद्धिः सदा नित्यः सुखरूपः स्वयंप्रभः ॥१३॥
अज्ञानमलपङ्कं यः क्षालयेज्ज्ञानतोयतः ।
स एव सर्वदा शुद्धो नान्यः कर्मरतो हि सः ॥१४॥

षष्ठ.' खण्डः

प्राणायामलक्षणम्

प्राणायामक्रमं वक्ष्ये सांकृते शृणु सादरम् ।
प्राणायाम इति प्रोक्तो रेचपूरककुम्भकैः ॥१॥
वर्णत्रयात्मकाः प्रोक्ता रेचपूरककुम्भकाः ।
स एष प्रणवः प्रोक्तः प्राणायामश्च तन्मयः ॥२॥

इडया वायुमाकृष्य पूरयित्वोदरस्थितम् ।
शनैः षोडशभिर्मात्रैरकारं तत्र संस्मरेत् ॥३॥
पूरितं धारयेत् पश्चाच्चतुःषष्ट्या तु मात्रया ।
उकारमूर्तिमत्रापि संस्मरन् प्रणवं जपेत् ॥४॥
यावद्वा शक्यते तावद्धारयेज्जपतत्परः ।
पूरितं रेचयेत् पश्चान्मकारेणानिलं बुधः ॥५॥
शनैः पिङ्गलया तत्र द्वात्रिंशन्मात्रया पुनः ।
प्राणायामो भवेदेष.' ततश्चैवं समभ्यसेत् ॥६॥
पुनः पिङ्गलया पूर्य मात्रैः शोडशभिस्तथा ।
अकारमूर्तिमत्रापि स्मरेदेकाग्रमानसः ॥७॥
धारयेत् पूरितं विद्वाण प्रणवं संजपन् वशी ।
उकारमूर्तिं स ध्यायन् चतुःषष्ठ्या तु मात्रया ॥८॥

मकारं तु स्मरन् पश्चाद्रेचयेदिडयानिलम् ।
एवमेव पुनः कुर्यादिडया पूर्य बुद्धिमान् ।।९।।

एवं समभ्यसेन्नित्यं प्राणायामं मुनीश्वर ।
एवमभ्यासतो नित्यं षण्मासाद् ज्ञानवान् भवेत् ।।१०।।
वत्सराद्ब्रह्मविद्वान् स्यात् तस्मान्नित्यं समभ्यसेत् ।
योगाभ्यासरतो नित्यं स्वधर्मनिरतश्च यः ।।११।।
प्राणसंयमनेनैव ज्ञानान्मुक्तो भविष्यति ।१२।

पूरकादिलक्षणम्

बाह्यादापूरणं वायोरुदरे पूरको हि सः ।।१२।।
संपूर्णकुम्भवद्वायोर्धारणं कुम्भको भवेत् ।
बहिर्विरेचनं वायोरुदराद्रेचकः स्मृतः ।।१३।।

प्राणायामसिद्धयः

प्रस्वेदजनको यस्तु प्राणायामेषु सो ऽधमः ।
कम्पनं मध्यमं विद्यादुत्थानं चोत्तमं विदुः ।।१४।।
पूर्वपूर्वं प्रकुर्वित यावदुत्थानसंभवः ।
संभवत्युक्तमे प्राज्ञः प्राणायामे सुखी भवेत् ।।१५।।
प्राणायामेन चित्तं तु शुद्धिं भवति सुव्रत ।
चित्ते शुद्धे शुचिः साक्षात् प्रत्यग्ज्योतिर्व्यस्थितः ।।१६।।
प्राणश्चित्तेन संयुक्तः परमात्मनि तिष्ठति ।
प्राणायामपरस्यास्य पुरुषस्य महात्मनः ।।१७।।
देहश्चोत्तिष्ठते तेन किंचिज्जज्ञानाद्विमुक्तता ।
रेचकं पूरकं मुक्त्वा कुम्भकं नित्यमभ्यसेत् ।।१८।।
सर्वपापविनिर्मुक्तः सम्यग्ज्ञानमवाप्नुयात् ।
मनोजवत्वमाप्नोति पलितादि च नश्यति ।।१९।।
प्राणायामैकनिष्ठस्य न किंचिदपि दुर्लभम् ।
तस्मात् सर्वप्रयत्नेन प्राणायामान् समभ्यसेत् ।।२०।।

रोगनिवर्तकप्राणायामभेदाः

विनियोगान् प्रवक्ष्यामि प्राणायामस्य सुव्रत ।
संध्ययोर्ब्रह्मकाले ऽपि मध्याह्ने वाथवा सदा ॥२१॥
बाह्यं प्राणं समाकृष्य पूरयित्वोदरेण च ।
नासाग्रे नाभिमध्ये च पादाङ्गुष्ठे च धारणात् ॥२२॥
सर्वरोगनिर्मुक्तो जीवेद्वर्षशतं नरः ।
नासाग्रधारणाद्वापि जितो भवति सुव्रत ॥२३॥
सर्वरोगनिवृत्तिः स्यान्नाभिमध्ये तु धारणात् ।
शरीरलघुता विप्र पादाङ्गुष्ठनिरोधनात् ॥२४॥
जिह्वया वायुमाकृष्य यः पिबेत् सततं नरः ।
श्रमदाहविनिर्मुक्तो योगी नीरोगतामियात् ॥२५॥
जिह्वया वायुमाकृष्य जिह्वामूले निरोदहयेत् ।
पिबेदमृतमव्यग्रं सकलं सुखमाप्नुयात् ॥२६॥
इडया वायुमाकृष्य भ्रूवोर्मध्ये निरोधयेत् ।
यः पिबेदमृतं शुद्धं व्याधिभिर्मुच्यते हि सः ॥२७॥
इडया वेदतत्त्वज्ञ तथा पिङ्गलयैव च ।
नाभौ निरोधयेत्तेन व्याधिभिर्मुच्यते नरः ॥२८॥
मासमात्रं त्रिसन्ध्यायां जिह्वयारोप्य मरुतम् ।
अमृतं च पिबेन्नाभौ मन्दंमन्दं निरोधयेत् ॥२९॥
वातजाः पित्तजा दोषा नश्यन्त्येव न संशयः ।
नासाभ्यां वायुमाकृष्य नेत्रद्वन्द्वे निरोधयेत् ॥३०॥
नेत्ररोगा विनश्यन्ति तथा श्रोत्रनिरधनात् ।
तथा वायुं समारोप्य धारयेच्छिरस्थितम् ॥३१॥
शिरोरोगा विनश्यन्ति सत्यमुक्तं हि सांकृते ।३२।

षण्मुखीमुद्राभ्यासादिना वायुजय.:

स्वसतिकासनमास्थाय समाहितमनास्तथा ॥३२॥
अपानमूर्ध्वमुत्थाप्य प्रणवेन शनै.: शनै.: ।

हस्ताभ्यां धारयेत्सम्यक् कर्णादिकरणानि च ।।३३।।
अङ्गुष्ठाभ्यां मुने श्रोत्रे तर्जनीभ्यां तु चक्षुसि ।
नासापुटावथान्याभ्यां प्रच्छाद्या कारणानि वै ।।३४।।
आनन्दाविर्भवो यावत् तावन्मूर्धनि धारयेत् ।
प्राणः प्रयत्यनेनैव ब्रह्मरन्ध्रं महामुने ।।३५।।
ब्रह्मरन्ध्रं गते वायौ नादश्चोत्पद्यते ऽनघ ।
शङ्खध्वनिनिभश्चादौ मध्ये मेघध्वनिर्यथा ।।३६।।
शिरोमध्यगते वायौ गिरिप्रस्रवणं यथा ।
पश्चात् प्रीतो महाप्रज्ञ साक्षादात्मन्मुखो भवेत् ।।३७।।
पुनस्तज्ज्ञाननिष्पत्तिर्योगात् संसारनिह्नुतिः ।
दक्षिणोत्तरगुल्फेन सेवनं पीड्येत् स्थिरम् ।।३८।।
सव्येतरेण गुलफेन पीड्येट्बुद्धिमान् नरः ।
जान्वोरधः स्थितां सन्धिं स्मृत्वा देवं त्रियम्बकम् ।।३९।।
विनायकं च संस्मृत्य तथा वागीश्वरीं पुनः ।
लिङ्गनालात् समाकृष्य वायुमप्यग्रतो मुने ।।४०।।
प्रणवेन नियुक्तेन बिन्दुयुक्तेन बुद्धिमान् ।
मूलाधारस्य विप्रेन्द्र मध्ये तं तु निरोधयेत् ।।४१।।
निरुध्य वायुना दीप्तो वह्निरूहति कुण्डलीम् ।
पुनः सुषुम्नया वायुर्वह्निना सह गच्छति ।।४२।।
एवमभ्यसतसतस्य जितो वायुर्भवेद्भृशम् ।४३।

वायुजयचिह्नानि

प्रस्वेदः प्रथमः पश्चात् कम्पनं मुनिपुङ्गव ।।४३।।
उत्थानं च शरीरस्य चिह्नमेतज्जिते ऽनिले ।४४।

वायुजयेन रोगपापविनाश्वैराग्यपूर्विका ज्ञानोत्पत्तिः

एवमभ्यसतस्तस्य मूलरोगो विनश्यति ।।४४।।
भगन्धरं च नष्टं स्यात् सर्वरोगाश्च सांकृते ।
पातकानि विनश्यन्ति क्षुद्राणि च महान्ति च ।।४५।।
नष्टे पापे विशुद्धं स्याच्चित्तदर्पणमद्भुतम् ।

पुनर्ब्रह्मादिभोगेभ्यो वैरग्यं जायते हृदि ।।४६।।
विरक्तस्य तु संसाराज्ज्ञानं कैवल्यसाधनम् ।
तेन पाशापहानिः स्यात् ज्ञात्वा देवं सदाशिवम् ।।४७।।
ज्ञानामृतरसो येन सकृदास्वादितो भवेत् ।
स सर्वकार्यमुत्सृज्य तत्रैव परिधावति ।।४८।।
ज्ञानस्वरूपमेवाहुर्जगदेतद्वि चक्षणाः ।
अर्थस्वरूपमज्ञानात् पश्यन्त्यन्ये कुद्धष्टयः ।।४९।।
आत्मस्वरूपविज्ञानादज्ञानस्य परिक्षयः ।
क्षीणे ऽज्ञाने महाप्राज्ञ रागादीनां परिक्षयः ।।५०।।
रागाद्यसंभवे प्राज्ञ पुण्यपापवि मर्शनम् ।
योर्नाशे शरीरेण न पुन: संप्रयुज्यते ।।५१।।

सप्तमः खण्डः

प्रत्याहारलक्षनं तद्भेदाश्च
अथातः संप्रवक्ष्यामि प्रत्याहारं महामुने ।
इन्द्रियाणां विचरतां विषयेषु स्वभावतः ।।१।।
बलादाहरणं तेषां प्रत्याहारः स उच्यते ।
यत्पश्यति तु तत्सर्वं ब्रह्म पश्यन्समाहितः ।।२।।
प्रत्याहारो भवेदेष ब्रह्मविद्भिः पुरोदितः ।
यद्यच्छुद्धमशुद्धं वा करोत्यामरणान्तिकम् ।।३।।
तत्सर्वं ब्रह्मणे कुर्यात् प्रत्याहारः स उच्यते ।४।

अथवा वित्यकर्माणि ब्रह्माराधनबुद्धितः ।।४।।
काम्यानि च तथा कुर्यात् प्रत्याहारः स उच्यते ।
अथवा वायुमाकृष्य स्थानात् स्थानं निरोधयेत् ।।५।।
दन्तमूलात्तथा कण्ठादुरसि मारुतम् ।
उरोदेशात् समाकृष्य नाभिदेशे निरोधयेत् ।।६।।
नाभिदेशात् समाकृष्य कुण्डल्यां तु निरोधयेत् ।

कुण्डलीदेशतो विद्वान् मूलाधारे निरोधयेत् ।।७।।
अथापानात् कटिद्वन्द्वे तथोरौ च सुमध्यमे ।
तस्माज्जानुद्वये जङ्घे पादाङ्गुष्ठे निरोधयेत् ।।८।।

प्रत्याहारो ऽयमुक्तस्तु प्रत्याहारपरैः पुरा

प्रत्याहारफलम्

एवमभ्यासयुक्तस्य पुरुषस्य महात्मनः ।।९।।
सर्वपापानि नश्यन्ति भवरोगश्च सुव्रत ।१०।

वायुधारणात्मकप्रत्याहारः

नासाभ्याम् वायुमाकृष्य निश्चलः स्वस्तिकासनः ।।१०।।
पूरयेदनिलं विद्वानापादतलमस्तकम् ।
पश्चात पाददवये तद्वत् मूलाधारे तथैव च ।।११।।
नाभिकन्दे च हृद्मध्ये कण्ठमूले च तालुके ।
भ्रूवोर्मध्ये ललाटे च तथा मूर्धनि धारयेत् ।।१२।।

वेदान्तसंमतप्रत्याहारः

देहे त्स्वात्मभुतिं विद्वान् समाकृष्य समाहितः ।
आत्मनात्मनि निर्द्वन्द्वे निर्विकल्पे निरोधयेत् ।।१३।।
प्रत्याहारः समाख्यातः साक्षाद्वेदान्तवेदिभिः ।
एवमभ्यसतस्तस्य न किंचिदपि दुर्लभम् ।।१४।।

अष्टमः खण्डः

पञ्चभूतेषु धारणा

अथातः संप्रवक्ष्यामि धारणाः पञ्च सुव्रत ।
देहमध्यगते व्योम्नि बाह्याकाशं तु धारयेत् ।।१।।
प्राणे बाह्यानिलं तद्वत् ज्वलने चाग्निमौदरे ।
तोयं तोयम्शके भूमिं भूमिभागे महामुने ।।२।।

हयरावलकाराख्यं मन्त्रमुञ्चारयेत् क्रमात् ।
धारणैषा परा प्रोक्ता सर्वपापविशोधिनी ।।३।।
जान्वन्तं पृथिवी ह्यंशो ह्यपां पात्वन्तमुच्यते ।
हृदयांशस्तथाग्न्यंशो भ्रूमध्यान्तो ऽनिलांशकः ।।४।।
आकाशाम्शस्तथा प्राज्ञ मुर्धांशः परिकीर्तितः ।
ब्रह्माणं पृथिवीभागे विष्णुं तोयंशके तथा ।।५।।
अग्न्यंशे च महेशानमीश्वरं चानिलांशके ।
आकाशांशे महाप्राज्ञ धारयेत्तु सदाशिवम् ।।६।।

आत्मनि धारणा

अथ वा तव वक्षामि धारणां मुनिपुङ्गव ।
पुरुषे सर्वशास्तारं बोधानन्दमयं शिवम् ।।७।।
धारयेद्बुद्धिमान् नित्यं सर्वपापविशुद्धये ।
ब्रह्मादिकर्यरूपाणि स्वेस्वे संहृत्य कारणे ।।८।।
र्वकारणमव्यक्तमनिरूप्यमचेतनम् ।
साक्षादात्मनि संपूर्णे धारयेत् प्रणवे मनः ।
इन्द्रियाणि समहृत्य मनसात्मनि योजयेत् ।।९।।

नवमः खण्डः

सविशेषब्रह्मध्यानम्

अथातः संप्रवक्ष्यामि ध्यानं संसारनाशनम् ।
ऋतं सत्यं परं ब्रह्म सर्वसंसारभेषजम् ।।१।।
ऊर्ध्वरेतं विरूपाक्षं विश्वरूपं महेश्वरम् ।
सो ऽहमित्यादरेणैव ध्यायेद्योगीश्वरेश्वरम् ।।२।।

निर्विशेषब्रह्मध्यानम्

अथ वा सत्रमीशानं ज्ञानमानन्दमद्वयम् ।
अत्यर्थम् अमलं नित्यमादिमध्यान्तवर्जितम् ।।३।।

तथास्थूलमनाकाशमसंस्पृश्यमचाक्षुषम् ।
न रसं न च गन्धाख्यमप्रमेयमनुपमम् ।।४।।
आत्मानं सच्चिदानन्दमनन्तं ब्रह्म सुव्रत ।
अहमस्मीत्यभिध्यायेद्देहातीतं विमुक्तये ।।५।।

ध्यानफलम्

एवमभ्यासयुक्तस्य पुरुषस्य महात्मनः ।
क्रमाद्वेदान्तविज्ञानं विजायेत न संशयः ।।६।।

दशमः खण्डः

समाधस्वरूपम्

अथातः संप्रवक्ष्यामि समाधिं भवनाशनम् ।
समाधिः संविदुत्पत्तिः परजीवैकतां प्रति ।।१।।
नित्यः सर्वगतो ह्यात्मा कूटस्थो दोषवर्जितः ।
एकः सन् भिद्यते भ्रान्त्या मायया न स्वरूपतः ।।२।।
तस्मादद्वैतमेवास्ति न प्रपञ्चो न संसृतिः ।
यथा ऽकाशो घटाकाशो मठाकाश इतीरितः ।।३।।
तथा भ्रान्तैर्द्विधा प्रोक्तो ह्यात्मा जीवेश्वरात्मना ।
नाहं देहो न च प्राणो नेन्द्रियाणि मनो न हि ।।४।।
सदा साक्षिस्वरूपत्वाच्छिव एवास्मि केवलः ।
इति धीर्या मुनिश्रेष्ठ सा समाधिरिहोच्यते ।।५।।

ब्रह्मात्रावशेषः

सो ऽहं ब्रह्म न संसारी न मत्तो ऽन्यः कदाचन ।
यथा फेनतरङ्गादि समुद्रादुत्थितं पुनः ।।६।।
समुद्रे लीयते तद्वत् जगन्मय्यनुलीयते ।
तस्मान्मनः पृथङ् नास्ति जगन्माया च नास्ति हि ।।७।।
यस्यैवं परमात्मायं प्रत्यग्भूतः प्रकाशितः ।

स तु याति च पुंभावं स्वयं साक्षात् परामृतम् ।।८।।
यदा मनसि चैतन्यं भाति सर्वत्रगं सदा ।
योगिनो ऽव्यवधानेन तदा सम्पद्यते स्वयम् ।।९।।
यदा सर्वाणि भूतानि स्वात्मन्येव हि पश्यति ।
सर्वभूतेषु चात्मानं ब्रह्म संपद्यते तदा ।।१०।।
यदा सर्वाणि भूतानि समाधिस्थो न पश्यति ।
एकीभूतः परेणासौ तदा भवति केवलः ।।११।।
यदा पश्यति चात्मानं केवलं परमार्थतः ।
मायामात्रं जगत् कृत्स्नं तदा भवति निर्वृतिः ।।१२।।

उपसंहारः

एवमुक्त्वा स भगवान् दत्तात्रेयो महामुनिः ।
सांकृतिः स्वस्वरूपेण सुखमास्थ तिनिर्भयः ।।१३।।

2. Pronunciation Guide

a	nut
ā	father
i	bit
ī	knee
u	hook
ū	sue
ṛ	hurt
e	net
ai	time
o	got
au	house
ṃ	hum
ḥ	h + preceding vowel
k	paprika
kh	ink horn
g	ago
gh	big hut
ṅ	anger
c	chat
ch	much harm
j	jog
jh	raj house
ñ	engine
ṭ	borscht
ṭh	borscht home
ḍ	fresh dill
ḍh	flushed heart
ṇ	rainy
t	tarp
th	scout hall
d	modern

dh	mud hut
n	banal
p	papa
ph	top half
b	maybe
bh	mob hall
m	chroma
y	young
r	merit
l	alas
v	lava
ś	shin
ṣ	sunshine
h	hut

3. Continuous Translation

Invocation

Let these verses bring fulfilment. Thus [there will be] peace.

First Section

Aṣṭāṅga yoga is the sādhana of the jivanmukta.

1.

The great yogin, Dattātreya, [is] the blessed one [who] promotes the welfare of all living beings. The four-armed great Viṣṇu initiated [him] into the brilliance of yoga.

2.

His devoted disciple, Sāmkṛti by name, who is the best of ascetics, asked his guru, in solitude, respectfully, his hands folded together in humility.

3.

O Lord, describe to me in detail the eight-limbed yoga. With this knowledge, I shall become a *jivanmukta.*

4, 5.

Listen, Samkriti, I will explain the system of the eight-limbed yoga. (Here follows) the account of the eight limbs: *Yama* and *niyama* and then *āsana* and *prāṇāyāma*, then *pratyāhāra*, then complete *dharana*, and then *dhyanam,* and *samadhi* is the eighth, oh Sage.

6.

Knowledge of the ten yamas; *ahimsā*, *satyam*, *asteyam*, *brahmacaryam*, *daya*, *arjavam*, *kṣamā*, *dhṛti,* *mitāhāra*, *śauca* are the ten *yamas*.

7, 8.

Non-violence: Except in the manner declared in the Vedas,

oh austere one, [there should] truly [be] no violence at all in body, speech and mind, or any other way. The *ātma* [is] all-pervading, indivisible [and] imperceptible. O Sage, this understanding is stated by those who know *vedānta*, [which is] the best authority on *ahimsā*.

9, 10.
Truth: O great Sage, that which is seen, heard and smelt through the sense organs of the eyes etc is said to be *satyam,* as *Brahman* is no different from that. The highest truth is that *Brahman* is everywhere and not elsewhere. This understanding leads to the highest truth as declared by those who have absorbed the wisdom of *Vedānta*.

11, 12.
Honesty: [When] the mind is free of thoughts of wealth, belonging to others, [such as] sacrificial grass, gold and pearls, the wise ones know this to be *asteyam*. O Great Sage, those who know the *ātma,* say that by being in the *ātma* [and] avoiding action, which arises from the ego, or lower self, this is said to be *asteyam.*

13, 14a.
Abstinence: Avoiding women in body, speech [and] mind, [and] his own wife during her periods, then this is called *brahmacarya*. O Supreme Ascetic, the mind attains *brahmacarya*, when absorbed in the Absolute.

14b, 15a.
Kindness towards all creatures in body, thought and speech, [as if] towards oneself, this is indeed called compassion by the one who knows *vedānta*.

15b, 16a.
Straight-forwardness: O Sage, continuously [viewing] the one form whatsoever in oneself, (in one's) son, friend, wife and enemy, is proclaimed by me as *arjavam*.

16b, 17a.
Patience: [When] one is tormented in body, thought and speech by enemies, and is free from agitation in the mind, that [is] *kṣamā*, o Eminent Sage.

17b, 18.
Equanimity: It is said that total liberation from the cycle of birth, death and rebirth comes indeed through the vedas, and not otherwise. Equanimity is said to be the outcome of this understanding, by those versed in the vedas. 'I am *ātman* and nothing else', says he, whose faith [is] steadfast.

19.
Moderate diet: A balanced, moderate diet has little fried food and one fourth [of the stomach] relatively empty. [This is] thus a suitable yogic diet.

20 to 23a.
Cleanliness: O Great Sage, removing dirt from one's body and cleaning it with water is external cleanliness. Knowing the mind through reflection: 'I am pure', this wisdom is *śaucam* of the very wise. The body is completely impure, and the embodied Self [is] completely pure. To one who knows the difference, which *śaucam* is prescribed? O Virtuous One, having abandoned purification through meditation, the man who delights in the external [is] a fool, who picks up a lump of earth, ignoring the gold.

23b to 25.
The way to know the supreme consciousness: Satisfied with the nectar of meditation and having fulfilled his duties, the yogin has nothing more to be done. Longing for something to do, he is not a knower of *Brahma*. For one who knows the supreme spirit, there is nothing more to be done in the three worlds. Therefore, o Sage, with every effort, with *ahiṃsā* and other practices, know *Brahma* as the imperishable self through meditation and higher knowledge.

Second Section
Knowledge of The Ten Niyamas, inner disciplines

1, 2a.
These are called the *niyamas.* Listen, I will describe these in order: (i) self-discipline, (ii) contentment, (iii) devotion, (iv) giving freely, (v) worship of a supreme reality, (vi) listening to the scriptures, (vii) remorse, and also (viii) desire for humility, (ix) repetition of *mantra,* and (x) commitment.

2b to 4a.
Austerity: Emaciating the body in the manner taught in the vedas, such as the penances performed, according to the moon's course, is called *tapas*, austerity, by the wise. What is *mokṣa*, liberation? How [and] from where [does it come]? The learned ones declare [that] understanding the sense of *tapas* is obtained by reflecting on the cycle of birth and death.

4b to 6a.
Contentment: When the joy [which] arises in men from obtaining any desire [is] constant, this is known as *santoṣa* by the wise [who are] solely intent on true insight. Becoming indifferent to obtaining one's desire, and free from attachment everywhere, until one has realised brahma, is known as the supreme santoṣa.

6b.
Faith in the higher reality: Faith in the *śrutis* and *smṛtis* is called *āstikyam.*

7.
Giving freely: When money acquired ethically is given away with reverence to another person [who is] distressed or versed in the vedas, this is declared *dānam* by me.

8.
Worship of *Īśvara*: When the heart is free from desire etc, the speech is not guilty of lying [and the] action is devoid of violence etc, this is *īśvara pūja,* worship of Īśvara.

9.
Hearing the knowledge of truth: Thus, knowing that the ultimate permanence of truth, infinite wisdom and supreme bliss is to be perceived inwardly is *vedānta śravaṇam*.

10.
Remorse: When action is blameworthy, according to the ways of the worlds of the gods, then there is remorse, and this [remorse] is called *hrīḥ*.

11.
Faith in the vedic teaching: That faith in all those teachings versed in the Vedas is *mati*. And if [another] system is advised by the guru, the connection [with him should be] terminated.

12 to 16.
Japa: The practice of *mantra* in the correct way of the vedas is known as *japa.* According to the *Kalpa Sūtras, Vedas*, *Dharma Śāstras*, *Purāṇas* and *Itihāsas*, this method is called japa by me. Then it is said there are two kinds of japa, vocal [and] mental. Vocal is divided into two kinds, whispered and aloud. Mental uses two kinds, differentiating between reflection [and] deep meditation. Whispered japa is said to be a thousand times better than japa [said] aloud. Likewise mental [japa] is said to be a thousand times better than whispered. Whereas it is said *ucchaiḥ japa* (uttered aloud) is rewarding in all [instances], *nīcaiḥ* japa (uttered in a low voice) is heard by the ear, and it has no results.

Third Section
Nine Āsanas

1, 2a.
O Eminent Sage, thus [these nine *āsanas* are]: *swastikāsana*, the auspicious pose, *gomukhāsana*, the cow-face pose, *padmāsana*, the lotus pose, *vīrāsana*, the hero pose, *siṃhāsana*, the lion pose, *bhadrāsana*, the gracious pose, *muktāsana*, the liberated pose, and indeed the *mayurāsana*, the peacock pose, and *sukhāsana*, the easy pose, is counted as the ninth.

2b, 3a.
One should always practise the auspicious pose, placing the neck, head [and] body in alignment, trying to put the knees exactly parallel with both feet.

3b, 4a.
One should place the right ankle on the left behind the back, and then the left on the right; this is called the cow face pose.

4b, 5.
O Distinguished Brahman, placing (the soles of) both feet upwards on the thighs, one should hold the ends of the big toes with the hands turned up. This is the lotus pose, O Wise One, which wards off all disease.

6.
One should put the left foot on the right thigh, the body straight and comfortable. This is called the hero pose.

6i, ii and iii.
One should place the ankles under the testes and beside the perineum, the right one with the left ankle, [and] vice versa, hands well-placed on the knees and spreading one's fingers. With open mouth, one should gaze intently at the tip of the nose. This is the lion pose, honoured always by the yogins.

7, 8a.
One should put the ankles under the testes and beside the

perineum, knees out to the sides, holding [them] firmly and still with the hands. This is the gracious pose, which removes poison [and] disease.

8b to 10a.
Pressing the perineum gently with the right ankle, [and the pubis] with the left ankle, this is the pose of liberation. Placing [the right ankle] and the left ankle one above the other, with the penis placed between the ankles, this [is] the pose of liberation, O Sage.

10b to 12a.
O Esteemed Sage, one should put the elbows in front against the sides of the navel, placing both hands on the ground, mind one-pointed, head raised, legs straight, placed in the air. This is the peacock pose, remover of all negativity.

12b to 13a.
By whatever way one becomes comfortable and steady, this is called the easy pose. One who is weak should resort to this.

13b, 14.
Result of mastery of āsana: Whoever is victorious in āsana attains victory over the three worlds. According to this principle, one who is intent [on āsana] should always do *prāṇāyāma.*

Fourth Section
The Subtle Body

1, 2.
The body is of a size consisting of ninety-six *aṅgulas*. In the centre of the body [is] the site of *Agni*, whose light glows like gold from the Jambū river. O Sāṃkṛti, there is truly a triangle here in men. It is two aṅgulas above the anus and two aṅgulas below the penis.

3 to 5a.
O Sāmkṛti, best of sages, in the centre of the human body [is] the location of the root of the nāḍīs, nine aṅgulas from *mūlādhāra cakra.* O Esteemed Sage, it is four *aṅgulas* in length, like the shape of a chicken egg, covered with skin etc. O Esteemed Sage, it is said by the wise that the navel [is] inside it.

5b to 8.
Enumeration of the nāḍīs: The nāḍī that is situated in the centre of the kanda is called suṣumnā. Around it are seventy two thousand nāḍīs, among which are the fourteen principal ones, o Esteemed Sage. The fourteen principal *nāḍīs* are called: *suṣumnā, piṅgalā,* also *iḍā*, and *sarasvatī, pūṣā* and *varuṇā,* as well as *hastijihvā, yaśasvinī, alambusā, kuhū* and also *viśvodārā, payasvinī, śaṅkhinī* and *gāndhārā.*

9, 10.
First of all, among them, three [are] the main ones; among the three [there is] one main [nadi]. This is called *brahma nāḍī*, by those who know *vedānta*, o Sage. Suṣumnā is at the centre of the back, straight as a *vīṇā* shaft, like a bone going right up to the head.

11 to 13a.
Location and qualities of the *kuṇḍalī*: The location of the kuṇḍalī is two aṅgulas below the root of the navel, o Sage. The kuṇḍalī [has] the form of the eight elements of nature, most venerable Sage. [When] one is constantly consuming water and food and the movement of air, just like [the kuṇḍalī] always located around the sides of the kanda, blocks the fontanelle mouth, surrounding [it] with her own mouth, o Sage.

13b to 17.
Locations of the nāḍīs: iḍā is on the left of suṣumnā; piṅgalā is on the right. Sarasvatī and also kuhū are on both sides of

suṣumnā. Gāndhārā is at the back and hastijihvā at the front of iḍā. Pūṣā is at the back and yaśasvinī at the front of piṅgalā. Viśvodarā is located between kuhū and hastijihvā. Varuṇā is fixed between yaśasvinī and kuhū. Yaśasvinī is said to be between pūṣā and sarasvatī. Śaṅkhinī is said to be between gāndhārā and sarasvatī. Alambusā goes right up to the anus from the kanda.

18 to 23a.
Kuhū is located at the upper part of suṣumnā, the full moon. [This] nāḍī goes up and down the southern nostril. Now iḍā is located at the left nostril, o esteemed Sage, and yaśasvinī goes to the toes of the left leg. Pūṣā [goes] right up to the left eye and is behind piṅgalā, and payasvinī is said by the wise [to go] to the left ear. Then sarasvatī goes up to the tongue, o Sage, and hastijihvā goes up to the toes [of] the left leg. The nāḍī called śaṅkhinī goes up to the left ear; gāndhārā is said by those versed in the Vedas [to go] up to the left eye. The nāḍī named viṣvodarā is situated at the centre of the kanda.

23b to 30a.
The movement of prāṇa in the nāḍīs: *prāṇa, apāna, vyāna, samāna, udāna,* and also *nāga, kūrma, kṛkara, devadatta* and *dhanaṃjaya* are the ten prāṇas, circulating in all the nāḍīs. Of these, five prāṇas are the most beneficial, o Virtuous One. Among [these] five prāṇas, called prāṇa and apana, prāṇa is to be worshipped, o Sage. Thus the vital air called prāṇa exists continuously within the face, the nostrils, the navel [and] the heart, o excellent Sage. Apāna is continuously in the anus, stomach, navel, and each hip and thigh up to the knees, o Virtuous One. Vyāna is within the ears, eyes, from the shoulders and also in the ankles, and even in the pranic area in the neck, o esteemed Sage. Udāna is known in the feet [and] also the hands. Samāna is without doubt contained in the whole body. The five (minor) prāṇas, beginning with nāga are located in the skin, bones etc.

30b to 34.

Functions of the prāṇas: Sighing, exhalation and coughing are the activity of prāṇa, o Sāṃkṛti. Now, feces and urine etc are evacuated by the vital air called apāna. Samāna acts in this whole region, o esteemed Sage. For sure udāna performs the upward movement. Vyāna is said by those who know vedānta to cause conflict [between them], o Sage. The one called *nāga* is said [to have] the attributes of belching etc, o great Sage. *Dhanaṃjaya* is said [to have] the effect [of] lustre, o Sāṃkṛti. Now *kūrma* [causes] shutting the eyes etc, and *kṛkara* [causes] hunger. It is stated that *devadatta* [is] the cause [of] sleep, o distinguished Brahman.

35 to 39a.

The nāḍī deities: Śiva is the deity of *suṣumnā*. Hari is the deity of *iḍā*, Virinca of *piṅgalā* and Virat of *sarasvatī*, o Sage. Adhidevata, the Supreme Deity, is said [to be for] *pūṣā* [and] Varuṇā, the deity of *vāyu*, is the deity of the one named *hastijihvā*. It is declared, o distinguished Sage, that Bhagavān Bhaskara [is the deity] of *yaśasvinī*, and Varuṇā [has] the nature of *alambusā*. The deity of *kuhū* is Hunger; the Moon is called the deity of *gāndhārī*. Likewise, *śaṅkhinī* has the Moon, *payasvinī* Prajapati and the one named *viśvodara* has the lord Bhagavan Pavaka.

39b, 40a.

The movement of the moon and sun in the nāḍīs: The lunar energy does always flow in *iḍā*, o Great Sage. Likewise, the solar energy [flows] in *piṅgalā*, o excellent Sage of those who know the Vedas.

40b to 43a.

The yearly flow of the solar (and lunar) energy in the nāḍīs: Now, when the vital airs move from piṅgalā into iḍā, that is called *uttarāyaṇam,* the northern path, by those who know vedanta, o Sage. However, the prāṇa moving from iḍā into piṅgalā is said to be *dakṣiṇāyanam*, the southern path, o

Sage, as it is stated in the Vedas about piṅgalā. When the prāṇas of iḍā and piṅgalā join, then *amavasya* is said [to be] in the body of living creatures, o eminent One.

43b to 47.
When the prāṇa enters mūlādhāra, o wise Pandit, this is called the beginning of the equinox by ascetics, o excellent Ascetic. When this prāṇa enters the crown of the head, o esteemed Sage, this is called the end of the equinox by ascetics who are conscious of the True Reality. Every month there is the coming together of the exhalation and inhalation. When the prāṇa reaches the site of the kundalini through iḍā, then it is said [to be] the eclipse of the moon by the knowers of the true reality, o excellent One. When the prāṇa enters the site of the kundalini through piṅgalā, then it is the solar eclipse, o esteemed Sage.

48 to 56.
Praise of the inner *tīrthas: Mt. Kailash* [is] within the head, *Kedāra* [is] in the forehead, *Vārāṇasī* [is] between the eyebrows and the nose, o wise One. *Kurukṣetra* [is] within the chest. *Prayāga* moves up in the heart. Now, *Cidambara* [is] in the heart centre. *Kamalālaya* [is] in the base. Whoever goes to external tīrthas, abandoning the inner tīrtha, seeks a piece of glass, while disregarding the precious jewel lying in his hand. *Bhāvatīrtha* is the highest tīrtha [and] proof of all actions. Either the wife or the daughter may be embraced. Yogins, because of understanding the self, do not need water tīrthas [or] gods made of wood or other [materials]. The inner tīrtha [is] the supreme tīrtha, [higher] than the external tīrtha, o great Sage; the tīrtha of the soul is the greatest tīrtha; another tīrtha [is] useless. Dirt concealed in the mind cannot be cleansed by baths in tīrthas, just as a container for alcohol [is] impure, even though it has been washed a hundred times. Always bathing in Vārāṇasī and such places, during all the solstices and other eclipses, a man becomes pure. Yet, having his feet washed for purity of mind by masters of *jñāna yoga*,

that is the tīrtha of the ignorant, o esteemed Sage.

57 to 59.
Vision of Śiva in oneself. The unconscious self always sees Śiva in tīrtha, charitable gifts, *japa*, *yajña*, movement of wind and cloud, stone [idols], whereas Śiva is established in the body. Thus, whoever worships the external, forsaking me, the internal, [is as if] he licks his own elbow, having cast away the food in this hand. The yogins see Śiva inside themselves, not in idols. Idols are designed for the benefit of ignorant people.

60 to 63.
Absorption in Brahman through insight into Brahma: Whoever sees Brahma [as] incomparable, unexcelled, true, non-dual, full of knowledge [and] bliss, he sees his own Self. Thus affirming 'Through the Self, I am the Self', having renounced the mass of nāḍīs [as] ever unimportant to the spirit of man, o great Sage, [and] having rejoiced with one's own eyes in the bodiless within the body [and] the imperishable bliss of the great all-pervading *Īśvara*, the wise one does not grieve. [When] the knowledge which has generated distinctions is destroyed by the forces of wisdom, o Sage, [there] being no difference between the Self and Brahman, what can it do?

Fifth Section

1 to 4.
Purification of the nāḍīs: O Brahman, describe to me exactly [and] succinctly the purification of the nāḍīs, [so that] always contemplating through this purity, I become liberated while in this body. O Sāmkṛti, listen! I will tell you concisely of the purification of the nāḍīs, according to ritual and set actions [and] devoid of personal desires and wishes. Serene, merged with the eightfold path, beginning with the yamas, [their] highest aim truth, and fixed on their true self, the wise

practise correctly. Having made a hut in a pleasant, clean place, on a mountain peak, on the bank of a river, at the base of a *bilva* tree, or else in a forest, one can withdraw the mind.

5 to 10.

And having begun āsana from the west, facing east or even facing north, neck, head [and] body aligned, [the body] covered [and] immobile, with well-focused mind on the nose tip, one should see with one's own eyes *turīya*, the flow of nectar in the crescent moon at *bindu*. Drawing the prāṇa in through iḍā, filling the belly, then meditating on the fire arising from the flames in the centre of the body, one should reflect upon the *bīja* of *agni*, together with the *nāda* of *bindu*. Next the sage emits the prāṇa completely through piṅgalā. Then, inhaling through piṅgalā, one should reflect upon the *bīja* of *agni*. Then, with full awareness, one should exhale very slowly through iḍā. One should practise six times for three or four days or else three or four times, and always in secret at sunrise, noon and sunset.

11, 12.

Indications of nāḍī purification: One obtains purification of the nāḍīs [when] different signs are perceived: lightness of the body, radiance of fire, moving in the digestive system. It is said the manifestation of *nāda* is the sign, indicating this *siddhi*. One should do the practices until one recognises these [signs].

13, 14.

Purification of one's own self: Or, having ceased this [practice], one should practise purification of one's own self. The *ātman* [is] always pure, ever delightful, and self-illumined. Whoever is cleansed of the dirt of ignorance by the water of knowledge, he is indeed completely pure and is not bound to other action.

Sixth Section: Aspects of Prāṇāyāma

1, 2.
Description of prāṇāyāma: Listen respectfully, Sāmkṛti. I will speak of the system of prāṇāyāma. It is declared [that] prāṇāyāma [is] by means of exhalation, inhalation and breath retention. Exhalation, inhalation and breath retention are said to consist of the three sounds; this is called *praṇava*, and prāṇāyāma is formed of this.

3 to 9.
Drawing the breath in through iḍā, and filling the abdomen, one should bring to mind the sound 'A', [counting] slowly for sixteen *mātrās*. Then, holding the inhalation for sixty four mātrās, [and] also contemplating here the form of 'U', one should repeat the praṇava. The sage should hold the inhalation as long as he can; following the repetition [of the praṇava], he should then expel the vital air with the sound 'M' slowly for thirty-two mātrās through piṅgalā again. This is prāṇāyāma, and therefore, one should practise correctly. Again, inhaling through piṅgalā for sixteen mātrās, one should also concentrate here on the form of 'A' with one-pointed attention. The knowledgeable one should hold the inhalation for sixty-four mātrās, repeating powerfully the praṇava, while meditating on the form of 'U'. Then, concentrating on 'M', he should expel the vital air through iḍā. Inhaling through iḍā, the wise one should repeat [the process] in this way.

10 to 12a.
O excellent Sage, one should practise prānāyāma regularly [and] correctly. Having practised regularly [and] correctly, one becomes a *jñāni* in six months. One will be a *brahmavit* in a year. Thus one should practise continually. Whoever is always engaged in the practice of yoga and devoted to his *svadharma*, by control of the prāṇa, will indeed become liberated through higher wisdom.

12b, 13.
Description of *pūraka:* So, filling the abdomen with vital air from outside [is] pūraka. Holding the vital air as if in a full pot is *kumbhaka*. Expelling the vital air from the abdomen is called *recaka*.

14 to 20.
Siddhis of prāṇāyāma: He who produces perspiration is at the lowest [level] of prāṇāyāma. Trembling is the middle [stage], and the most accomplished one [who] levitates is the highest. When this is done repeatedly, the highest stage is attained, [and] the wise one becomes joyful in prāṇāyāma. O virtuous One, through prāṇāyāma there is purification of the mind. When the mind is purified, the bright inward light is clearly established. Having united the prāṇās with the mind, he rests in the supreme spirit. This supreme prāṇāyāma [is] the spirit of the great soul. The body rises and thus [there is] loss of any [mundane] knowledge. Leaving exhalation and inhalation, he should practise breath retention regularly. Released from all sins, he obtains correct knowledge. He gains swiftness of thought and grey hair etc disappears. Nothing [is] hard to obtain for one who is singularly intent on prāṇāyāma. Thus, one should practise prāṇāyāma with total effort.

21 to 32a.
The various prāṇāyāmas [which] eradicate disease: O virtuous One, I will explain the uses of prāṇāyāma at dawn and dusk, before sunrise, at noon, or else at all times. Inhaling the external prāṇa [until] the abdomen [is] full, and by concentrating on the nose tip, navel or the big toe, released from all disease, a man can live a hundred years. [Prāṇa] can be conquered by holding it at the nose tip, o virtuous One. All diseases disappear, when it is held at the navel. If it is confined to the big toe, o wise One, the body [becomes] light. The man who continuously drinks the vital air, having drawn it in through the tongue, is a yogin [who]

attains good health, free of fatigue and heat. Drawing the vital air in through the tongue [and] holding [it] at its root, one should drink the nectar steadily, [thus] obtaining total happiness.

Drawing the vital air in through iḍā [and] holding it at the eyebrow centre, whoever drinks pure nectar will surely be freed from sickness. O you, who understands the essence of the Veda, [drawing the breath in] through iḍā, or even through piṅgalā, and holding it at the navel, then a man will be freed from sickness. Inhaling the air through the tongue at [these] three points for a whole month, he should drink the nectar and hold it very gradually at the navel. Without doubt the disorders caused by *vāta* and *pitta* disappear, after drawing in the vāyu [and] retaining [it] in both eyes. The more he holds the breath for a long time, having placed [it there], the more will diseases of the eyes be annihilated, [and diseases of] the ears destroyed. Diseases of the head will be annihilated. I declare this the truth, o Sāmkṛti!

32b to 43a.
Control of *vāyu* through the practice of *ṣaṇmukhī mudrā*: Seated in *swastikāsana*, the mind steady, then, raising the *apāna* upwards very slowly with *praṇava*, he should completely cover the ears and other sense organs with his hands. Having covered the sense organs well, o Sage, with the thumbs on the ears, the index fingers on the eyes [and] then two others on the nostrils, he should hold the *prāṇa* with effort at the roof of the palate until he experiences the bliss of the *brahmarandhra*, o Great Sage. When the vāyu reaches the brahmarandhra, the *nāda* comes forth, o Faultless One, and that is like the sound of a conch, inside like thunder. When the vāyu goes inside the head, [it is] like a waterfall coming down from the mountains. Afterwards there is delight in the sight of the appearance of the *ātman,* o Great Wise One. When he is again in possession of that knowledge, which has come forth, there is repudiation of the material

world. He should press the suture firmly, with the right and left ankles. The wise man should press with the right ankle, contemplating its site at the junction above the knees, and then also meditating on the deities Triyambaka, Vināyaka and Vāgīśvarī. Drawing vāyu from the front, o Sage, having contracted the urethra, united with praṇava and *bindu*, the wise one should hold it in the centre of *mūlādhāra*, o Chief of Brahmins. Having been restrained by the vāyu, the brilliant fire ascends the *kuṅḍalī;* then, together with the fire of vāyu, it goes through *suṣumnā*. Thus, with his regular practice, he definitely becomes the conqueror of vāyu.

43b, 44a.
Signs of the conquest of vāyu: At first [there is] excessive perspiration, then trembling, o esteemed Sage, and raising of the body, this sign vanquishes the air [element].

44b to 51.
The conquest of *vāyu* gives rise to the knowledge of *vairagya*, non-attachment, and removal of disease and sins: Thus, with constant practice, the root cause of disease is eradicated. [Even] a fistula can be destroyed. All diseases and sins, both small and large, disappear, o Sāmkṛti. With the removal of sin, the mind becomes pure [and] wondrous [like] a mirror. Then, because of delight in Brahma and other [gods], vairagya is produced in the heart. Indifferent to the material world, [this] knowledge is the means for liberation. Through it, when one has known the god *Sadaśiva*, the snare is removed. Thus, he who has tasted the nectar of immortality, of *jñāna* once, having renounced all actions, hastens straight there. Because of ignorance of the purpose of their own true nature, others see with defective eyesight the appearances of this crooked world, not the true form of jñāna. When there is realisation of the true nature of the atman, that is the end of ignorance. When ignorance is eroded, great wise One, that is the end of desires and other [afflictions]. When

desires and other [afflictions] are absent, o wise One, [there] is no inquiry into virtue and vice. With the destruction of these, one is no longer attached to the body.

Seventh Section
Pratyāhāra

1 to 4a.
Description of *pratyāhāra* and its modifications: Now I will explain pratyāhāra, o great Sage. The senses move about naturally in the sense objects. Wilfully withdrawing [the senses] from them is called pratyāhāra. Seeing in this withdrawn state, whatever one sees, all that [is] Brahma. This is pratyāhāra, as formerly declared by knowers of Brahma. Whatever one does, [be it] pure or impure, until the end of this life, all this one should do in [the awareness of] Brahma; this is called pratyāhāra. Or one should perform regular and desired actions, knowing [that they are] homage to Brahma; this is called pratyāhāra.

4b to 8.
One should perform daily actions and desired (actions) while knowing Brahma and (paying) homage to Brahma. This is called pratyāhāra. Or, having inhaled the *vāyu,* one should hold [it] from place to place. Thus, having drawn in the vital air, one should retain [it] from the root of the teeth to the throat, from the throat to the chest, [and] from the chest to the navel. Drawing [it] in from the navel, the wise one should retain [it] in the *kuṇḍalī,* from the place of the kuṇḍalī in *mūlādhāra.* Thereupon, one should retain the *apāna* in the waist, and then in the hips and thighs, from there in the knees, lower legs [and] toes.

9, 10a.
This is said [to be] *pratyāhāra* by those accomplished in pratyāhāra in ancient times. Thus, [whenever] a great being [is] engaged in regular practice, all sins and worldly disease

vanish, o virtuous One.

10b to 12.
Pratyāhāra by holding the prāṇa within: Inhaling through the nostrils [while sitting] steadily in *svastikāsana*, the wise one should fill [the body] from the soles of the feet to the top of the head. Next it is held also in both legs, then at mūlādhāra, at the knot of the navel, the heart centre, throat pit, palate, eyebrow centre, forehead and then the top of the head.

13, 14.
Pratyāhara, according to vedānta: Withdrawing the attachment to his body, the wise one is withdrawn into the true self, non-dual [and] thoughtless. [This is] clearly called pratyāhāra by knowers of vedānta. For one who practises thus, nothing [is] difficult to attain.

Eighth Section
Dhāraṇā

1 to 6.
Dhāraṇā, or concentration, on the five elements: Thus I shall describe the five forms of concentration, o virtuous One. Now, one should concentrate on the external ether in the atmosphere, contained in the centre of the body; also on the external air in the *prāṇa*, and on the fire burning in the belly, water in the watery part [and] earth in the earthy place, o great Sage. One should utter in sequence the sounds [of the] names [of the] mantras: *Ham*, *Yam*, *Ram*, *Vam*, *Lam*. This [is] declared the supreme concentration, purifying all sins. For it is said the earth section is down from the knees, water [is up from the knees], then fire section in the area the heart centre, air section at the eyebrow centre [and] ether section is at the top of the head; thus it is proclaimed, o wise One. Then one should concentrate on Brahma in the earth place, Viṣṇu in the water area, Maheśa in the fire section, Īśvara in the air portion and Sadāśiva in the ether section, o great wise One.

7 to 9.
Concentration on the self: Now shall I describe to you [this] concentration, o esteemed Sage? This [is] in the *puruṣa*, (who is) Śiva, the ruler of all, blissful [and] all-knowing. The wise one, for the purification of all sins, should always concentrate on the forms [and] deeds of Brahma and other [gods], absorbing [them] into one's own cause, [concentrating on] the unmanifest, without form [and] indefinable [which is] the cause of everything. One should fix the mind clearly [and] completely on the *praṇava* in the *ātman*; having withdrawn the senses, one should merge the mind with the self.

Ninth Section
Dhyāna

1, 2.
Meditation on the attributes of Brahma: Now I shall describe *dhyāna*, [which] destroys the illusory world, [which is] divine harmony, truth, the supreme Brahma, the remedy for all delusions. Saying reverently 'I Am That', the yogin should meditate on the Lord of Lords, [whose] seed [is] contained, [who is] Śiva of many forms, of the cosmic form, [and] Maheśvara, the highest reality.

3 to 5.
Meditation on Brahma without attributes: Now [this is] Śiva, the possessor of truth, [whose] knowledge [and] bliss [are] non-dual, [who is] beyond meaning, pure, eternal, without beginning, middle [and] end. Thus, [being] without matter, space, touch, sight, taste and smell, [he is] immeasurable [and] incomparable. Brahma [is] the soul, infinite existence-consciousness-bliss, o Virtuous One. Being absorbed in the mantra *iti aham asmi,* 'Thus I Am', one transcends the body [and] is liberated.

6.
Fruits of dhyāna: Without doubt there should gradually bring forth in a great soul, [who] engages thus in regular practice, knowledge of *vedānta.*

Tenth Section
Samādhi

1 to 5.
Nature of samādhi: Now I shall describe *samādhi*, the destroyer of worldly existence. Samādhi gives rise to knowledge [and] hence oneness with other beings. The ātman is, for sure, eternal, everywhere, unchangeable [and] devoid of faults. Being one, it differs from the mistaken illusion, [but] not in its own form. Therefore, there is really no duality, no phenomenal world, no transmigration, just as, it is said, the space in a pot or hermitage is obtained from the ether element. So, because of false notions [of] duality, the ātman is called *jīva* [and] *Īśvara*. Indeed I am not the body, nor the prāṇa, nor the senses, nor the mind. I am Śiva alone, ever the witness [of my] true form. This wisdom is said [to be] samādhi in this life, o excellent Sage.

6 to 12.
Here Brahma Remains: I am this Brahma, not the worldly being. [There is] nothing other than me. Just as the foam [of the] waves, arising from the ocean, is absorbed back into the ocean, in the same way the world is absorbed in me. Thus, the mind is not separate, nor is the material world. He, whose supreme self has been purified within [and] illumined, immediately reaches maturity and his own immortality. When the all-pervading consciousness shines continually [and] without interruption in the mind, then the yogin becomes absorbed in himself. When indeed he sees all creatures in himself and himself in all creatures, then he merges with Brahma. When, absorbed in samādhi, he does

not see all creatures [as many], but [as] one, then that pure consciousness is attained. And when he sees the self alone [as] the true reality, then he is set free from the whole world, [which is] merely an illusion.

13.
Epilogue: The great sage Lord Dattātreya having spoken thus, Sāṃkṛti [is] joyfully [and] fearlessly established in his own true nature.

ABOUT THE AUTHOR

Swami Satyadharma is a senior sannyasin, a yoga acharya, and a versatile teacher of yogic meditation and allied philosophies, having a Master of Arts in Yoga Philosophy with First Class Honors from Bihar Yoga Bharati, India. She wrote the commentary on the *Yoga Chudamani Upanishad*, while living in India, which was published by Yoga Publications Trust in 2003. In 2015 she published her commentary on *Yoga Tattwa Upanishad.*

Born in Connecticut USA, she lived in India for over 35 years under the direct tutelage of her yoga master, Swami Satyananda Saraswati, where she imbibed the traditional yogic teachings, and became Director of the Department of Undergraduate Studies at Bihar Yoga Bharati. She has compiled and edited many major yoga publications, such as *Yoga Darshan, Sannyasa Darshan, Dharana Darshan* and the *Teachings of Swami Satyananda.* Now based in Australia, she lives a life of sadhana and introspection, while continuing to elucidate the ancient teachings of yoga in the form of the 20 Yoga Upanishads.

ABOUT THE TRANSLATOR

Srimukti (Ruth Perini) was for many years a teacher of yoga and meditation. Already a linguist, having graduated in French, Italian and Japanese from the Universities of Sydney and Queensland, Australia, she undertook four years of studies in Sanskrit at the Australian National University (ANU) with Dr McComas Taylor. She was invited to join the Golden Key International Society for outstanding academic achievement, as she was awarded High Distinctions throughout her Sanskrit studies. She is the translator of *Yoga Tattwa Upaniṣad*, commentary by Swami Satyadharma. She has also translated the *Nāda Bindu*, *Dhyānabindu, Yoga Kuṇḍalī Upaniṣads*, and is currently working on the *Varāha Upaniṣad.*

Ruth (Srimukti) may be contacted on yoga.upanishads@yahoo.com.